Small Space Big Ideas

Small Space Big Ideas

Philippa Pearson
Australian Consultant Jennifer Wilkinson

LONDON, NEW YORK, MUNICH,
MELBOURNE, DELHI

Editor Holly Kyte
Project Art Editor Vicky Read
Senior Editor Alastair Laing
Senior Designer Sonia Moore
Pre-production Producer Rebecca Fallowfield
Senior Producer Alex Bell
Jacket Designer Rosie Levine
Senior Jacket Creative Nicola Powling
Managing Editor Penny Warren
Art Director Jane Bull
Publisher Mary Ling
Australian Managing Editor Rosie Adams
Australian Editor Nigel King
Delhi CTS Sunil Sharma, Pushpak Tyagi

Project Photography Will Heap,
Debbie Patterson, Andy Crawford
Illustrations Bryony Fripp

First published in Australia in 2014 by
Dorling Kindersley Australasia Pty Ltd
707 Collins Street, Melbourne, Victoria 3008
(a division of Penguin Australia Pty Ltd)

Copyright © 2014 Dorling Kindersley Limited
2 4 6 8 10 9 7 5 3 1
001–196187–Aug/2014

First published in Great Britain in 2014 by
Dorling Kindersley Limited

All rights reserved. No part of this publication may be
reproduced, stored in a retrieval system, or transmitted in
any form by means, electronic, mechanical, photocopying,
recording, or otherwise, without the prior permission
of the copyright owner.

A CIP catalogue record for this book is available
from the National Library of Australia.
ISBN 978-1-74033-964-3

Colour reproduction by Altaimage UK
Printed and bound by Leo Paper Products Ltd.

Discover more at
dk.com.au

Contents

SMALL SPACE, BIG POTENTIAL	06

MICRO GARDEN

Vertically Mounted Air Plant Canisters	18
Mexican-style Tin Can Cacti Planters	22
Moroccan-style Lantern Garden	26
Pots and Pots of Gourmet Microgreens	28
Cut-and-come-again Colourful Salad Colander	32
Closed Glass Terrarium	38
Instant Bonsai	44
Moss Pots	49
Miniature Tabletop Water Garden	52
Kids' Miniature Farmyard Garden	56

LET IT ALL HANG

Hanging Plant Pot Mobile	64
Kokedama Hanging Garden	68
Saddle Bag Balcony Planters	74
Edible Planted Wall	80
Hanging Ball of Succulents	84
Vintage Teatime Alpine Planter	90
Upside-down Lampshade Chilli Planter	96
Plastic Cup Air Plant Chandelier	100

GROW UP

Strawberry Picture Frame Planter	106
Succulents Living Mirror Frame	112
Succulents Living Picture Frame	118
Air Plants Living Picture Frame	124
Pea and Broad Bean Shooter Shelves	128
Vertically Mounted Miniature Greenhouse	132
Funky Abstract Bamboo Trellis	138
Homegrown Bean Feast	142
Brightly Painted Terracotta Pot for Climbers	146
Upcycled Stepladder Tiered Planter	150

CONTAIN YOURSELF

Summer Drinks Tiered Planter	156
Make-it-yourself Slate Box Planter	160
Rock Strata Alpine Planter	164
Grow Your Own Fruit in Tubs	170
Make-it-yourself Concrete Planters: Sleek White Bowl	176
Make-it-yourself Concrete Planters: Carnivorous Garden	180
Make-it-yourself Concrete Planters: Slate-grey Window Box	184
Two Ways to Decorate Your Terracotta Pots	190

GO WILD

Portable Hanging Insect House with Green Roof	198
Vintage Drawer Wildflower Meadow	204
Bee and Butterfly Wildlife Hamper	210
Cup-and-Saucer Bird Stations	216

PLANT PRACTICAL

Choosing Plants	224
Ornamental Plants Directory	226
Get the Look	234
Small Space, Big Harvest	236
Fruit, Vegetables, and Herb Directory	238
Essential Garden Kit	244
Caring for Your Plants	246
Index and Suppliers	252
Acknowledgements	256

SMALL SPACE BIG POTENTIAL

Maximizing Your Space

Even if your gardening space is tiny to non-existent, you can still fill it with greenery and bring plants into your life. We've created over 40 inspiring and fun gardening projects that will add colour, interest, and a "wow!" factor to your home, whether you've the tiniest courtyard, a balcony, or just an outside step.

Grow in Miniature

Small is beautiful, so think big and put eye-catching plants in unusual and interesting containers. You'll be surprised at what will grow in a teacup, tin can, or kitchen utensil – all great sizes for placing on tables, windowsills, steps, and ledges for a miniature gardening world to enjoy inside and out.

Terrariums are miniature gardens enclosed in glass and designed to be easy to look after.

Create a tiny farmyard garden in a cake tin. Fun for all the family!

Garden in the Air

Look up! The space above your head needn't be bare; it can be transformed into a hanging garden. With the right plants and innovative airborne containers, you can plant ceilings, walls, railings, porches, and window frames with a whole range of flowering and edible plants, so that even the tiniest balcony or verandah can be blooming.

Kokedama is the Japanese art of hanging plants in moss balls tied with string.

TOPSY-TURVY

Make use of limited space and grow plants in lampshades for a fun feature. These chillies thrive on being planted upside down.

Air plants are perfect for growing in hanging arrangements as they don't need soil to thrive.

Take the Vertical Challenge

If your only space is vertical, climbing plants needn't be your only option. Get creative and upcycle your upwards space with unusual vertical planters, such as picture frames and stepladders. With the right planter, your vertical space can be opened up to all sorts of different plants.

Guttering and old picture frames make good use of vertical space, while wooden boxes can be turned into a miniature greenhouse.

Customize Your Containers

Make the most of terracotta pots by painting them in bright colours and decorating with prints and patterns. Or try making your own containers: drill a few drainage holes and all sorts of charming vintage objects can be used for growing plants, while wooden boxes can be given a contemporary makeover by cladding them in slate.

Transform terracotta pots with paint and decoupage decoration.

You'll be surprised how easy it is to create your own stylish and contemporary planters out of simple concrete – give it a try!

PERSONALIZE POTS

With a little creativity, an ordinary pot can be turned into a stunning and useful container for showing off your favourite plants.

Gardening in a small space needn't restrict your ideas or planting opportunities. Accept the challenge and discover new possibilities!

High-impact Planting

You may be surprised by the sheer range of plants it's possible to grow in small spaces. Enjoy your plants to the full by choosing ones with interesting flowers, scent, foliage, architectural shapes, or edible elements.

Bonsai, herbs, planting for wildlife, fruit, succulents, and carnivorous plants can easily be grown in small spaces.

Small Space, Big Potential

Play Host to Wildlife

By selecting the right plants and creating habitats, even the smallest garden patch can become a special place for wildlife, attracting insects like bees, butterflies, and ladybirds that will also help you out by pollinating and keeping pests in check. And happily, insects seem to share our love of brightly coloured flowers!

Make a pretty insect hotel for friendly creatures to hibernate in, with a roof space for plants as well.

A wildflower meadow is surprisingly well suited to growing in an old drawer, while you can both feed the birds and feast your eyes with these decorative bird stations.

Practical Checklist

Before you start to fill your space with plants, get kitted up with the right tools and equipment (see pages 244–5), and take time to learn about different plants and their needs (see pages 224–43). Consider how much time you can allocate to looking after your plants and jobs like watering, feeding, and pruning. Here are some essential pointers to help you get started.

CONTAINERS
- Choose a container that is big enough for plant growth and pot on plants when roots get bigger.
- Make sure there are drainage holes in the container and make some if there aren't.
- Add extra drainage like gravel or crocks to the bottom of containers.
- Avoid metal and plastic containers for hot sites.

WATERING AND FEEDING
- Containers can dry out quickly in warm, sunny, and exposed sites and, unless you choose drought-tolerant plants, will need watering frequently, sometimes twice a day.
- Try to ensure easy access to water, or work out a strategy that will lessen the burden of watering.
- Put drip trays under containers to protect surfaces and retain moisture.
- Most plants need regular watering and feeding in their growing season, but winter-dormant plants won't need any during dormancy.

RIGHT PLANT, RIGHT PLACE
- Assess the growing conditions in your garden space before planting up. Does it get a lot of sun? Does it get wet when it rains or is it sheltered? Is it in a windy position?
- Once you know the growing conditions of your site, choose plants that will survive and thrive in these conditions; a plant that loves the sun, for example, may not grow happily in the shade.
- Planting high up in an exposed position where it is dry and windy, such as on a balcony, will need plants that are suited to these conditions.

KEEP THINGS SMALL
- Look out for plants that are grown especially for smaller spaces, such as dwarf forms of larger plants like fruit trees.
- With regular pruning, many larger plants can be kept in check and given a compact form, which is better suited to a small site.

Choose the right plants and containers, then just add your creativity for fabulous small space gardening.

STORAGE FEATURE
Make a feature out of storing garden tools by upcycling a storage chest or cupboard. Simply decorate with exterior paint and place a planted container on top.

MICRO GARDEN

Vertically Mounted Air Plant Canisters

TOOLS & EQUIPMENT

sandwich cake tins in several sizes (make sure they are not the loose-bottomed variety)

clear-drying superglue

thick clear acetate

scissors

spoon

small gravel & sand in several different colours & grades

florist's ornamental Spanish moss (optional)

pencil

Velcro adhesive pads

PLANT LIST

selection of small air plants (a type of bromeliad available from a specialist nursery), such as:
Tillandsia bulbosa
Tillandsia caput medusae
Tillandsia ionantha
Tillandsia pruniosa
Tillandsia streptophylla

Great fun and simple to make, these planted canisters look like miniature desert landscapes and provide a novel means of decorating a wall, fence, or even your front door with some quirky living greenery.

 **TIME IT RIGHT** Spring is a good time to plant up your canisters as air plants aren't frost hardy. Put the canisters outside, but in cold regions bring them indoors from late autumn.

1 Apply a small amount of superglue around one half of the outside rim of a cake tin. Be careful not to apply too much.

2 Press a rectangle of acetate over the glued half of the rim so that it covers it completely with sufficient overlap.

Project Steps

3 Leave to dry completely overnight, then neatly cut around the cake tin rim with a pair of scissors to remove the excess acetate.

4 Spoon layers of sand and gravel into the "planting chamber"; this is for decorative purposes as air plants don't need soil to grow. Build up contrasting layers until the plants will be able to sit comfortably and longer leaves can extend over the rim of the acetate. Top with florist's ornamental moss for extra decoration, if you like.

5 Select your air plants, choosing different shapes, colours, and leaf textures for interest. Don't overfill the canisters; the smallest canisters work best with a single bold plant, while two or more plants in larger canisters look better if plants contrast in style or have similar qualities that work well as a group.

Micro Garden 21

6 Position the air plants so that they are stable and evenly spaced. Hold the canisters up to the wall or fence and create an arrangement that works for you. With a pencil, mark where the tops of each canister will be positioned.

7 Stick half a Velcro pad near the top of each canister, then stick the other half at the matching point on the wall or fence, ensuring all pads are level. Press the canisters on to the wall so that the pads are exactly aligned.

Care Advice

Where to site Air plants like warmth but not direct sunlight and are happy outdoors where the weather is mild. In cold districts, bring inside before temperatures drop below 8°C (46°F). Place where light levels and air circulation are good. Do not place near heat sources; a damp atmosphere is preferable.

Watering Air plants absorb moisture through their leaves and should be sprayed 2–3 times a week (ideally with rainwater), more frequently during summer or in dry conditions. If plants look dry, submerge them in room temperature water for a little while, then shake off any excess water and replant.

General care Remove any dead, diseased, or dying foliage and do not to let any water sit in the base of the plant as this could cause it to rot.

Feed with a diluted special air plant liquid fertilizer misted on leaves once a week in spring and summer, fortnightly in winter.

TOOLS & EQUIPMENT

collection of tin cans with appealing designs printed onto the metal

masking tape

electric drill & drill bits

scoria or gravel

cacti potting mix

horticultural grit

small scoop or spoon

dibber, chopstick, or pencil

decorative gravel

PLANT LIST

selection of succulents, such as:
 Aloe aristata
 Aloe brevifolia
 Echeveria species
 Haworthia species
 Pachyphytum species
 Rebutia species
 Sedum species
 Sempervivum species

Mexican-style Tin Can Cacti Planters

For a taste of Mexico without leaving your garden, create a desert scene with architectural cacti and juicy succulents grouped together in bright food tins for a brilliant table display.

 **TIME IT RIGHT** Best to plant at the start of the growing season from mid-spring. Plants will last 1–3 years before needing to be potted on, depending on the size of plant and can.

1 Clean the tin cans thoroughly before using. Drill drainage holes in the bottom of each can with an electric drill. Use masking tape to prevent the drill slipping.

2 Add a layer of drainage material, such as scoria or gravel, to the bottom of each can. Good drainage is vital so that the roots don't sit in water and rot.

Micro Garden

4 Place plants on a layer of potting mix and then fill in around the root ball, working in the mix with a dibber to reduce air pockets. Tap the container on the work surface to distribute the potting mix evenly. Top with a layer of decorative gravel. Place on a saucer or similar if you need to protect the table surface.

3 Create a free-draining, gritty potting mix by mixing horticultural grit and cacti potting mix in 3:1 proportions. Remove plants from their pots and gently break up the root ball, teasing out the roots and removing soil. Take care not to damage the roots.

Care Advice

Where to site Cacti and succulents need morning sun, but also shade from hot summer sun. You can leave them outside in mild climates, as long as there is protection from wind and rain. In cold regions, bring inside during winter and place on a sunny windowsill in a warm room.

Watering and feeding The easiest way to water these is to place the tins in a shallow container of water, leave until the surface of the mix is moist, then lift out and leave to drain. Water regularly in the growing season – every 10 days or so – and add a diluted liquid feed to the water during spring and summer. Do not feed or water in autumn and winter.

Repot plants into large containers when roots start to show through the tin's drainage hole. Repotting is best done in spring, and watering plants a couple of days before keeps roots moist.

Create a theatrical scene matching the shape of plants to the design and size of the tins

Moroccan-style Lantern Garden

A glass lantern is easily adapted to house a miniature display of succulents for a stylish centrepiece that works both indoors and out.

TOOLS & EQUIPMENT

large glass lantern with opening
electric drill & drill bits (optional)
waterproof liner
strong outdoor adhesive
strip of thick, clear plastic
2 contrasting types of gravel
cacti potting mix mixed 3:1 with horticultural grit
dibber, chopstick, or pencil

PLANT LIST

selection of succulents, such as:
 carpet moss (optional)
 Crassula species
 Echeveria species
 terrestrial bromeliad such as *Abromeitiella* species

Care Advice

General care Water every 10 days from spring to early autumn by wetting the soil with a water mister; include a diluted liquid feed. Position in a protected but well-lit spot, and leave the door open for air.

 **TIME IT RIGHT** This project can be completed in an hour and is best started in spring or summer when the plants will be actively growing.

1 Drill drainage holes in the base of the lantern, if required, then apply a waterproof liner. Glue the plastic strip across the bottom third of the open side. Add a layer of gravel then a layer of potting mix.

2 Arrange a selection of plants inside to suit the height and space of the lantern, then plant them up with the help of a dibber. Dress the surface with gravel.

3 If you like, line the top rim too and plant with moss, but make sure the moss doesn't dry out.

Pots and Pots of Gourmet Microgreens

Make your own mini windowsill propagators with plastic cups and their domed lids, perfect for growing a collection of tasty, nutritious microgreens in the smallest of spaces.

TOOLS & EQUIPMENT
plastic drinks pots with domed lids
metal skewer or similar
garden twine
scissors
all-purpose adhesive
small parcel labels
seed-raising mix

SEED LIST
beetroot 'Bull's Blood'
mustard green 'Osaka Purple'
silverbeet 'Bright Lights'
lots of other strong-tasting crops are suitable for growing as microgreens, including: radishes; herbs such as basil, coriander, and fennel; other Asian greens like mizuna; and even less exotic brassicas like broccoli and kale

 **TIME IT RIGHT** Seeds are best sown from early spring to early autumn, when they will germinate quickly and you should be snipping leaves in 1–2 weeks. Germination in winter willl be slower and more erratic.

1 Wash your drinks pots and lids thoroughly, leave to dry, then assemble the ingredients to make your mini propagators.

Project Steps

2 Drainage is vital to prevent the seedlings from sitting in too much water and rotting. Carefully pierce the base of each container a few times to create drainage holes.

3 Decorate each pot by tying bands of garden twine around the top and bottom, and add a parcel label on the top band. Glue the string in place at several points and leave for a couple of hours while the glue dries.

4 Fill the plastic pots with seed-raising mix, leaving a gap of 3–4cm (1¼–1½in) below the rim for watering.

5 Gently tap the whole pot on a hard surface to remove any air pockets that may prevent water from being distributed evenly through the soil. This also lets the mix settle and creates a nice even growing surface for you to sow your seeds.

Micro Garden 31

6 Put some seeds in the cradle of your palm and lightly sprinkle them over the surface of the mix. You are aiming to create an even spread, so the seeds are sown closely, but are not clumped together.

7 Sprinkle a thin layer of mix over the seeds – just enough to cover them – then water your pot, put the domed lid on top, and write the plant's name on the label. Place a container under the pot to prevent water from damaging surfaces and position on a sunny windowsill or outside in a warm sheltered spot.

Care Advice

Where to site and watering Place on a sunny windowsill in a warm room to aid germination. In warmer weather, you can leave the pots outside in a warm sheltered spot but not in hot sun. Do not overwater, especially in the early stages as this will prevent seed germination. Water pots regularly once shoots are growing.

Harvesting You need to harvest quickly and regularly. The optimum harvest time ranges from 7–14 days after sowing, depending on the variety. Crop by snipping the small leaves with scissors just before you are ready to serve. If you need to harvest shoots earlier, place in a polythene bag with a little water and put in the fridge to keep fresh.

Take the lid off your pot once shoots are beginning to grow so plants have more air circulation and space to grow.

Cut-and-come-again
Colourful Salad Colander

Sow red and green lettuce seeds in a vintage colander for a stunning effect inspired by patchwork. It makes an impressive display at dinner parties where guests can cut their own fresh salad leaves.

TOOLS & EQUIPMENT
colander with feet
card
pencil
scissors
hanging-basket liner
general-purpose potting mix
large scoop or trowel
watering can

SEED LIST
loose-leaf lettuce varieties such as 'Green Coral', 'Royal Oak', and 'Salad Bowl'

 **TIME IT RIGHT** Sow cut-and-come-again lettuce from spring to early autumn. Nursery grown seedlings can be planted close together in cooler months. First harvest should be cut in 4–5 weeks.

1 Place your colander upside down on some thick card and draw around the rim. Then draw another circle inside the outline, 2–4cm (¾–1½in) smaller.

2 Within the smaller circle, draw your stencil design. Keep it simple; we divided the circle into four quadrants. Cut out your stencil, and keep all the shapes.

Project Steps

3 Place a hanging-basket liner inside the colander – this will help to keep soil and moisture inside the container. Cut to shape, to just below the rim for a cleaner look.

4 Fill with general-purpose potting mix to just under the level of the liner, then gently tap the colander down on a hard surface to get rid of any air pockets and to level the mix surface.

5 Water the potting mix well at this stage so as not to disperse the seeds in the design.

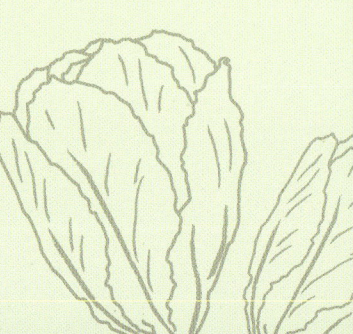

Care Advice

Watering You won't need to water for a few days to start with as you have watered the potting mix before sowing; it is then best to spray with a mister to stop seeds from dispersing before germination and disrupting the design. Make sure the mix doesn't dry out. Water overhead once seeds have germinated using a watering can with a rose attachment, but do not overwater as the small seedlings may die off in too much moisture. In very dry summer conditions, place the colander in a container filled with water up to the level of the colander's base so that it takes water from underneath; this method will also stop seeds from dispersing before germination.

Feeding Use light liquid feed between harvesting to encourage more leaves to grow back for cutting.

Thin out after germination by lightly pulling seedlings from the mix. This increases air circulation and helps to keep the plants less congested and the design more structured.

6 Cover alternate sections of the design with stencils and sow lettuce seeds of one colour, then cover the sown areas with stencils and sow the remaining areas with the other lettuce seeds.

7 Remove stencils and sprinkle a layer of fine potting mix over all the seeds to cover them lightly, then place in a warm, bright place. Note that red lettuce seedlings will be green at first and then change to red as the plants mature.

More Salad Planting Ideas

Why not try growing lettuce in other containers? Wicker baskets are great because, like the colander, they allow drainage. Zinc containers add a vintage look, while for something quirky cut the base off plastic milk bottles, plant up and hang on a wall. Lettuces can be decorative; they're perfect to plant on the edges of beds and with other herbs and ornamental plants in containers.

As well as lettuce leaves, there are plenty of edible flowers you can grow that will add a splash of colour to your planting and an unusual zing to your salads, such as calendula (top centre), nasturtiums, and French marigolds.

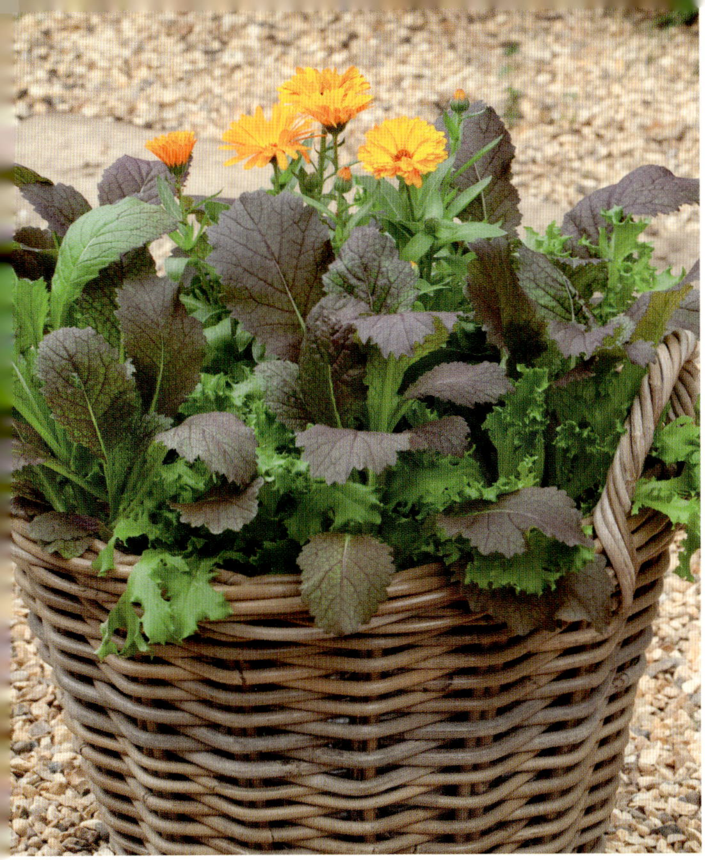
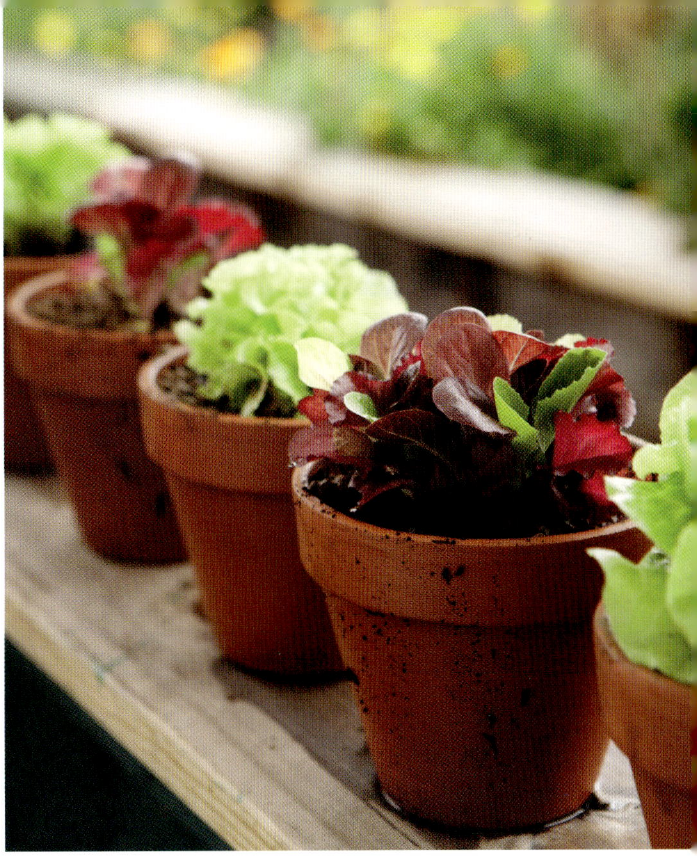
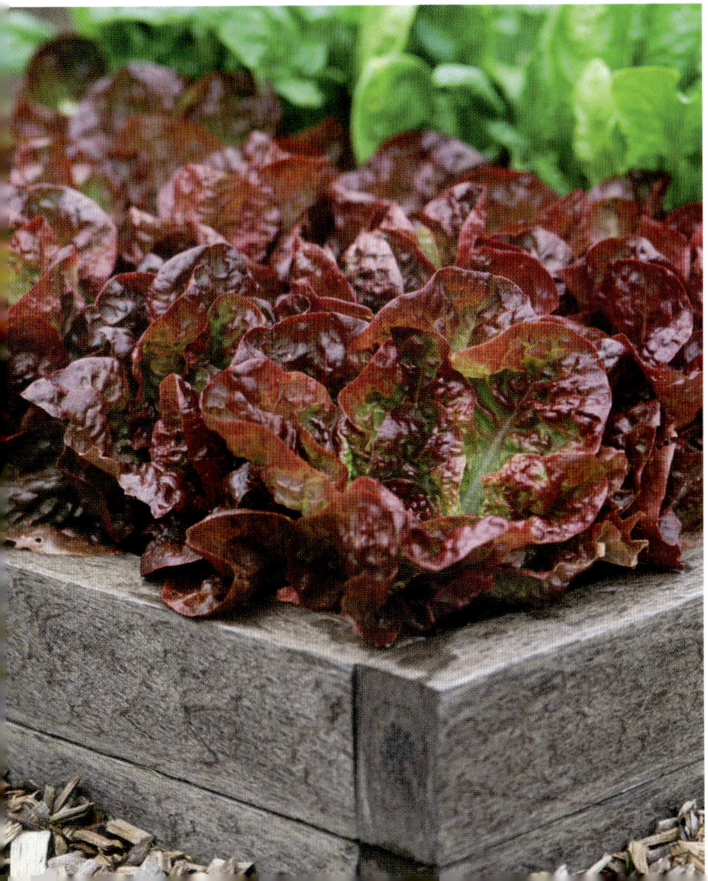
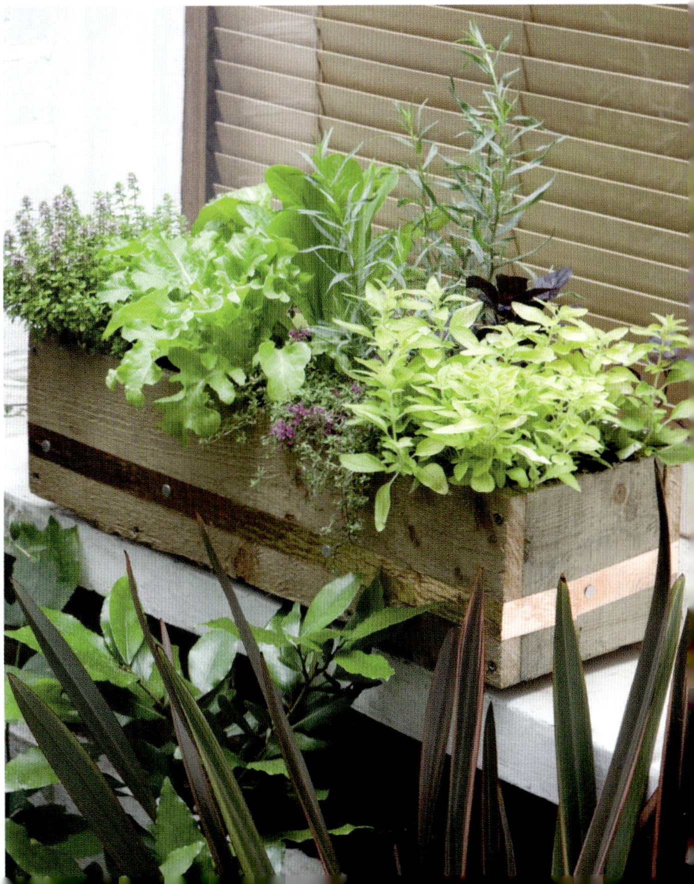

Closed Glass Terrarium

A mini garden encased in glass, a terrarium makes an eye-catching display and is the perfect choice if you lack space and time for a real garden. They are easy to look after, so even better if you lack green fingers.

TIME IT RIGHT Plant in spring or summer when plants are actively growing. Plants should last 2–3 years without needing to be transferred to a larger container and can be kept smaller by pruning.

TOOLS & EQUIPMENT

- clear glass container with lid or dome, such as a hurricane lamp, preserving jar, bell cloche, or cake cover
- gravel or small pebbles
- small scoop or spoon
- activated carbon granules
- orchid potting mix
- dibber, chopstick, or pencil
- bonsai or ordinary tweezers
- water mister

PLANT LIST

selection of carnivorous plants and foliage plants, such as:
- carpet moss
- *Dionaea muscipula*
- *Hosta* species
- *Nepenthes* species
- *Ophiopogon planiscapus*
- *Scleranthus uniflorus*

1 Choose a transparent container and lid appropriate to the size of your plants, with room for the planting medium and growing. Terrariums have no drainage holes so, to keep roots from rotting, it is vital to include a generous layer of gravel for excess water to collect.

2 Use a spoon to sprinkle a thin layer of activated carbon granules (available from aquatic suppliers) over the gravel. This will help to keep the container smelling sweet by filtering out impurities. Wash the carbon granules first to remove any residue.

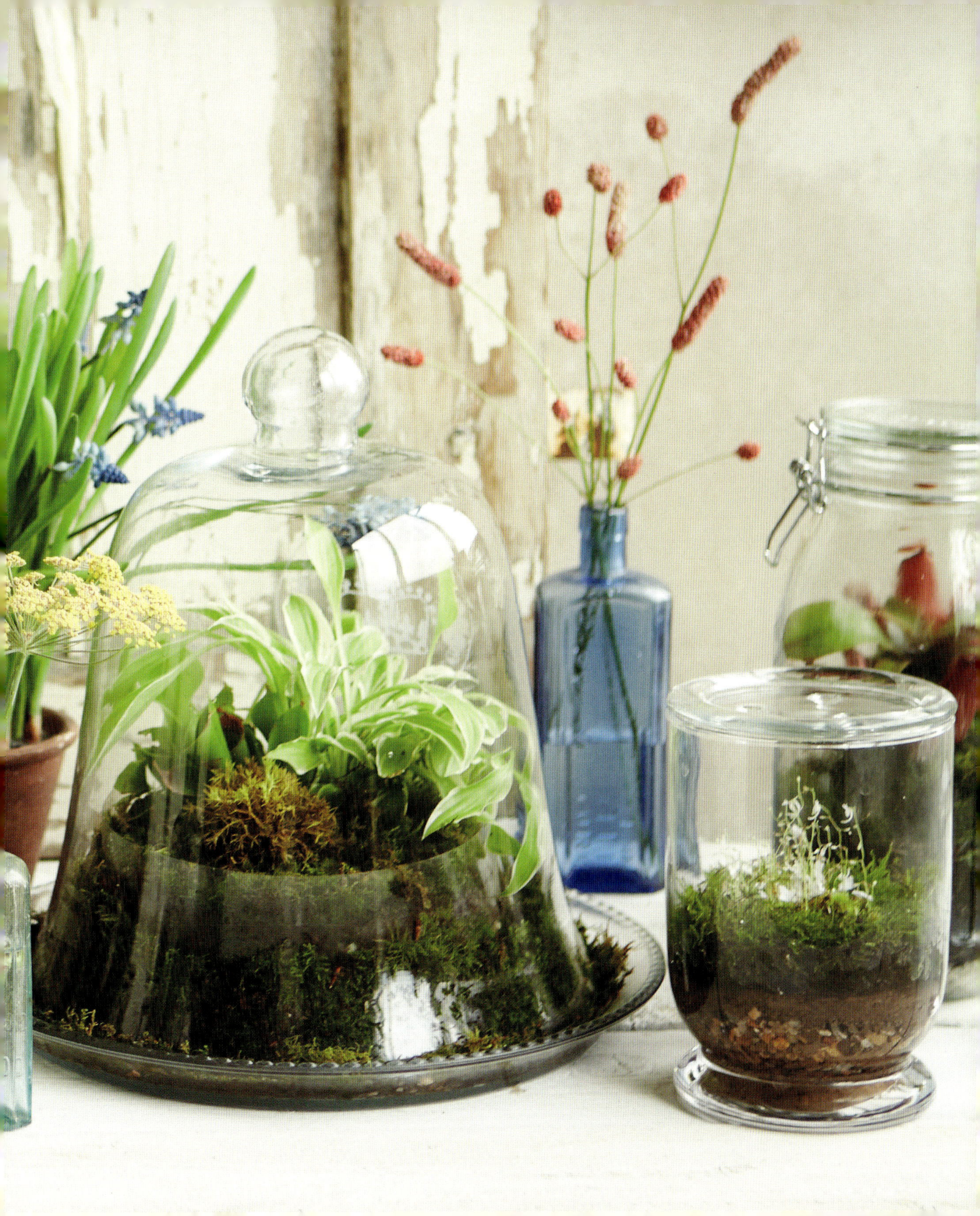

Project Steps

3 Next, add some planting medium. What you put in depends on the plants you choose, but a peat-like potting mix that retains moisture and allows drainage is a good choice. Add a layer of the mix and lightly pat down with a dibber, chopstick, or pencil.

PLANTING TIPS

Choose plants that will remain small and prefer low light and high humidity. Ferns, dwarf hostas, bog plants, carnivorous plants, and tropical plants are good choices. Avoid succulents and cacti as they prefer a drier, sunnier environment.

4 Get your plants ready for planting by removing any loose soil and gently teasing any pot-bound roots. Make a small depression in the mix, then carefully position your plant in the soil.

5 Add more mix around the sides of the plant, gently tapping this into position with a dibber, chopstick, or pencil. Make sure you are happy that there is enough soil for roots to grow before going on to the next step.

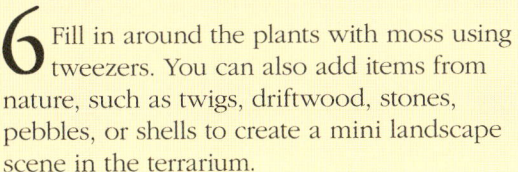

6 Fill in around the plants with moss using tweezers. You can also add items from nature, such as twigs, driftwood, stones, pebbles, or shells to create a mini landscape scene in the terrarium.

7 Remove soil from the sides of the glass with a mister. Water then seal and leave the terrarium to create its own atmosphere. If the glass mists up inside, it is working!

Care Advice

Where to site You must place your terrarium out of direct sunlight, so don't choose a sunny windowsill. They need low light, but enough to be able to grow without becoming straggly.

Watering The key to a terrarium is that it is self-sufficient. Plants form condensation in the enclosed environment, water drips down the sides and they water themselves. If the condensation stops or the soil looks dry, water plants by misting the inside. Don't overwater, especially in winter. Tropical or carnivorous plants need a bit more water, preferring rainwater, and while they do not enjoy being soggy they must always be wet, so maintain the water level at 5cm (2in) below the surface of the soil. Add more sand to the planting medium for these plants, too.

General care Air the terrarium every 2–3 weeks for a few hours, especially in the spring and summer. If you've chosen the right plants and the right container size to match, the terrarium will keep going for a while, without needing replacement plants. You can keep plants in shape by pruning; make sure you remove any trimmed foliage and any plant that begins to rot. Plants rot because of too much moisture, so you will need to redress the balance by opening the lid more frequently. The soil can be refreshed after a while by scraping off the surface layer and replacing it with fresh potting mix.

Terrariums were originally used by early plant hunters to transport their living specimens thousands of miles home

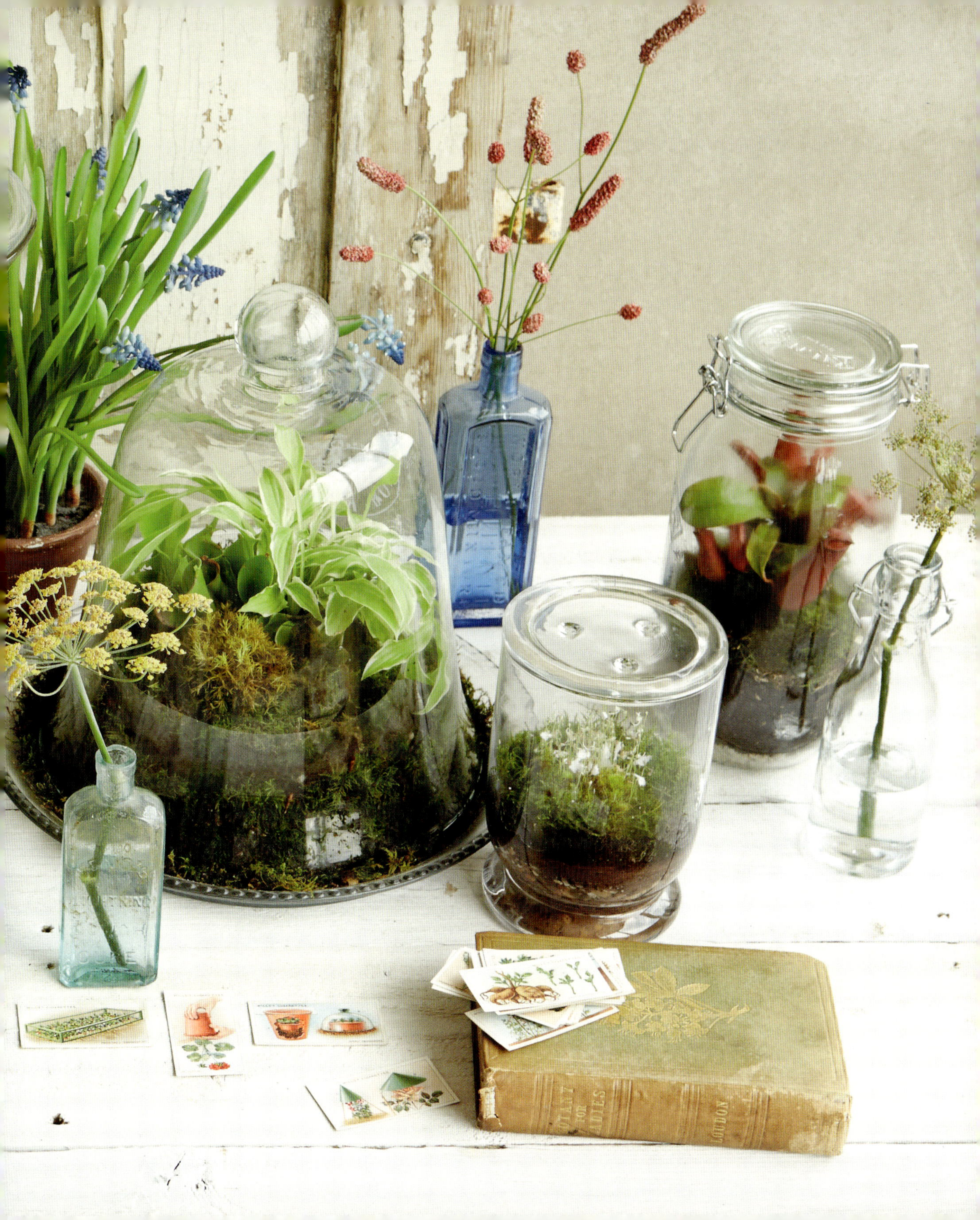

Instant Bonsai

Instant bonsai is all about creating a natural miniature landscape using moss and readily available plants. Delicate but bold, it makes a dynamic impact.

TIME IT RIGHT Early spring is the best time to pot up your plant, not when the plant is dormant in winter. You can choose evergreen or deciduous sapling trees, shrubs, or perennials.

TOOLS & EQUIPMENT

- coarse sand
- sandy loam
- organic material (half well-rotted manure, half leaf mould)
- large bowl for mixing soils
- slow-release fertilizer
- container with drainage hole
- plastic mesh
- scissors
- aluminium wire
- wire cutters
- bonsai or ordinary tweezers
- small pruners or bonsai scissors
- small scoop
- dibber, chopstick, or pencil
- spatula
- water mister

PLANT LIST

- a compact moss, such as carpet types found beside shaded paths
- a seedling tree, such as *Pinus thunbergii* (Japanese Black Pine)

Coarse sand
Sandy loam
Leaf mould and manure

1 Prepare the soil ingredients: wash and sieve the sand, sieve the loam, and pulverize the organic material. These materials suit smaller containers because they absorb and retain moisture but also allowing excess water to drain.

2 Mix 2 parts sand to 2 parts organic material and 1 part sandy loam, and then add 1 teaspoon of slow-release fertilizer. Make sure the pot has a drainage hole in the bottom.

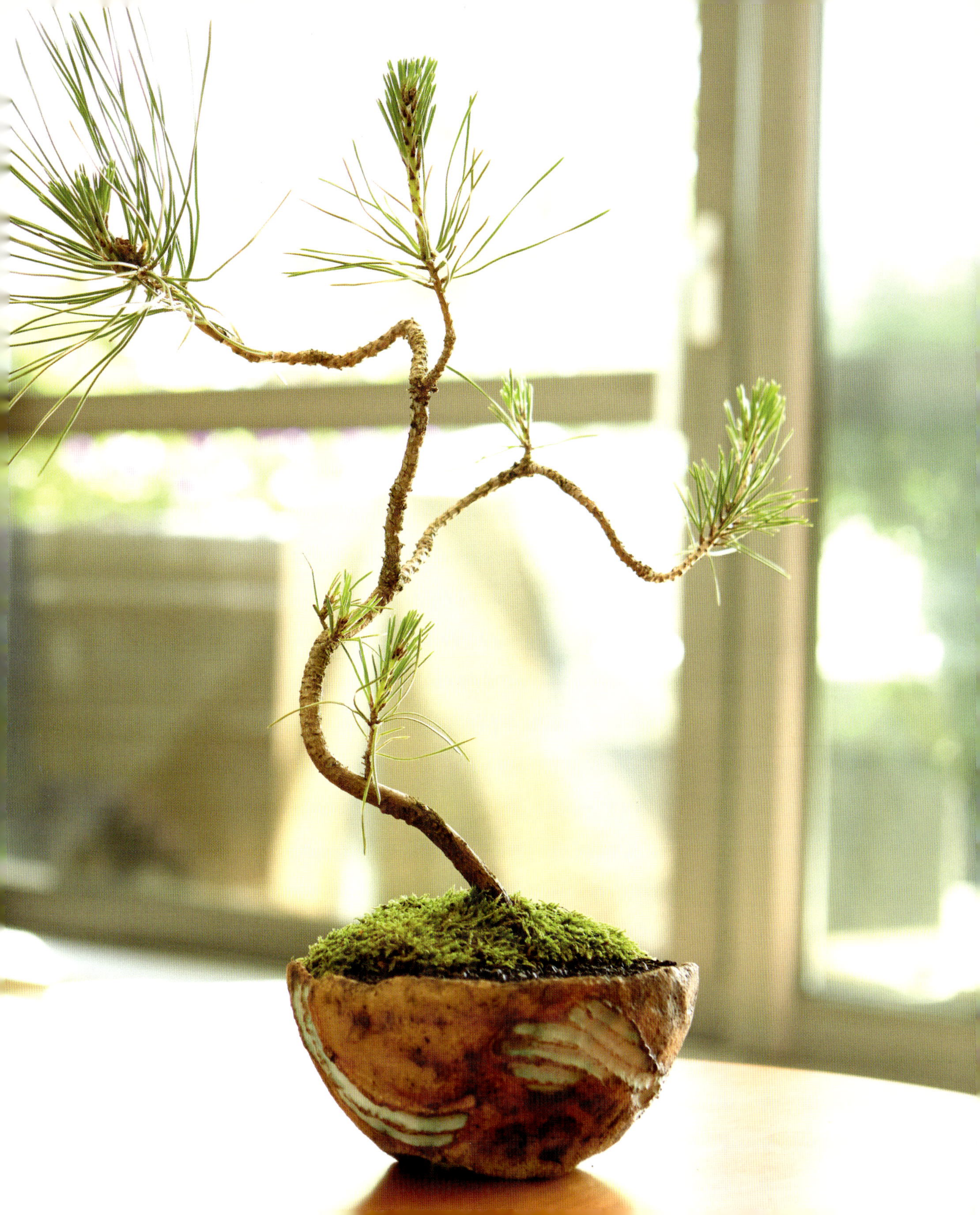

Micro Garden

🌱 Project Steps

3 Cut out a square of mesh to size and position it over the drainage hole; this will stop the soil from falling through and prevent clogging, enabling vital airflow. Cut a short section of aluminium wire with wire cutters and bend it into a U-shape.

4 Insert the wire through the middle of the mesh. Make sure the wire ends come through the drainage hole, then bend them so that they are flush with the bottom of the bowl to fix the mesh in place.

5 Carefully take your plant out of its pot. We have used a Japanese Black Pine.

6 Using tweezers, carefully remove as much of the soil from the surface and root ball as possible, then tease out the roots. Prune back any very long roots.

7 Put a layer of soil mix in the base of the pot to the correct height for the root ball of your plant. Bonsai look most authentic when set high in the container.

8 Position the plant to fit your miniature landscape design – it doesn't have to be central. Here, we're recreating the look of a tree growing out of a mossy hill.

9 Once you're happy with your plant's position, start to fill in around it with the soil mix.

10 Using a dibber, chopstick, or pencil, work the mix into the pot and then press it down with a spatula.

Project Steps

11 Moisten and clean up pieces of moss and position them around the base of the pine. Check if the moss is growing in a particular direction and try to add pieces in contrasting directions. Leave a portion of the soil uncovered.

12 To finish, pour a top dressing of coarse sand over the bare piece of soil to create the effect of water and add interesting texture. Smooth over the sand with a spatula and water everything well. A water mister is useful for the moss.

Care Advice

Where to site Place your bonsai outdoors, as it needs direct but not strong light; if kept inside, you'll need a well-ventilated room. Position where the plant won't dry out. It shouldn't be kept somewhere too wet or too shady, or where it receives hot sun.

Watering and feeding Small containers dry out quickly so require regular watering. In spring and autumn, water once a day; in summer, twice a day. During winter, water every 2–3 days.

The fertilizer used at planting should last 1–2 years. You can add additional fertilizer by gently mixing it into the soil, but only use a tiny bit, as the idea is to prevent the plant growing too much.

General care To keep your bonsai plant small, prune long growth back to a branch or secondary bud that is going to continue growing; this is especially important with pines. Every 2–3 years in early spring, tip the tree out of its container and trim back long roots. Re-pot when the plant fills the pot and roots come through the drainage hole.

Moss Pots

Celebrate nature in a teacup by creating miniature moss hills and mountains adorned with trees. These whimsical gems are perfect to enjoy in the smallest of spaces at home or at work.

TOOLS & EQUIPMENT

coarse sand, sandy loam, & organic material (well-rotted manure & leaf mould), mixed at a ratio of 2:1:1

large bowl for mixing soils

slow-release fertilizer

teacups with drainage holes drilled into the bottom using an electric drill & ceramic drill bit

plastic mesh

scissors

aluminium wire

wire cutters

bonsai or ordinary tweezers

small scoop

dibber, chopstick, or pencil

water mister

PLANT LIST (see page 51)

compact moss, such as woodland or carpet types (top right)

Cotoneaster horizontalis (bottom right)

Cyclamen hederifolium (bottom left)

Rhus succedeana (Japanese Sumac; top left)

Project Steps

1 Mix your soils, then add a little slow-release fertilizer. Take your teacup. Cut a square of mesh to size. Then, cut a short section of aluminium wire, bend it into a U-shape and insert through the middle of the mesh.

2 Position the mesh over the drainage hole and bend the ends of the wire so that they are flush with the bottom of the cup. Put a layer of soil mix in the base of the container; the depth will depend on the size of the plant.

3 Gently remove soil from the root ball and tease out the roots of the cyclamen with tweezers. Scoop enough soil into the cup so that the plant sits proud of the rim.

4 Build up the soil into a "hill" around the plant. Moisten and clean up pieces of moss and press them over the soil, tucking them into the rim. Mist everything well.

Select teacups that show off the plants and work well as a set

TOOLS & EQUIPMENT

selection of aquarium gravel in contrasting colours and sizes

large, transparent glass or plastic bowl

selection of pebbles

smaller bowl or other container

rainwater or distilled water

shells

PLANT LIST

selection of aquatic plants, such as:
 Juncus species
 Marsilea drummondi
 Sisyrinchium angustifolium

Miniature Tabletop Water Garden

This little container garden means you can enjoy a water feature in the smallest of spaces. Ask your aquatics supplier for advice on plants suitable for smaller containers and shallow depths of water.

TIME IT RIGHT Best to plant in growing season during spring and summer. Plants will last 1–2 years before needing to be transferred to a larger container. Floating plants may outgrow the space more quickly.

1 Carefully take plants out of their pots and remove as much soil as you can while minimizing any damage to the root systems.

2 To loosen the soil and make it easier to remove, you can also soak the plants in room temperature water.

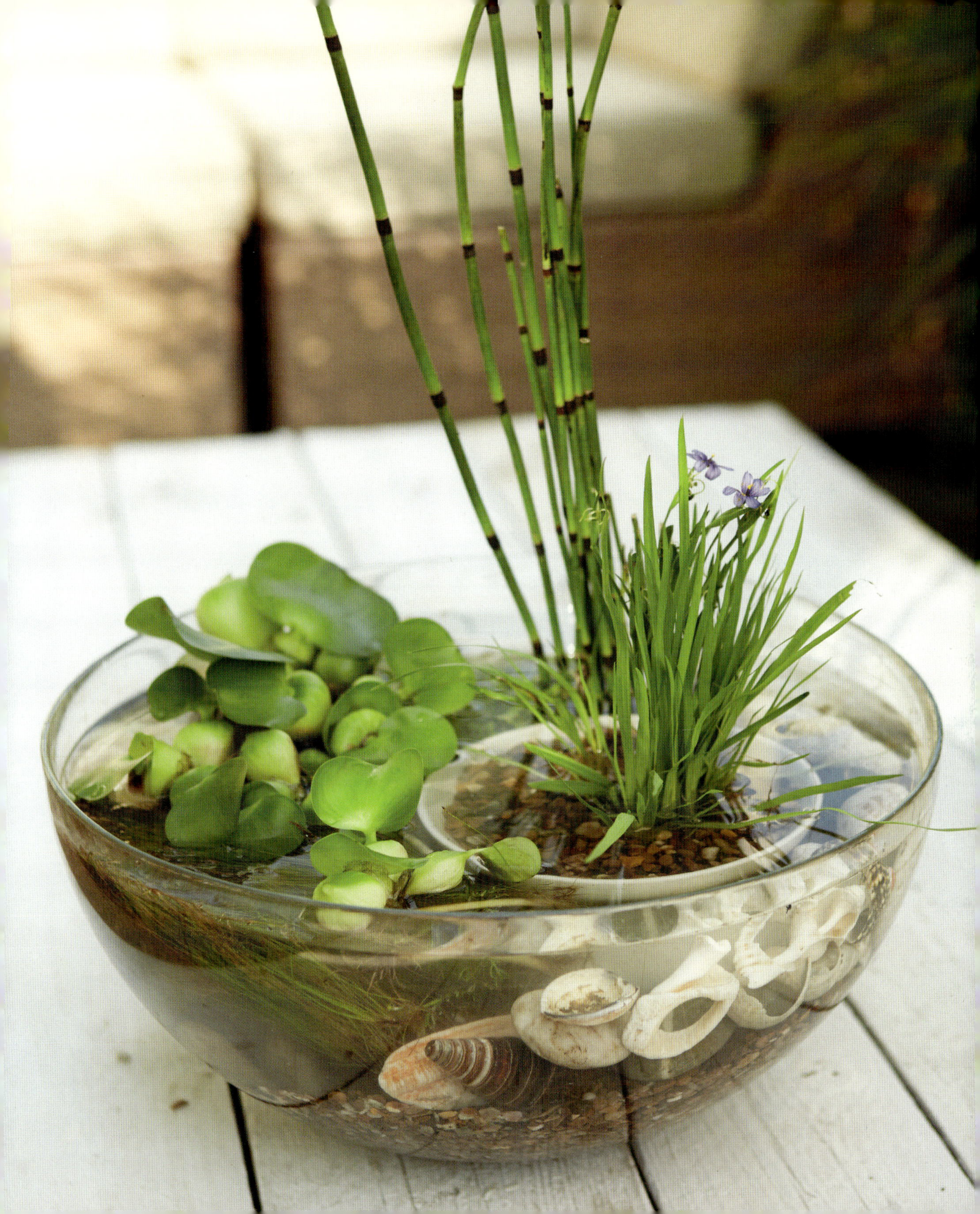

Project Steps

3 Keeping them separate, thoroughly wash the gravels to remove any mud on them that would dirty the water. Add one type of gravel to the large bowl. Build it up on one side to create a platform for marginal plants that don't sit in deep water.

4 Once you have your built-up area of gravel, use washed pebbles to help hold it in place and to separate the two areas in your container.

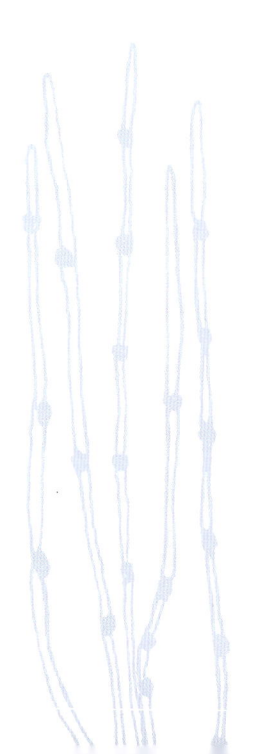

5 Position a smaller bowl or other container, also filled with gravel, on top of the built-up section of gravel to create the planting area for your marginal plants.

6 Add the second, contrasting gravel to your large bowl on the other side of the pebble divide.

Micro Garden

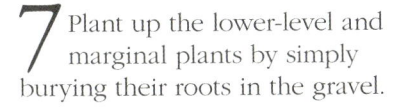

7 Plant up the lower-level and marginal plants by simply burying their roots in the gravel.

8 Fill the container with rainwater or distilled water; it will look cloudy at first, but will turn clear as the particles settle. Drop the floating plants into the water and decorate with more pebbles and shells until you are happy with the finished result.

Care Advice

Where to site Place the water garden where it will receive 4–6 hours of sunlight a day, but do not put it in direct sunlight as this may turn the water green. You can keep the water garden outside but position it in a sheltered spot.

Feeding and general care Use a slow-release aquatic fertilizer capsule placed directly under the plant in early spring or at planting. Liquid fertilizers tend to discolour the water. Do not feed in autumn and winter when plants are dormant. Remove leaf litter or other debris, pull off any dead roots from floating water plants, and keep the water levels topped up. Try adding activated carbon granules occasionally, which remove impurities to keep the water clear and sweet smelling.

Occasionally, the water may turn green or brown from foliage decay. When this happens, empty the water out and refill as quickly as possible with rainwater or distilled water.

Kids' Miniature
Farmyard Garden

From a tiny farmyard to a dinosaur landscape or a beach scene – let children get creative and enjoy gardening on a small scale. Use tiny plants and rooted cuttings for trees and bushes, or sow seeds that will grow into a crop for your farm.

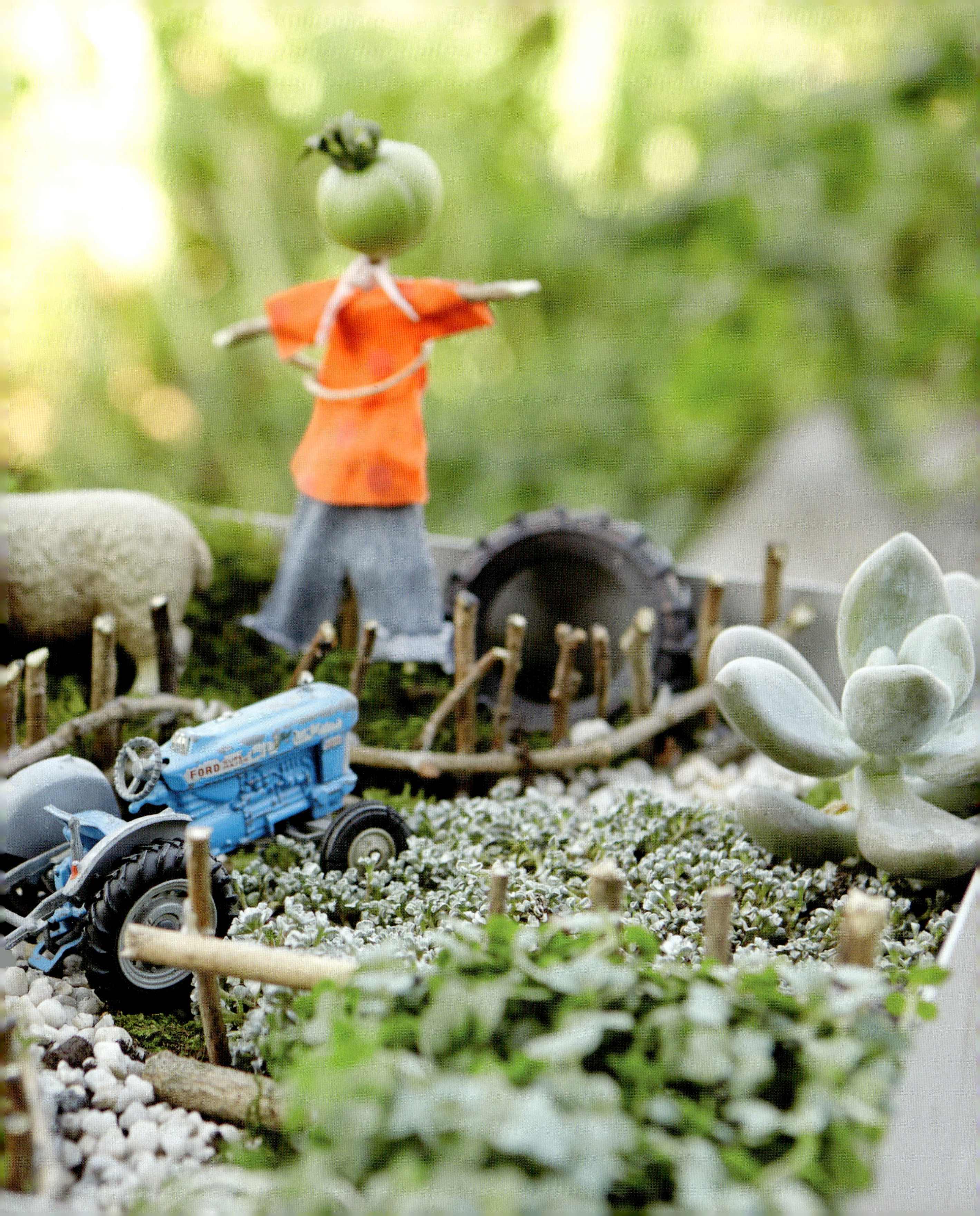
FORD

TOOLS & EQUIPMENT

high-sided loose-bottomed square cake tin

gravel

general-purpose potting mix

small glass or plastic container, for the pond

blue glass pebbles

small twigs & sticks

scissors

glue gun or multi-purpose glue

small aquarium gravel

scraps of material

unripe cherry tomato

selection of small farmyard toys & animals

PLANT LIST

carpet moss

cress

Sedum species

Thymus creeping species

selection of small foliage plants and succulent cuttings

Project Steps

1 A cake tin with a loose bottom is perfect for drainage, but add drainage holes if using a different container. Cover the base with a layer of gravel for extra drainage.

2 Add a layer of potting mix over the gravel, gently tapping the container when all the mix is in to disperse any air and allow it to settle evenly. Create a mound for the hill and leave a gap of about 7cm (2¾in) from the top of the container to help with watering.

3 Make a space in the potting mix and add the container you are using for the pond.

4 Add blue glass pebbles to the bowl to create your "water".

5 Make a fence by cutting twigs to similar sizes for the uprights, with longer pieces for the crossbars, and glue it all together; a glue gun is useful for this but not essential.

6 Start to lay out your landscaping features, such as the fence, and add pathways made from small aquarium gravel, before you start adding plants.

7 Use carpet moss as your "grass" and start to cover hills and fields, leaving spaces for plants.

8 To make a scarecrow, use a twig for the body, glue two twigs at one end for the legs, then glue another twig horizontally to make the arms. Lay the scarecrow on scraps of material and cut around it to make the clothes. Cut out two identical shapes for each item, dab with glue around the edges and stick together. Pop a green tomato on top of the stick for the head.

9 Add plants in scale with your other decorations to act as trees, shrubs, and crops. Finally, add your scarecrow and selection of small toys, and pour some water into the pond.

Care Advice

Watering Plants will need watering once or twice a week, more often in the summer, but do not overwater.

Feeding Add a liquid feed to the water monthly in spring and summer, but do not feed plants during their dormant season and water only sparingly. Place the farmyard on a tray to protect surfaces.

General care Depending on the plants used, you can keep your miniature farmyard outside during spring and summer, but bring inside or keep in a cool place during hot weather. Keep plants trimmed, aiming to maintain as natural a shape as possible. Some plants will eventually need to be moved to larger containers when they outgrow their space; simply replace them with smaller plants.

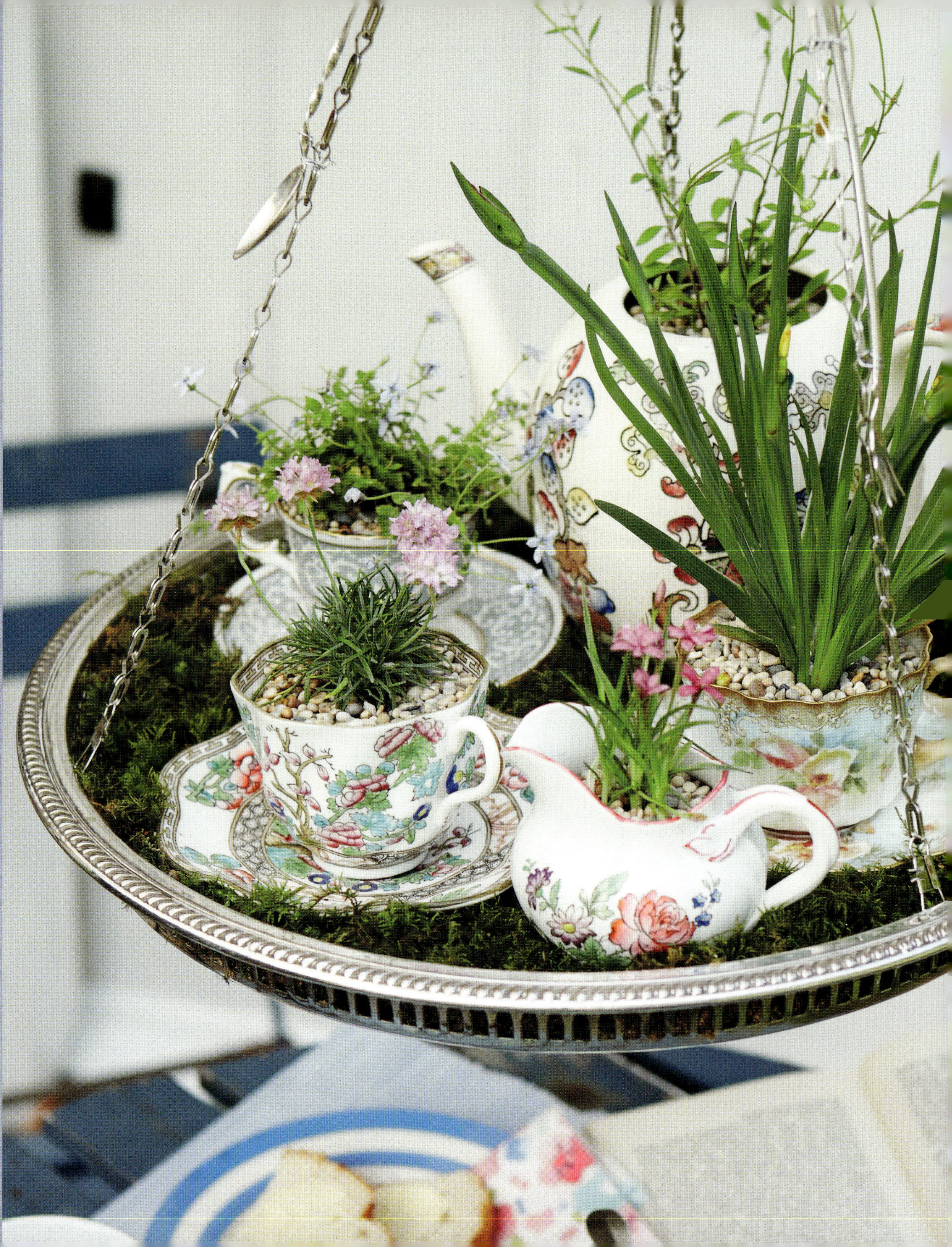

LET IT ALL HANG

Hanging Plant Pot Mobile

A stylish alternative to hanging baskets, this mobile is easy to make and can be personalized by painting the holders, pots, and even the rope. We have used architectural plants for a contemporary effect.

TIME IT RIGHT We've grown plants with interesting foliage that can be planted all year round, but it's best done in autumn or early spring. Try annuals, herbs, and small evergreen shrubs, too.

TOOLS & EQUIPMENT

- planks of wood
- handsaw
- 3 terracotta pots with lips, all the same size
- tape measure & pencil
- electric drill & drill bits
- fretsaw or jigsaw
- wood clamp
- exterior wood paint & paintbrush
- clear yacht varnish (optional)
- blackboard paint & white chalk
- crocks or gravel
- general-purpose potting mix
- watering can
- 4 lengths of strong but not too thick rope, each at least 2m (6ft 6in) long
- carabiner or other strong metal hoop
- strong metal hanging bracket, fixed securely to a wall
- heavy-duty scissors
- PVC tape

PLANT LIST

Eucalyptus gunnii
Festuca glauca 'Intense Blue'
Juncus spiralis (corkscrew rush)

1 Cut the planks into three equal squares, 3–4cm (1¼–1½in) larger than the circumference of your pots. Position a pot in the centre and draw round the top edge.

2 Draw another circle within this first circle to match the circumference under the lip of the pots, approximately 1.5cm (½in) inside the larger circle.

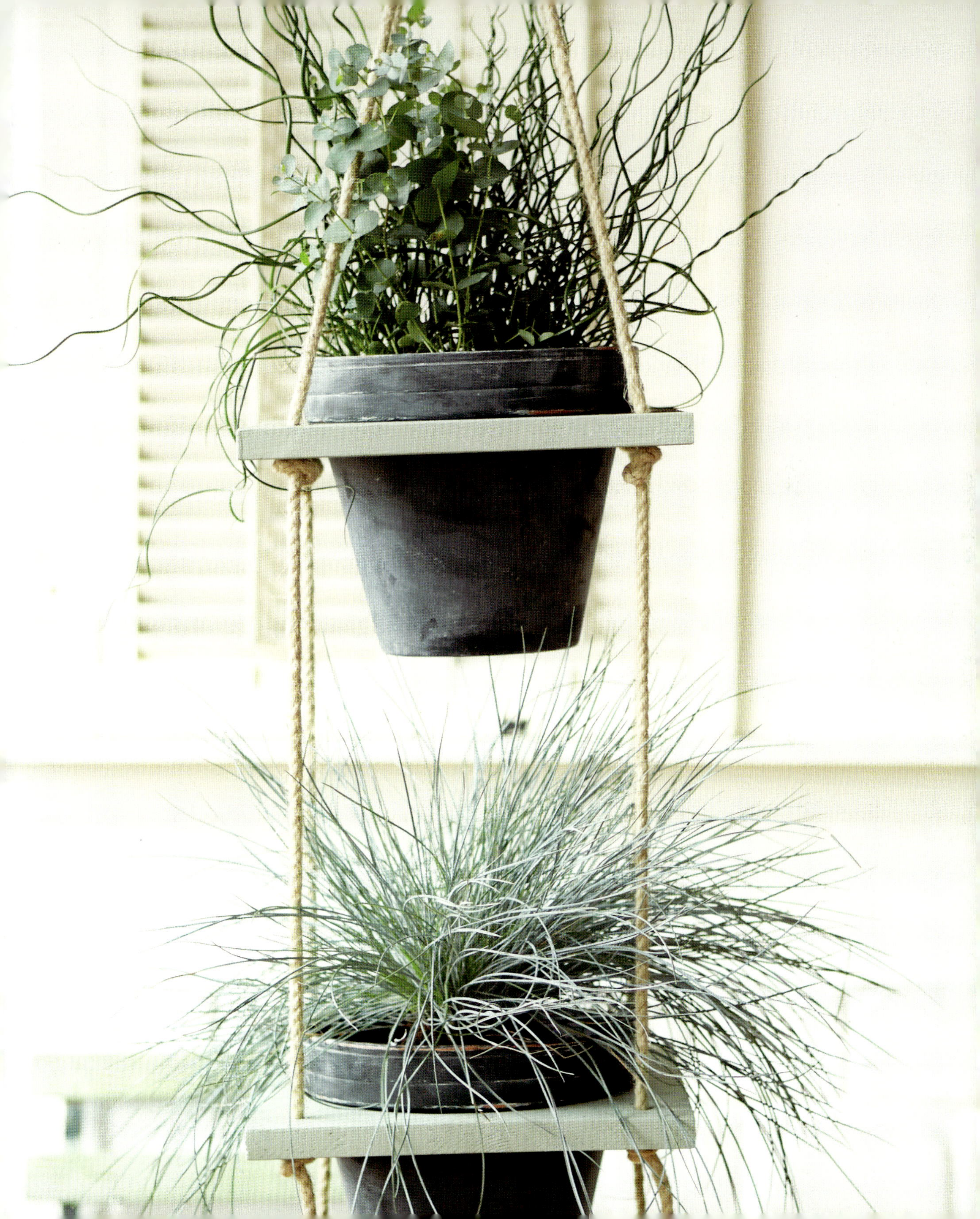

66 Let It All Hang

Project Steps

3 Drill holes slightly wider than your rope into the four corners of each wooden square.

4 Take a square and clamp it to a sturdy work surface to keep it steady. Drill a pilot hole at a point just inside the smaller circle, large enough to accommodate the fretsaw or jigsaw blade. Thread the blade through the hole and cut all the way round the inner circle. Repeat for the other squares.

5 Paint each pot holder with exterior wood paint and leave to dry. You can also add a coat of clear yacht varnish for extra protection. Paint your pots at the same time; we used blackboard paint and chalk (see page 194).

6 Before planting up your pots, first add a layer of crocks or gravel for drainage, and then fill about halfway with potting mix.

7 Remove plants from their pots and tease out the roots if they are encircling a little. Place in the pots. Fill around with potting mix and firm in. Water thoroughly.

8 Gather together the four ends of your rope, form a long loop, and then tie this off with a strong knot to leave a 10cm (4in) loop at the top. Attach to the carabiner or metal hoop and hook this onto the bracket where you will be hanging the mobile. A sheltered, part-shade position is ideal for the plants.

9 Take a pot holder and insert the rope ends through the corner holes, feeding through until the holder is roughly where you want the top plant. Tie knots in each rope under the holder to keep it in position. Place the plant in the hole. Adjust the rope knots until level. Repeat with the remaining holders. Cut the rope ends and wrap with PVC tape for a neat finish.

Care Advice

Watering and feeding Water often in the growing season, especially if hot and dry. Add diluted liquid feed monthly from mid-spring to early autumn. In winter, reduce watering and do not feed.

General care Remove damaged foliage throughout the growing period. The eucalyptus will need repotting into a larger container eventually. Do not cut back the grass or rush in spring.

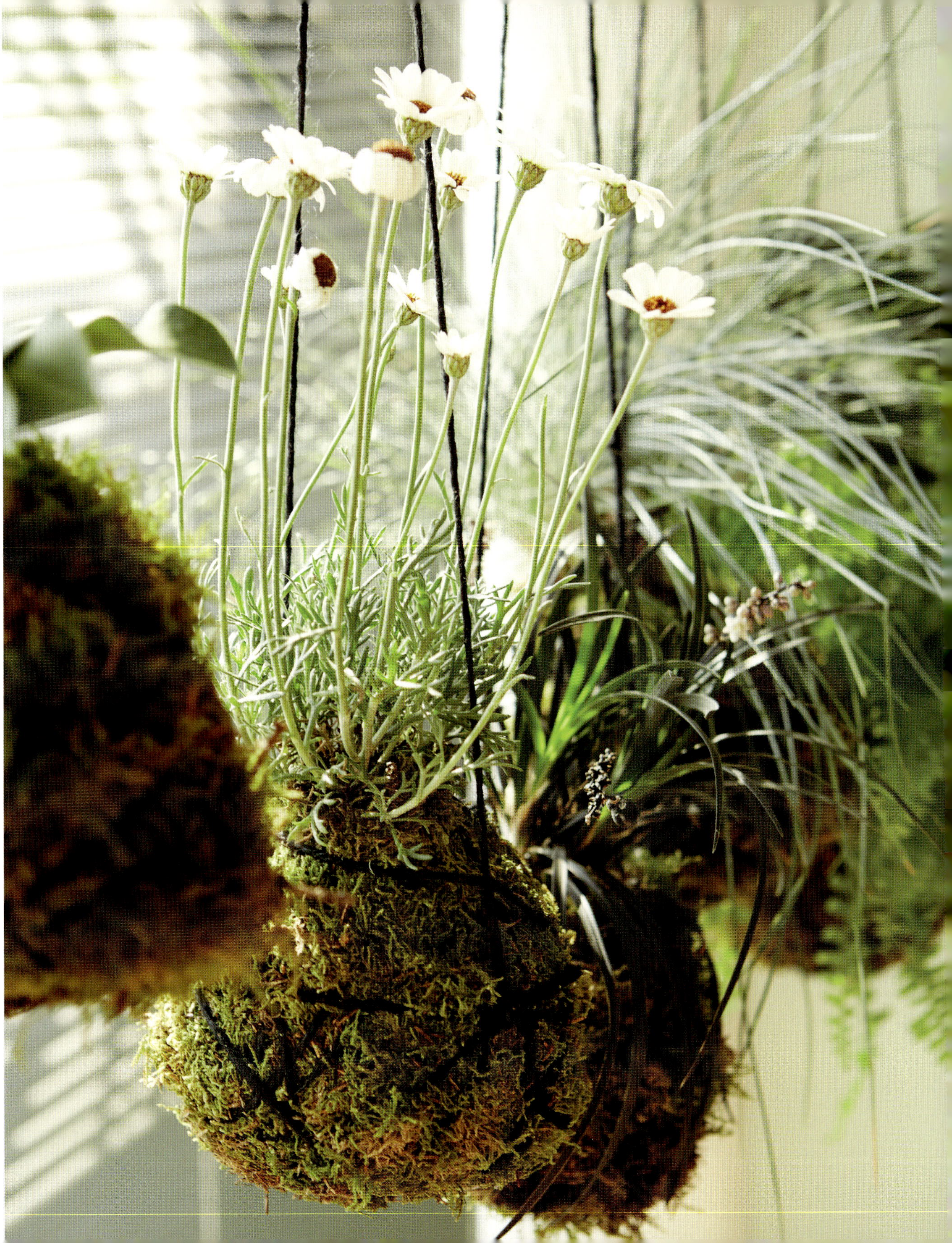

Kokedama
Hanging Garden

Meaning "moss" (koke) and "ball" (dama), kokedama is a Japanese art form that offers a whole new way of displaying indoor plants. It's intriguing, tranquil, and thoroughly enjoyable to make.

TIME IT RIGHT Plants should last 1–2 years and can be kept small by pruning. If roots start to show through, it's time to pot on. Almost any plants can be grown but remember some will die off or go dormant in winter, while evergreens provide year-round interest.

TOOLS & EQUIPMENT
- 2 large bowls
- general-purpose potting mix
- coarse sand
- jug of water
- water mister
- natural string or jute twine
- scissors
- secure hook

PLANT LIST
- carpet moss
- *Davallia* species
- *Erigeron karvinskianus*
- *Hosta* species
- *Miscanthus sinensis* 'Gold Bar'
- *Nephrolepis* species
- *Ophiopogon nigrescens*
- *Platycerium bifurcatum*
- *Rhodanthemum* 'African Eyes'
- sphagnum moss (if dried, soak for at least 1 hour first and squeeze out excess water before using)

1 Take plants out of their pots and remove as much soil as you can over a bowl without damaging the root systems. The aim is to keep the root ball as small as possible, though plants with fibrous roots (such as ferns) will need to retain some soil.

2 Taking a small amount of sphagnum moss, make a "moss wrap" by rolling the plant's roots in it. Set aside in a shady place and make the potting mix ball.

Project Steps

3 In a large bowl, mix together 70% potting mix with 30% coarse sand.

4 Now add water a little at a time and shape into a wet clay-like ball that holds together but is porous, and is large enough to take your plant's root ball.

5 Make a space in the centre of the ball with your thumbs to take the plant's moss-covered root ball. Insert the root ball and mould back into a ball or teardrop shape.

6 Start to cover the outside of the ball with carpet moss; both this and sphagnum moss are available from florists and florist suppliers. Dampen the moss with a water mister before using.

7 Take your string or twine and wrap it around the moss ball so that everything is held securely in place. Leave two long strands at either side, or one central strand, for hanging. Then simply hang your kokedama on a secure hook and enjoy.

Care Advice

Where to site Most indoor plants prefer to grow in bright but indirect light, although you can place the kokedama plants outdoors in mild weather. As the plants might drip a little after watering, be mindful not to hang them above anything that might be damaged by this. Make sure the place you choose to hang them has easy access for removal, watering, and care.

Watering and feeding You will need to water your kokedama plants regularly in the spring and summer growing season, and sparingly during autumn and winter. You can tell by the weight of the ball if it needs watering; if it feels light, then it does. Fill a bucket or bowl with water and immerse the ball to just below the base of the plant and let it soak for 3–5 minutes. Remove the ball and gently squeeze out the excess water, then leave to hang over a sink or bowl for any additional water to drain out. This method will be sufficient watering for several days, depending on air temperature. Add liquid fertilizer, such as seaweed extract, to the water during spring and summer, but do not feed in autumn and winter.

General care Keep the plants in shape by trimming and pruning, making sure you remove any trimmed foliage. Check that the binding string is secure and not rotting; replace with new string if necessary. Remove any dead, diseased, and dying foliage to keep the plant healthy. Repot any plant that is outgrowing the moss ball into a larger container, or plant outside in a border.

To water your kokedama plant, fill a bucket or bowl with water and fully immerse the moss ball for 3–5 minutes.

Remove the ball and gently squeeze out excess water, then leave it to drain over a sink or bowl before re-hanging.

Rhodanthemum 'African Eyes'

Ophiopogon nigrescens

Nephrolepis exaltata

Erigeron karvinskianus

Miscanthus sinensis 'Gold Bar'

Platycerium bifurcatum

Davallia humata tyermanii 'Bunny'

Hosta 'Blue Mouse Ears'

Saddle Bag
Balcony Planters

Just got a balcony as your garden space? These no-sew, easy-to-make saddle bag planters will give you lots of planting space for flowers, herbs, and edibles, and they look stylish and colourful, too.

TIME IT RIGHT We used a selection of herbs and flowers that can be planted in early spring and summer. Add spring bulbs for colour and small evergreen shrubs for year-round interest.

TOOLS & EQUIPMENT
- plastic-coated cloth
- tape measure
- metal rivet kit for fabrics, with post long enough to penetrate several layers of the oilcloth
- hammer
- plastic-coated motifs in attractive designs (we cut motifs from a woven carrier bag) (optional)
- scissors
- waterproof PVA glue or superglue, jar, & paintbrush (optional)
- hanging-basket liner, cut from a roll
- water-retaining gel
- general-purpose potting mix
- watering can

PLANT LIST
- Busy lizzie
- English lavender
- French lavender
- *Nemesia denticulata* 'Confetti'
- *Pelargonium* dwarf species
- rosemary
- sage 'Tricolor'
- strawberry 'Elan'
- *Viola* 'Blue Beacon'

1 Use a piece of plastic-coated cloth measuring 100 x 120cm (3ft 3¼in x 3ft 11in) and fold in half neatly along the shorter edge with the pattern on the outside.

2 Fold in one of the short ends by 2cm (¾in) and repeat twice more to create a seam.

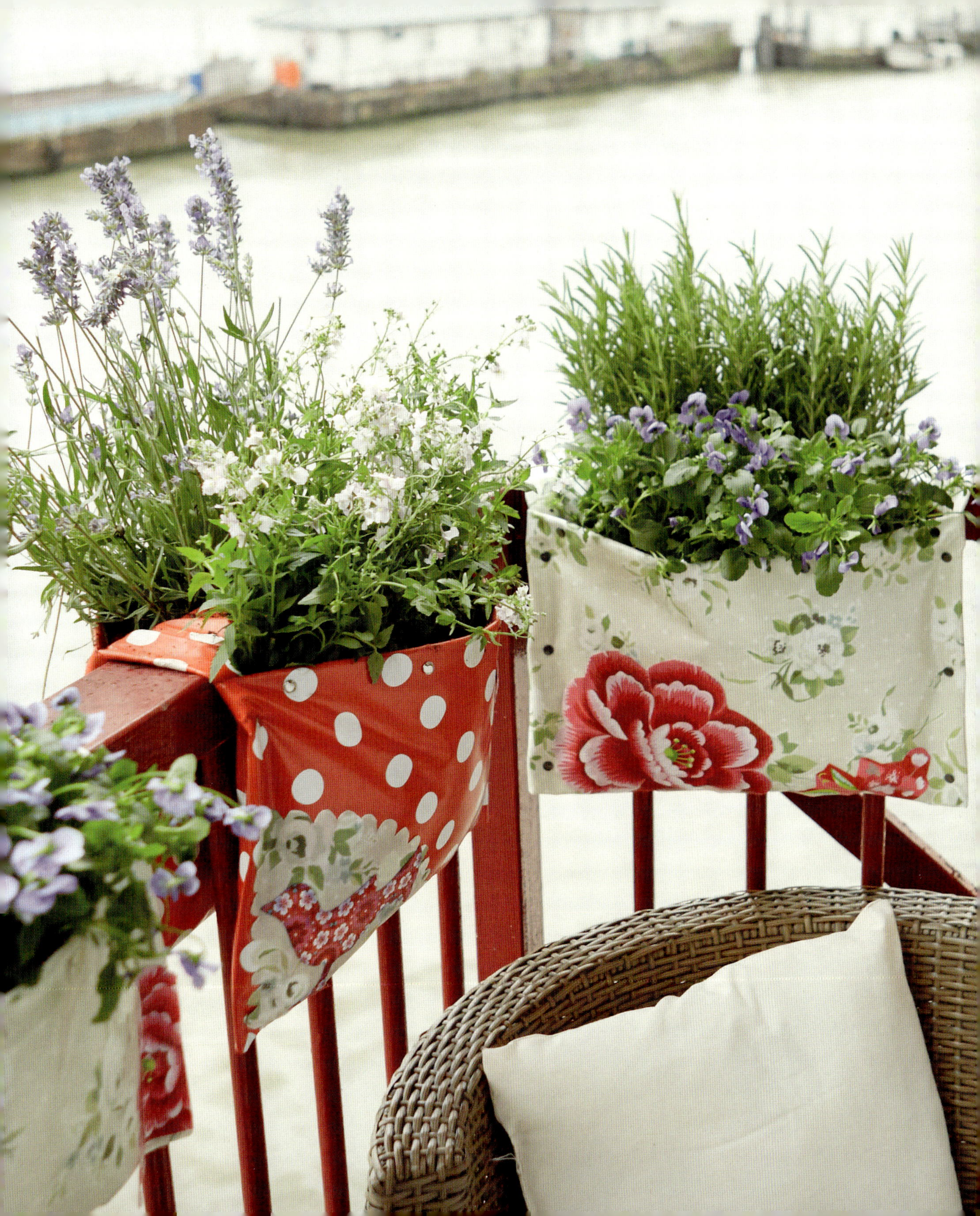

Project Steps

3 Rivet the seam in place, starting 10cm (4in) in from the edge. To make a rivet hole in the cloth, place the plastic disc underneath and hammer the recessed end of the hole punch through the cloth.

4 Push the rivet post through the hole from underneath and tap the cap in place with the hammer. Add three more evenly spaced rivets to the seam, finishing 10cm (4in) in from the other side. Repeat steps 2–4 at the opposite short end.

5 Fold in the riveted ends, leaving enough material in the middle to allow for the width of your balustrade, so the bags can hang comfortably with the tops of the pockets just below the balustrade.

6 Flip the cloth over. Fold in a long side twice, including the pocket flaps, to make a 3cm (1¼in) seam. Weight the seam down to hold it as you rivet it in place.

7 Repeat with the other long side. Flip the cloth back over and you have made your saddle bag planters. Repeat to make as many as you need.

8 For extra ornamentation, you can cut out some motifs from attractive reusable shopping bags to add to the saddle bags.

Let It All Hang **77**

9 Glue the designs on to the saddle bags with a waterproof PVA glue or superglue and then leave to dry.

10 Take a length of hanging-basket liner and line each of the planting pockets, cutting the liner to size with scissors. The liner should sit just below the lip of the pocket. This will help keep the potting mix moist in the pockets. To conserve moisture further, add 5g (¼oz) of water-retaining gel to every 5 litres (1 gallon) of potting mix.

11 Hang the bags in their final positions. Remove plants from their pots, tease out any circling roots, then position them in the pockets. Fill around with potting mix and firm in. Water thoroughly.

Care Advice

Watering Containers above ground level are more exposed and plants tend to dry out more easily, so water often in the growing season, especially if hot and sunny, and while plants are establishing.

Feeding Add diluted liquid feed to the water once or twice a month in the main growing season. You can also mist plants in hot weather, but not when in direct hot sunlight as the leaves might scorch.

General care Remove any damaged, diseased, or dying foliage throughout the growing period. Some plants are not frost hardy and will die back if left outside in winter. Reduce watering to a minimum in winter and top up or change the potting mix in spring.

Balconies can be blooming with these easy, pretty, and practical saddle bag planters

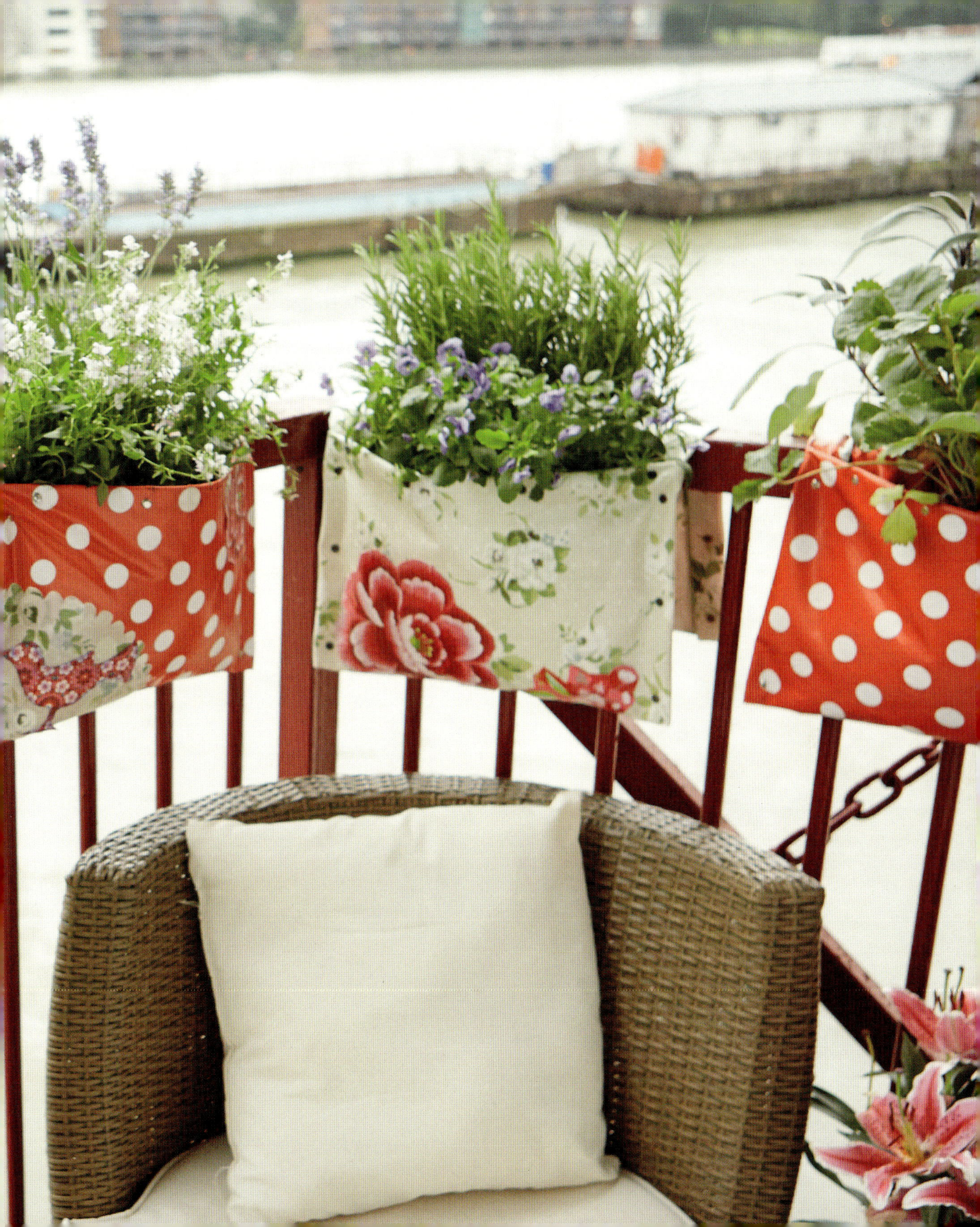

Edible
Planted Wall

A wall in a porch, verandah, balcony, or walkway needn't be left bare of plants. Think vertically and hang a carpet of pretty plants up the wall, all growing in their own special, individual pockets.

TIME IT RIGHT We've grown a mix of herbs, soft fruit, and ornamental plants with edible flowers that can be planted in early spring to allow them to mature for summer and autumn interest.

TOOLS & EQUIPMENT

- pack of fabric pocket planters (our wall required 6 panels)
- cable ties
- strong bamboo cane or wooden pole
- handsaw or lopper
- exterior wood paint & paintbrush
- strong garden wire
- wire cutters
- strong metal hanging brackets, fixed securely to a wall
- general-purpose potting mix
- water-retaining gel
- watering can

PLANT LIST

- alpine strawberry
- *Campanula* prostrate variety
- garlic chives
- golden oregano
- lemon thyme
- rosemary
- sage 'Tricolor'
- *Viola* 'Johnny Jump-up'
- *Viola* prostrate variety
- wild oregano

1 Take two panels of fabric pocket planters and overlap them along one of their long edges.

2 To join them together, align the top set of metal eyes and thread the end of a cable tie through them. Tie it off at the back for a neater finish. Tie securely but not too tightly or you risk bunching up the fabric.

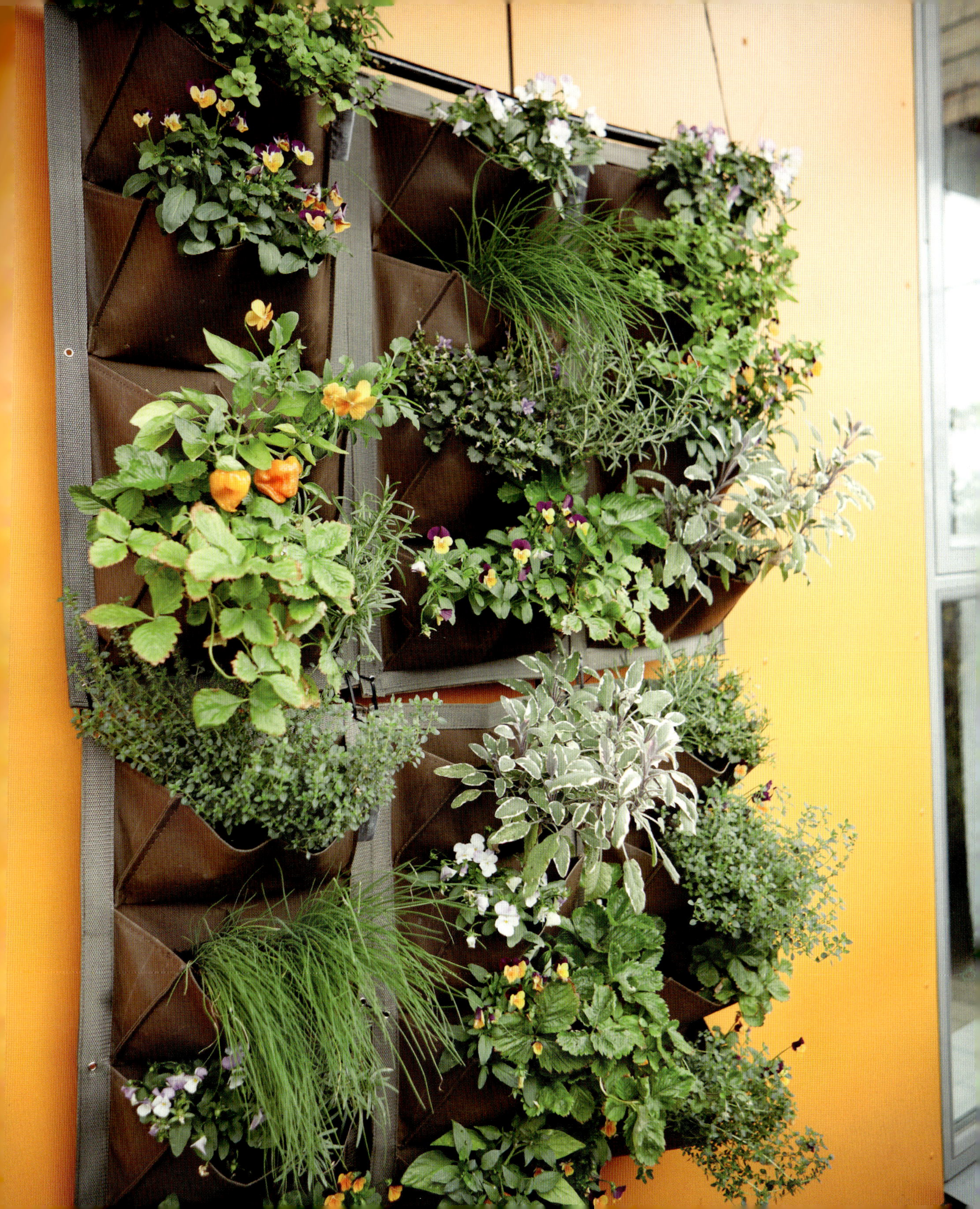

Project Steps

3 Repeat with the middle eyes, but leave the bottom eyes free for now; you will need to overlap the second row of panels before tying off. Build up the panels until you have a "wall" the size you want.

4 Cut a sturdy bamboo cane or wooden pole to size with a handsaw or lopper and paint it in a matching colour using exterior wood paint. Leave to dry, then attach the pole to the top of the planting wall with cable ties threaded through the free eyes along the top row of the panels.

5 Loop strong garden wire several times around the pole at either side of the hanging wall, leaving long lengths of wire at each end. Tie these ends securely to sturdy brackets and hang the planting wall in a sunny but sheltered spot shaded from hot afternoon sun.

6 The soil in the pockets can quickly dry out, so to help conserve moisture add 5g (¼oz) of water-retaining gel to every 5 litres (1 gallon) of potting mix.

7 Remove each plant from its pot, gently teasing out the roots if they are circling. Insert into a pocket; you may need to reduce the root ball by removing some of the earth for it to fit. Fill around with potting mix and firm in. Water well.

Let It All Hang **83**

Care Advice

Watering Water often during the growing season, especially if hot and sunny and while plants are establishing. Use a watering can with a long spout to get water directly into each pouch, but do not overwater so that soil spills out. Mist for extra moisture, but not when in direct hot sunlight as the leaves might scorch.

Feeding Add diluted liquid feed to the water monthly in the growing season and also mist with the mixture, avoiding any scorching sun.

General care Remove damaged foliage in the growing period. Some plants will need to be planted into larger containers eventually. Reduce watering in winter to minimal. Top up or change the potting mix in spring.

Deadhead flowering plants regularly to encourage production of more flowers.

Our edible plants include fragrant herbs, alpine strawberries, and tiny viola flowers. They make a living tapestry to adorn walls and vertical spaces.

TOOLS & EQUIPMENT

- 2 coir-lined hanging baskets
- plastic bucket
- small bag of vermiculite or perlite
- wooden board or sheet of stiff cardboard
- garden wire
- wire cutters
- long-handled screwdriver
- chopstick, dibber, or pencil
- hairpins or florist mossing pins
- heavy-duty chain & swivel hook

PLANT LIST

about 100 cuttings or offsets from 10–15 succulent plants, choosing a mix of shape and colour from the following genera:
- *Echeveria*
- *Graptopetalum*
- x *Graptoveria*
- *Sedum*
- *Sempervivum*

sphagnum moss

Hanging Ball of Succulents

Why just hang a basket when you can hang a living ball of contemporary art? Stylish and undemanding, succulents are perfect if you want a high-impact display, but don't have much time for plant care.

TIME IT RIGHT Plants will start to root quickly, but it will take 4–6 months for the ball to fill out completely. A smaller ball will take less time. Do not plant in winter when succulents become dormant.

Project Steps

1 Gather your materials and find a firm, level surface to work on. Remove the metal chains from the hanging baskets and set them aside as they are not required for this project. Position one of the wire baskets in a plastic bucket just big enough to hold it.

2 If using dried sphagnum moss, soak it in water for at least an hour before using. Remove from the water and squeeze out any excess, then pack a layer of moss at least 5cm (2in) thick into the base and sides of the basket.

3 Thoroughly wet the perlite or vermiculite then fill the basket, packing it in tightly to just below the top of the moss. The vermiculite provides a lightweight filling for the ball; the plants will root into the moss as they grow.

Project Steps

Succulents are plants that store water in their fleshy leaves and naturally thrive in dry climates

4 Cover the top of the vermiculite with another thick layer of moss. Pack it in well and then set aside the first basket. Repeat the process with the second basket. Place a wooden board (or sheet of stiff cardboard) over the first basket and carefully flip it upside down, then place it over the second basket and align the sides. Working quickly but carefully, pull the board out from between the two baskets.

5 Firmly tie together the baskets by cutting a length of flexible garden wire using wire cutters and threading it round the two edges. Secure with several tight knots.

Echeveria 'Topsy Turvy'

Graptopetalum 'Paraguayense'

Sempervivum 'Pippin'

Echeveria shaviana

Sedeveria 'Letizia'

Sedum commixtum

Echeveria elegans

x Graptoveria 'Fred Ives'

Sedum morganianum

Sempervivum 'Kelly Jo'

6 Cuttings of little plants called offsets, which grow from the main plant, are used. You need to make the stem as long as you can on the offset, then pare the end to a point. Ideally, take cuttings two days in advance to allow the cut ends to dry a little before planting as this helps with rooting. Twist together a length of garden wire around any short stems.

Project Steps

PLANTING TIPS

Adding twisted wire "tails" to cuttings with short or floppy stems will help to anchor them. A chopstick or dibber is perfect for teasing the stems into the planting holes. Fix any loose cuttings in place with hairpins or mossing pins.

7 Plant up the top half of the ball first. Make planting holes by inserting the end of a long-handled screwdriver. Position the holes roughly 5cm (2in) apart. Leave the ball for 10 days in a bright position to allow the cuttings to set roots; if you try planting both sides at once the cuttings will fall out when you turn it over.

8 When ready to plant up the second half, first immerse the whole ball in water for a minute and let it drip. Then, with the bare side uppermost for planting, attach a heavy-duty metal chain at the top centre of the basket. Fix a swivel hook to the other end of the chain so the ball can rotate. Hang in a secure place and finish planting.

Let It All Hang **89**

Care Advice

Where to site Succulents don't like a lot of humidity. They are happy outside if sheltered from rain, but they can't withstand very hot sun or prolonged wet conditions. Ideally, keep your hanging succulent ball in a bright sheltered position either inside, on a balcony or sheltered porch, or hanging from a tree in the garden. Remember, do not water the hanging ball during winter dormancy as this could cause the succulents to rot.

Watering Give the ball a thorough soaking in the growing season by immersing in a bucket of water for no longer than 20 minutes, then allow to drain before rehanging. Start with one immersion in September, then repeat monthly until the end of November and fortnightly in summer. Take care not to overwater. Immerse monthly again from March, but not from May to September as the plants are then dormant.

Feeding Apply a diluted feed to the plants by adding liquid fertilizer (such as seaweed extract) to the water when you immerse the ball. Measure how much water your bucket will hold and check the manufacturer's instructions on the liquid feed label to ensure the correct dilution. Only feed during spring and summer and at the same time as watering. Do not feed in autumn and winter.

General care Trim or prune plants to keep the ball neat and maintain its shape. Plants may need pruning as they start to produce offsets and outgrow their position. Snip off any excess plant material and use as cuttings, potting them into free-draining gritty potting mix after allowing two days for them to dry out. Trim any spent flowering stalks back to the plant base and remove any dead material before winter as this could attract disease if left.

Immerse your succulent ball completely in a bucket of water with added liquid feed. Leave to drain afterwards.

Snip off spent flower heads and remove overgrown plants. Tweezers are excellent for picking off dead leaves.

Vintage Teatime Alpine Planter

Enjoy traditional "afternoon tea" in the garden with this delicate tray and vintage tea set filled with dainty alpine plants. This fun project is quick and easy to make and brings a welcoming touch to your home.

TOOLS & EQUIPMENT

- old metal tray
- plastic pond liner & scissors
- strong outdoor adhesive & paintbrush
- vintage teacups, teapot, & milk jug
- masking tape
- electric drill & ceramic drill bit
- gravel & small scoop or spoon
- orchid potting mix
- horticultural grit
- water-absorbing crystals
- slow-release fertilizer granules
- strong galvanized chain
- wire cutters
- 3 small galvanized metal hooks
- large galvanized metal ring
- strong metal hanging bracket, fixed securely to a wall
- vintage cutlery (optional)
- silver florist wire or similar (optional)

PLANT LIST

- *Armeria* dwarf variety
- carpet moss
- *Erigeron karvinskianus*
- *Pratia peduncularis*
- *Rhodohypoxis deflexa*
- *Sisyrinchium* dwarf variety

TIME IT RIGHT Enjoy your tea set all year round with seasonal planting: alpine bulbs in spring and autumn; mossy alpines or dwarf ivy in winter. Add fairy lights at Christmas for a festive look.

1 Cut a piece of pond liner (or heavy-duty plastic sheeting) to fit the base of the tray. Glue into place with water-resistant adhesive.

2 Take your cups, teapot, and milk jug and make a cross with two pieces of masking tape over the centre area where you intend to drill a hole; this helps prevent the drill from slipping and creates a clean cut. Drill drainage holes in the base of the items using an electric drill with a ceramic tile drill bit.

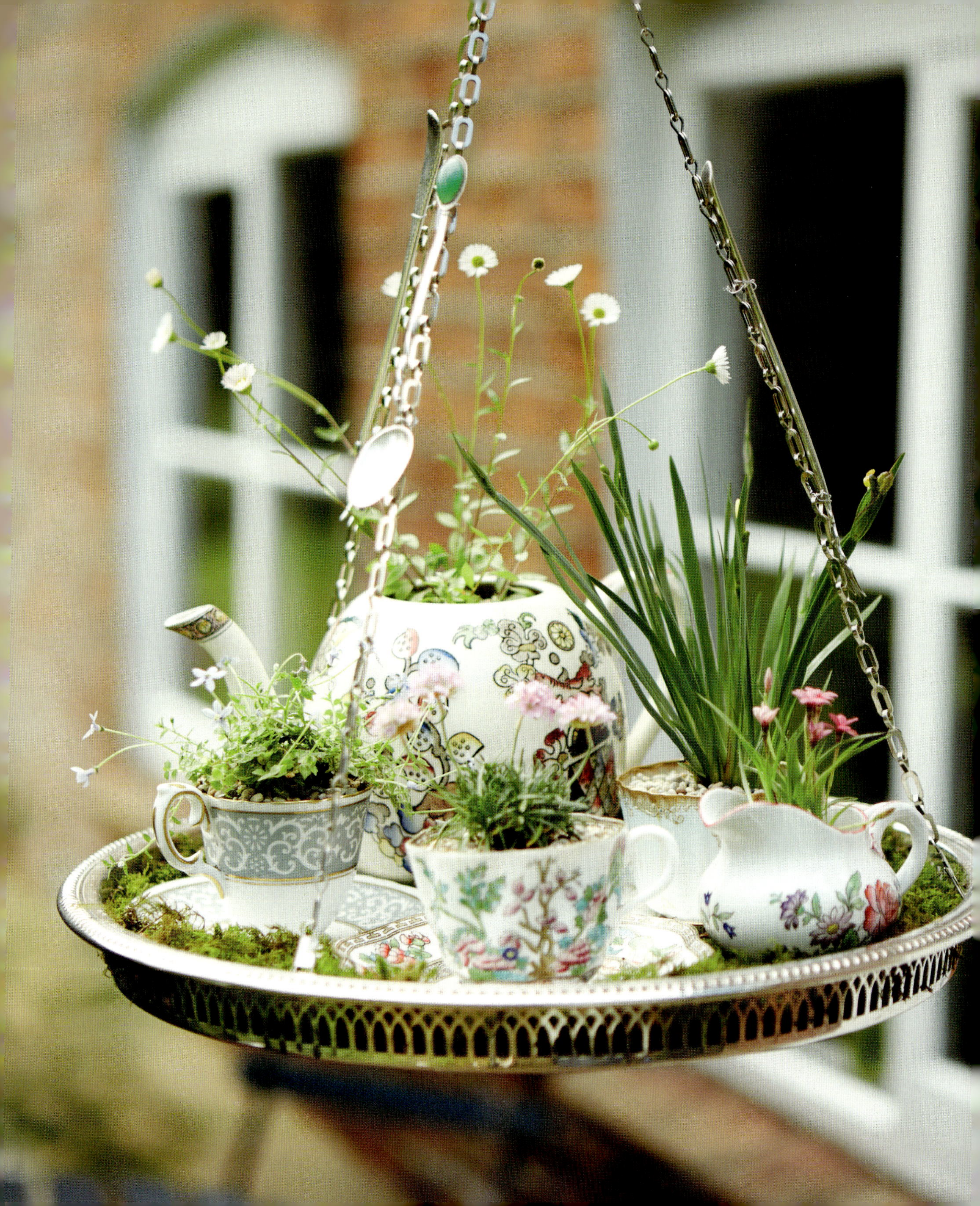

3 Select alpine plants to fit in the crockery. Look for different heights, leaf shapes, and flowers.

Project Steps

4 Create an attractive arrangement with your crockery on the lined tray and then glue the saucers in place and remove the cups, teapot, and jug for planting up.

5 Alpines need good drainage, so to plant up first fill the base of the crockery with a layer of gravel. Next, make a soil mix suitable for alpine plants by blending potting mix with horticultural grit at a ratio of 3:1. At the same time, mix in a small amount of water crystals and also slow-release fertilizer.

6 Add potting mix to your crockery until the plant sits at the right height. Fill around it with more mix, finishing with a layer of gravel. Water in using a fine rose.

Project Steps

7 Place the planted cups on saucers and the other items on the tray and glue in place; just dab glue on one or two spots on the bottom of the cups to leave space for water to drain into the saucers. Fill around the crockery with moss.

Care Advice

Where to site Alpines prefer a spot in morning sun and afternoon shade and, ideally for this arrangement, one that has shelter from wind. For occasional decoration, you can bring your teatime planter indoors, but keep it in a cool, light place.

Watering and feeding Alpines thrive in dry conditions in the natural world so don't overwater – just when needed from mid-spring to early autumn, with occasional watering at other times. Do not let plants sit in water for long periods of time as this could lead to rot. Alpines do not need a lot of feed so it is best to give a weak diluted liquid feed during the growing season. Do not feed when the plants are dormant.

General care Trim or prune plants with small scissors or secateurs to remove spent flower stalks and dead material. Plants will eventually outgrow their teacups so plant up into larger containers or plant out elsewhere in the garden.

8 To hang, cut three lengths of chain to the desired hanging height using wire cutters. Attach to hooks and then to the edge of the tray. Gather the chains and fix the free ends to a ring. Hang from a strong bracket. If you like, decorate the chains by attaching vintage pieces of cutlery with fine silver wire.

Succulents, such as the sempervivums shown top left and bottom right, also look pretty in teacups and require similar growing conditions and care.

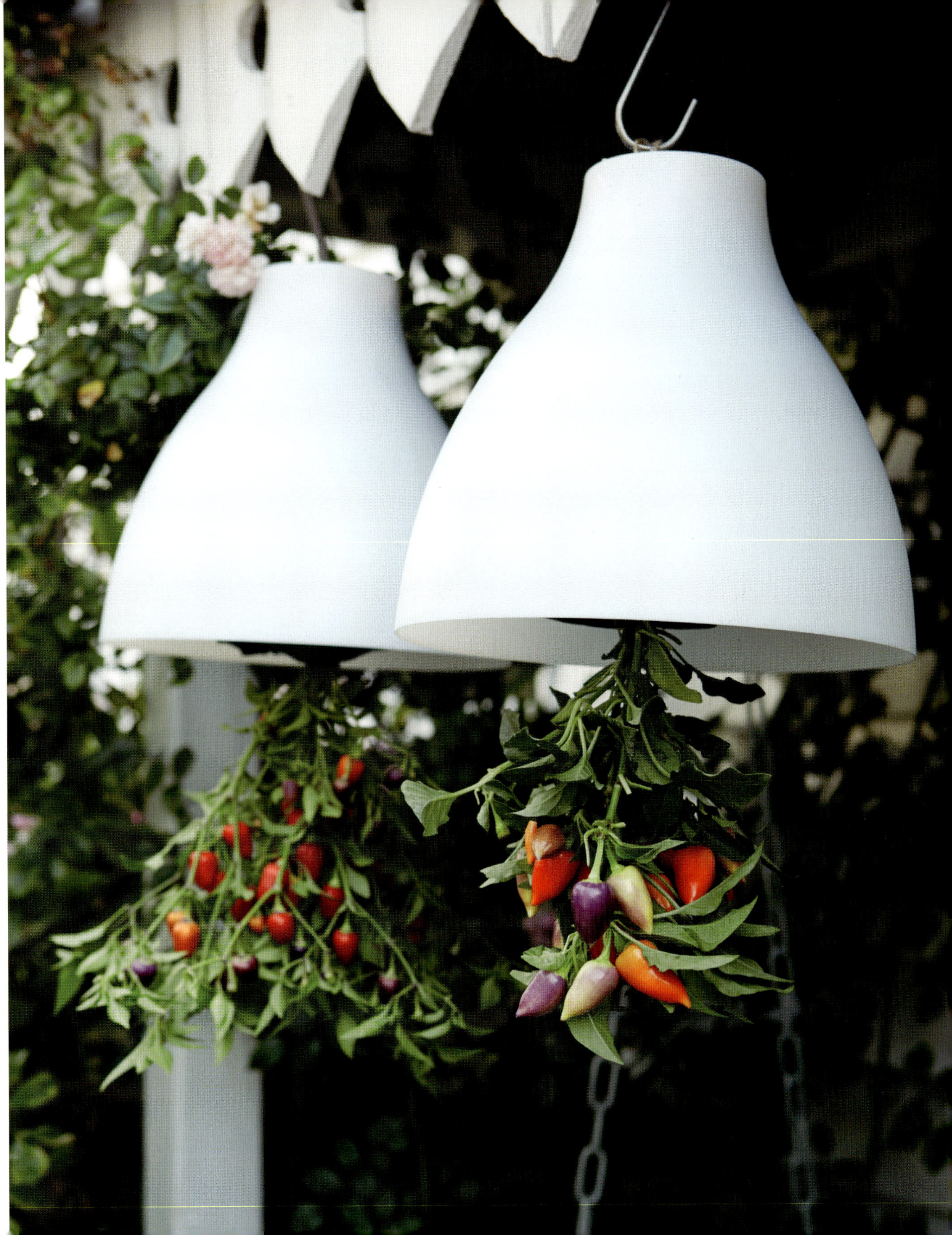

Upside-down Lampshade Chilli Planter

TOOLS & EQUIPMENT

- pendant lampshade in opaque plastic, large enough to fit a small plant bag – ours was 38cm (15in) in diameter and 180cm (71in) in height
- tape measure
- small hacksaw
- wooden dowel, 1.5cm (½in) in diameter
- electric drill & drill bits
- wood screws
- large metal cup hook
- small plant bag with handles
- scissors
- hanging-basket liner
- general-purpose potting mix
- slow-release fertilizer granules
- s-hook
- garden wire
- wire cutters

PLANT LIST

chilli, dwarf, and ornamental varieties

Turn your plants on their heads by growing them upside down in a lampshade. It may look quirky, but some vegetables thrive on this method, and it's ideal if you have limited space to grow things.

TIME IT RIGHT Young, small plants or seedlings are easier to plant up in early to mid-spring. Depending on what you're using, hang in a sheltered place until the cold, wintry weather has passed.

1 Measure the internal width of the top opening of the lampshade and, using a small hacksaw, cut a section of wooden dowel to fit this space.

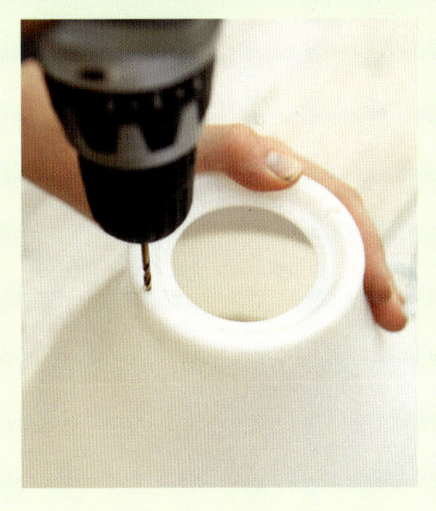

2 Match a drill bit to the size of your screws and drill two holes opposite each other through the lip of the top opening of the lampshade, near the outer edge.

Project Steps

3 Holding the section of dowel under the drilled holes and flush against the top opening, drill screws through the holes and firmly into the dowel.

4 Turn the lampshade over. Match a drill bit to the width of the cup hook and drill a shallow hole into the centre of the dowel, to help screw in the hook.

5 Take the plant bag and cut a small cross in the centre of the base, just large enough to fit the root ball of your plant.

6 Insert your plant through the cross. Carefully turn the bag over, resting it at the edge of the work surface so the plant hangs over the side.

7 If necessary, "sew" together the seams of the opening in the plant bag with garden wire to make the plant more secure. Cut a cross in the hanging-basket liner to match the one in the plant bag. Ease the liner over the root ball of the plant, making sure it fits snuggly around where the stem comes out of the opening. Trim the liner so it fits inside the bag.

Let It All Hang **99**

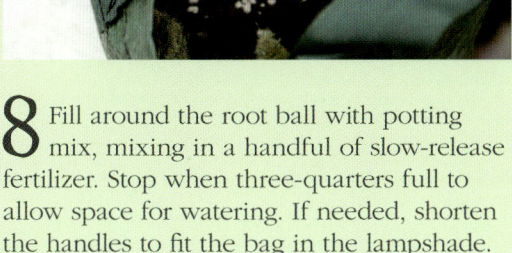

8 Fill around the root ball with potting mix, mixing in a handful of slow-release fertilizer. Stop when three-quarters full to allow space for watering. If needed, shorten the handles to fit the bag in the lampshade.

9 Lift the plant bag into the lampshade and hang it by the handles from the cup hook. Put an S-hook under the dowel, or fix it firmly with garden wire, and use the top of the S-hook to hang from a sturdy support.

Care Advice

Where to site Chillies need a good amount of sun to ripen, so place the lampshade planter in a sunny but sheltered place, where you can easily access the top for watering.

Watering and feeding Water frequently during the growing season and while the plant is establishing, especially if the weather is hot and sunny. Add some diluted liquid feed to the water once or twice a month in the main growing season. Watering is done through the open top of the lampshade directly into the plant bag, so use a watering can with a long spout. You can also mist the plants in hotter weather.

General care Remove damaged or dying foliage during the growing period. Chillies are not frost hardy and will die back if left outside in winter. You could try to overwinter your chilli plant in a light, frost-free place, or simply hang it inside by a sunny window. Reduce watering in winter and change potting mix in spring – your plant may start to grow new shoots!

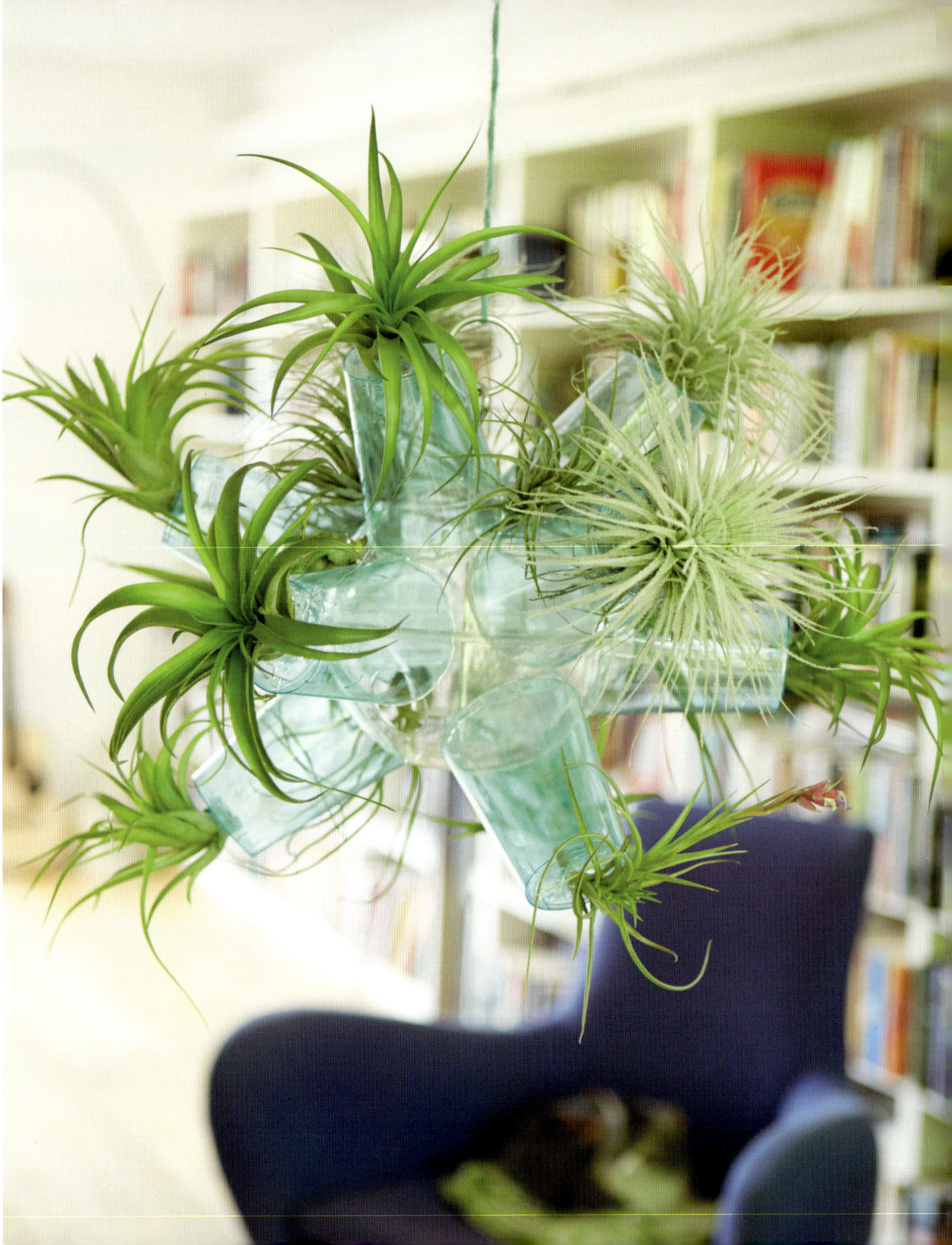

TOOLS & EQUIPMENT

clear strong plastic cups (ours were coloured turquoise)

soldering iron (optional)

clear-drying superglue

bird feeder globe with hanger, the two hemispheres superglued together and left to dry

air plant fixative (silicone rubber sealant)

masking tape

garden twine, ideally in a colour to match the cups

scissors

PLANT LIST

selection of small air plants – the spikier ones look good:
Tillandsia aeranthos
Tillandsia brachycaulos multiflora
Tillandsia ixioides
Tillandsia tectorum

Plastic Cup
Air Plant Chandelier

Versatile, fun, and quirky, air plants (a type of bromeliad) don't need any soil to grow in and as such are perfect for growing in unusual decorative features, like this stylish chandelier.

TIME IT RIGHT Plant up your chandelier at any time of the year if you are keeping it inside. Air plants aren't frost hardy, but you can hang it outside for summer, bringing it back indoors from mid-autumn.

1 We made holes in the base of the cups using a hot soldering iron, so that when "planted" the air plants seem to sprout from the ends. If you prefer not to do this, simply attach the plants straight to the cup base with silicone glue (see step 3).

2 Work out the best positions of the cups on the globe, so they cover the surface evenly and fit closely together. Apply superglue around the rim of each cup and press in place, holding them until bonded. Leave to dry completely.

Project Steps

3 Attach an air plant to the base of each cup using a silicone rubber sealant (other glues can harm plants). Apply sealant around the rim of the hole, if made, or apply a generous dab in the centre. Press the plants in place and avoid getting sealant on the stem end.

4 You can also stick further plants on to the globe in the spaces between the cups for a fuller effect. The sealant takes several hours to dry and you will need to hold each plant in place as it dries by sticking one or two leaves down with masking tape.

5 Once the sealant has dried completely and the air plants are secure, carefully remove the strips of masking tape. To hang the chandelier, cut a length of garden twine, thread it through the hook of the globe and tie it off with a secure knot.

Care Advice

Where to site Air plants like warmth but not direct sunlight so you can hang your chandelier outdoors in a bright, sheltered position. Bring inside or under a verandah during winter when the weather turns cold and frost is likely. Plants are fine in many areas of the house as long as light levels and air circulation are good, and they are kept moist (see below). Do not place them near heaters or other heat sources.

Watering and feeding Air plants absorb moisture through their leaves and generally need spraying 2–3 times a week, more frequently during summer or in dry conditions, and ideally with rainwater. Give plants a generous soak at least once a month by submerging the entire chandelier in room temperature water for a little while, making sure you shake off excess water afterwards. Feed with a diluted special air plant liquid fertilizer misted on leaves once a week in spring and summer, fortnightly in winter.

General care Remove any dead, diseased, or dying foliage throughout the year and be careful not to let any water sit in the base of the plant as this could cause it to rot. Plants will produce offsets, which can be removed when half the size of their mother plant and then used in other displays.

More Ideas for Air Plant Hangers

You can buy ceramic or clear glass aeriums and terrariums specifically designed for displaying air plants. Simply fill the base with a little sand or gravel for the air plant to sit in, or wire on or glue the plants in place with silicone rubber sealant.

Wicker balls also make effective hanging globes. Attach a long piece of florist wire to a plant, position it on one side of the ball, thread the wire through to the other side, pull gently, and tie off.

Hang aeriums and terrariums together in a group to create a tiny air plant world. Try adding florist's moss, shells, or bark to produce a miniature hanging landscape.

You could also fix plants to the ball with silicone sealant. Don't forget to keep your air plants regularly sprayed with water, and immerse the entire ball in water at least once a month.

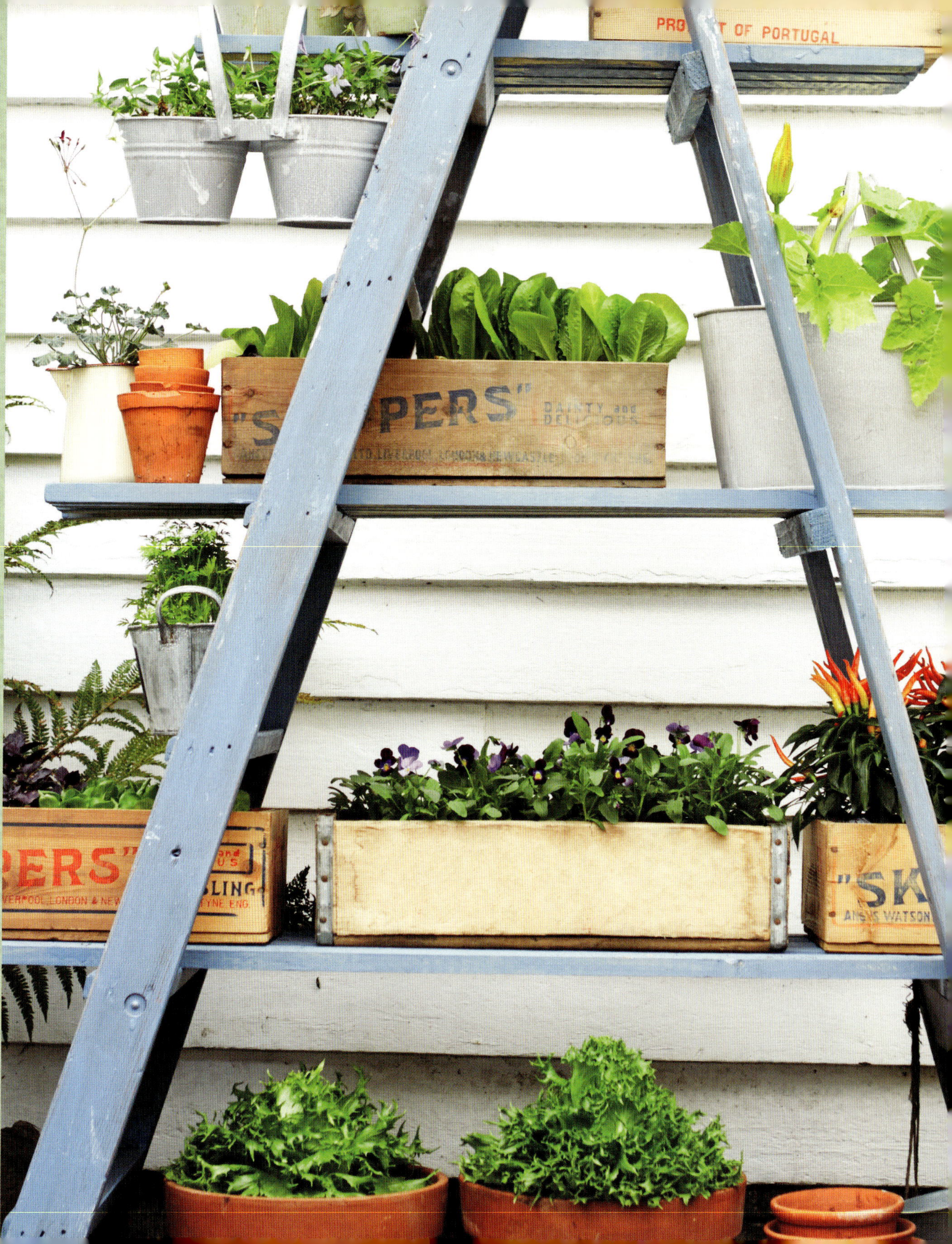
OF PORTUGAL
DAINTY and

GROW UP

Strawberry Picture Frame Planter

Bring life back to an old picture frame by creating planting pockets and filling them with strawberry plants. The "picture" changes as the plants grow, while flowers and fruit add extra interest and colour.

TOOLS & EQUIPMENT

- tape measure, pencil, & ruler
- handsaw
- marine plywood
- old picture frame
- electric drill & drill bits
- screws
- 6 heavy-duty metal hanging brackets
- PVA glue & water solution (mixed at a ratio of 1:10), jar, & paintbrush
- clear yacht varnish (optional)
- green garden wire
- water-retaining gel
- general-purpose potting mix
- 2 pairs of opaque tights
- scissors
- absorbent kitchen cloth
- cable ties
- hanging-basket liner, cut from a roll

PLANT LIST

- strawberry – small-leaf varieties look best

TIME IT RIGHT Create the planting pockets at any time of year, but late winter to early spring is best for planting up strawberries. Choose potted plants rather than bare-root plants for an instant effect.

1 Measure and cut a piece of marine plywood to fit the back of the picture frame. Screw in place, then screw brackets to the plywood at each corner and at the centre of the top and bottom edge.

2 Brush the PVA solution over the frame and plywood to help protect them from the elements. Leave to dry. You could also add a final coat of clear yacht varnish for extra protection.

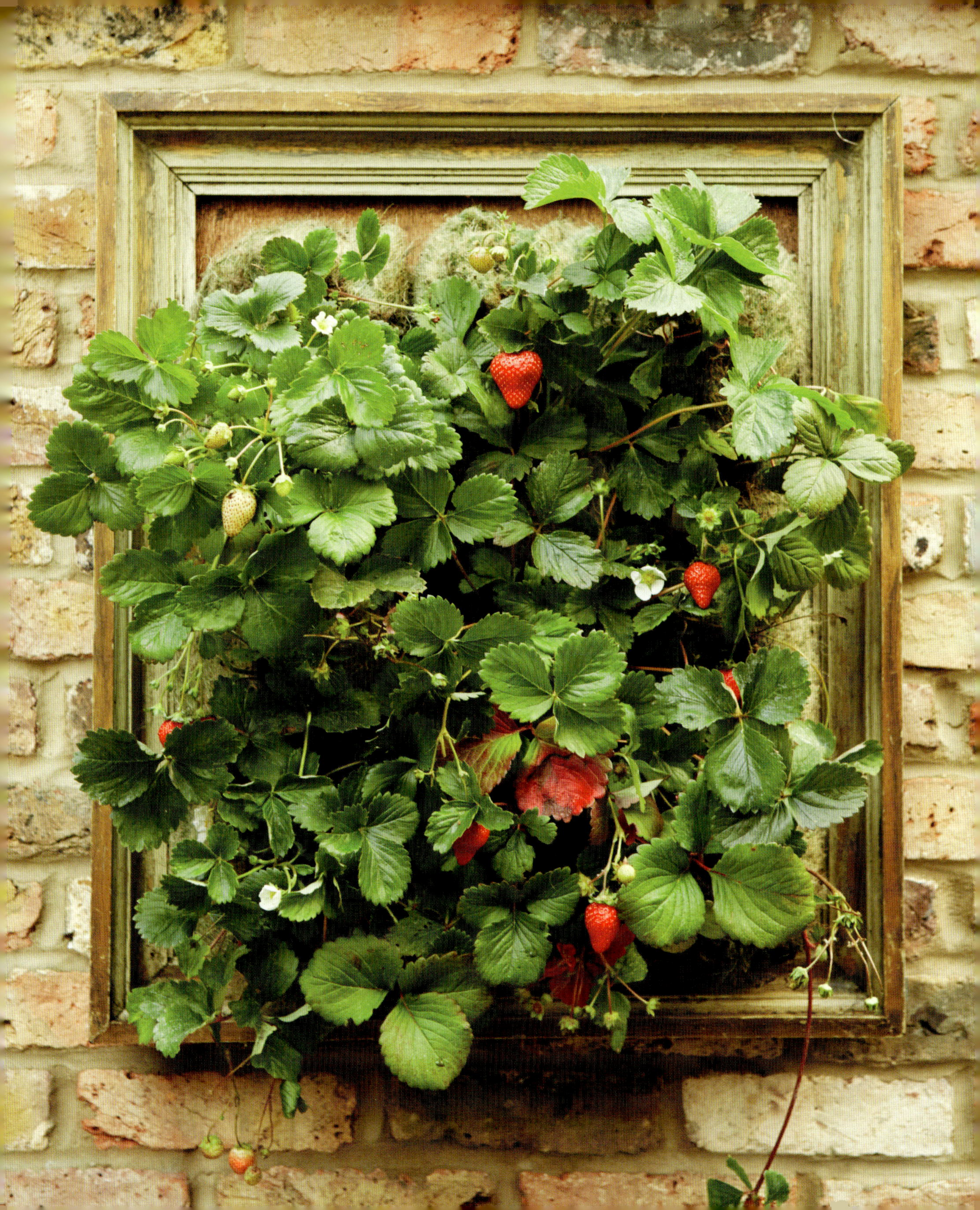

Project Steps

3 Mark on the plywood a straight vertical line of four crosses, evenly spaced along one of the long edges of the frame. The lowest cross should start just in from the bottom corner. Repeat at the opposite long edge and then twice more at equal intervals in between. You should have a grid of 16 crosses. Drill a hole, wide enough to hold two lengths of garden wire, at each cross.

PLANTING TIPS

Dainty alpine strawberries are a good choice if your frame is smaller. Alternative plants include tumbler-style tomatoes, trailing annuals, and herbs. Small-leaf ivy provides year-round greenery, and variegated forms add interest.

4 Add water-retaining gel to the potting mix at a ratio of 5g (¼oz) of gel to every 5 litres (1 gallon) of mix. Mix in thoroughly. This will help to hold moisture in the planting tube, but do not use more than necessary as it will push plants out of the mix.

5 Cut a pair of tights into separate legs and feed the potting mix into one of them until you have made a planting tube. The tube should be the same length as the inside long edge of the picture frame and should fit comfortably between the lines of holes drilled in the plywood.

6 Cut a piece of absorbent cloth 3–4cm (1¼–1½in) wide and the same length as the planting tube. Feed the cloth down what will be the back of the planting tube – this will act as a wick to help distribute the moisture.

7 Tie off the open end of the tube with a cable tie, then squeeze the potting mix to divide it into four equal sections. Tie off between sections with cable ties. This prevents soil from sinking down the tube.

8 Cut planting holes in the centre of each section with scissors and gently open them out a little with your fingers.

Project Steps

9 Cut a piece of hanging-basket liner large enough to wrap around the planting tube, allowing a little overlap on the side and a larger overlap at the bottom end.

10 Wrap the tube with the liner. Feel where the planting holes are and cut matching holes through the liner with scissors.

11 To attach the planting tube to the picture frame, thread lengths of garden wire over the tube and through the holes in the plywood on either side of it. Pull tight and tie off firmly at the back of the frame. The planting tubes are also held in place at the bottom, so make sure the bottom end of the hanging-basket liner is tucked underneath the tube and held firmly in place when tied to the frame. The top end of the tube is left open for watering.

12 Remove the strawberry plants from their pots and carefully pull off most of the soil attached to the root ball. Gently ease each plant into a planting hole and firm in around it.

13 "Stitch" planting holes with wire if too wide. Repeat steps 5–13 twice more to make three tubes. Water well while flat. Wait for excess water to drain. Attach the frame to your surface by screwing through the brackets.

Care Advice

Where to site Strawberries need a fair amount of sun for crops to ripen, so choose a sunny but sheltered spot.

Watering and feeding Water frequently in growing season and while plants are getting established. Add diluted liquid feed to the water once or twice a month. In winter, reduce watering and do not feed. Use a watering can with a long spout to water. You can also mist plants in hotter weather.

General care Remove damaged or dying foliage or fruits in the growing period. Cut back after fruiting and pot up any runners (see page 159). You may need to net the frame to protect fruit from birds.

Use a watering can with a long spout to get water directly into the soil at the top of each planting tube.

Succulents

Living Mirror Frame

Succulent plants are easy to look after and demand little attention. This stunning living wreath provides a glamorous frame to a mirror and creates impact wherever it is placed.

TIME IT RIGHT Plants will root quickly but it will take 3–5 months for the frame to fill out completely. Best started in mid-spring when plants come out of their winter dormancy and will be actively growing.

TOOLS & EQUIPMENT

compass & pencil
electric jigsaw
piece of MDF larger than the mirror
round mirror
exterior wood paint & paintbrushes
clear yacht varnish (optional)
shadecloth (preferably black)
craft knife
staplegun
chopstick, dibber, or pencil
hairpins or florist mossing pins
garden wire & wire cutters
strong outdoor adhesive
nails & sturdy brass picture hook
hammer

PLANT LIST

about 50 cuttings or offsets from a range of succulent plants, choosing a mix of shape and colour from the following genera:
Echeveria
Graptopetalum
Pachyphytum
Sedum
Sempervivum

sphagnum moss

1 Using a compass and pencil and a jigsaw, cut a piece of MDF to the shape of your mirror, allowing a 17cm (6¾in) border all round. Paint the MDF, leave to dry, then apply a coat of yacht varnish for added protection, if preferred. Once dry, draw around the mirror onto the MDF to create a guideline, but do not attach it at this stage.

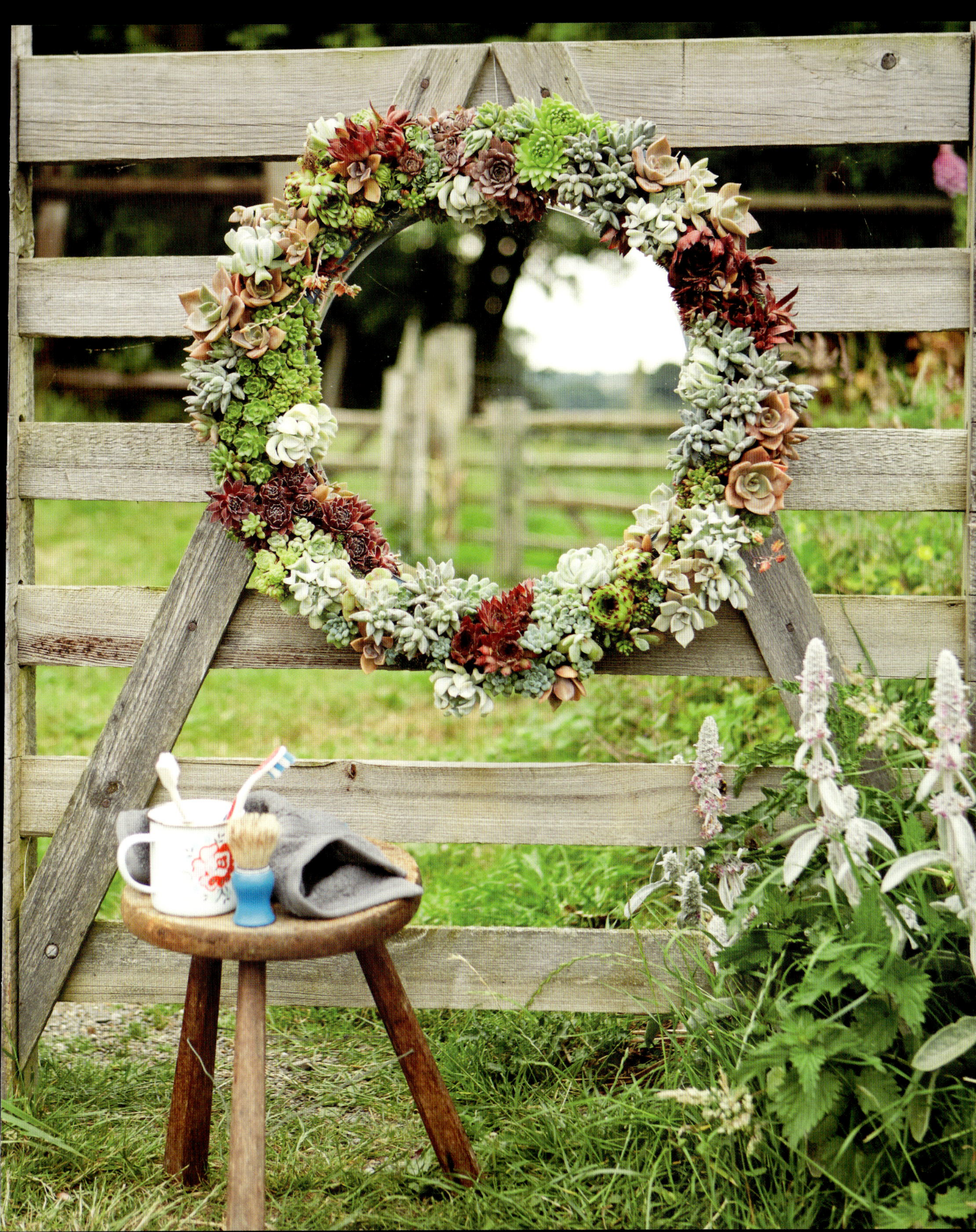

Sedum brevifolia

Sedum dasyphyllum

Sempervivum 'Grapetone'

Sempervivum 'Dark Cloud'

Sempervivum 'Rosie'

Echeveria elegans

Sedum sexangulare

Sedum album 'Coral Carpet'

Project Steps

2 To make the planting tube, use a craft knife to cut the shadecloth to twice the width of your border. Aligning one edge with the guideline, attach the shadecloth using a staplegun, pleating it to fit the circle.

3 Fold over the shadecloth and start to form the planting tube shape. Fill with dampened sphagnum moss and, as you do so, fold over the cloth, tuck under the loose edge, and staple down to form the tube.

4 Ideally, prepare plants a few days before planting to dry the stems and aid rooting. Take the plants out of their pots and remove most of the planting mix; with crowded pots it may be easiest to slice off any root ball beyond the planting depth required.

5 Separate plants into offsets or cuttings so you are left with a single longish stem. Using a craft knife, cut the stems to size, then pare the ends to a point. Fix short or floppy stems with hairpins or by attaching twists of wire as "tails".

Care Advice

Watering and feeding Use a water mister to squirt gently between the plants into the sphagnum moss, trying to avoid getting water on the leaves if possible. Water about every 10 days in summer; add a diluted liquid feed to the water during spring and summer. Do not feed through autumn and winter.

General care We used *Echeveria*, which isn't frost hardy, so the frame should overwinter on a verandah or sheltered porch; if very wet and cold, move somewhere more protected, cool, and bright. Plants may need pruning as they start to produce offsets and outgrow their position. Simply snip off excess plant material and use as cuttings. Remove spent flower stalks and dead material before winter as this could attract disease.

Excess plant trimmings are ideal for cuttings. Pot into free-draining gritty potting mix after you've left them for a couple of days to dry out.

6 Use a dibber to pierce planting holes 5cm (2in) apart, through the shadecloth and into the moss. Plant up the frame, making sure the cuttings sit flush with the cloth.

7 Once planted, leave the frame somewhere flat for two weeks to allow the plants to root in. Attach the mirror using a strong outdoor adhesive and nail a brass picture hook onto the back of the frame to hang your succulent mirror.

Succulents
Living Picture Frame

Easy to look after and, once rooted, happy growing vertically, succulents are a good choice for living pictures. Start your decorative display by using small succulent cuttings or offsets, then watch your picture grow and evolve over the seasons.

TIME IT RIGHT Plants will start to root quickly but it will take 4–6 months for the frame to fill out and be completely covered. Do not plant in winter when succulents become dormant.

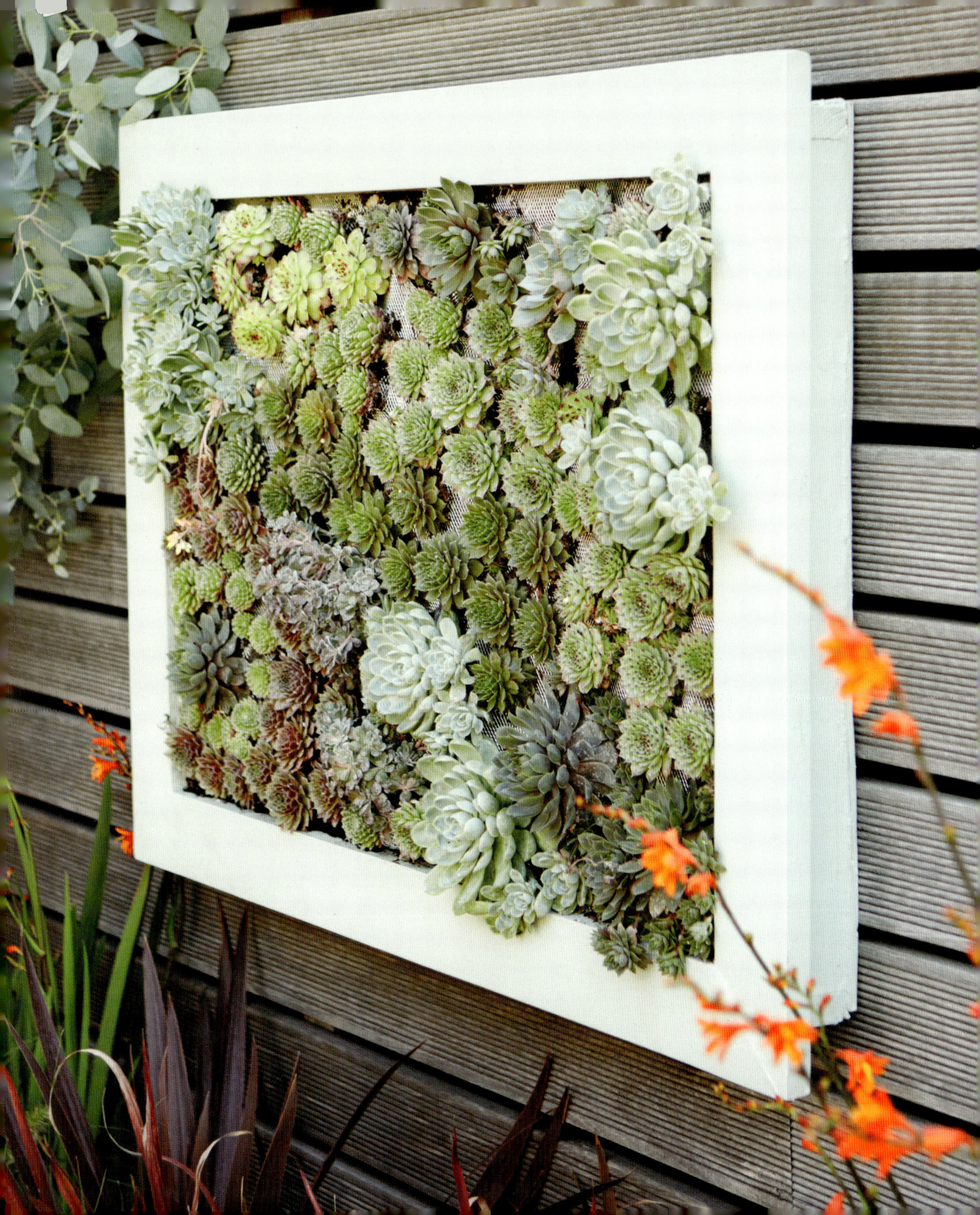

Project Steps

TOOLS & EQUIPMENT

wooden box-style picture frame in 2 parts, ideally 5cm (2in) deep and with an overlapping front

4–6 strong metal hanging brackets

electric drill & screws

emulsion paint mixed 2:1 with PVA

paintbrushes

clear yacht varnish (optional)

heavy-duty plastic liner & scissors

exterior glue or staplegun

tape measure

wooden batten & handsaw

cacti potting mix & perlite

bucket & trowel

tulle fabric

wood filler & sandpaper (optional)

dibber, chopstick, or pencil

PLANT LIST

selection of succulent cuttings:
  Echeveria elegans
  Echeveria secunda glauca
  Sedum spathulifolium 'Purpureum'
  Sempervivum 'Atropurpureum'
  Sempervivum 'Blue Boy'
  Sempervivum tectorum

sphagnum moss
  (soaked 1 hour, if dry)

1 Buy or make your own box frame, 5cm (2in) deep to allow space for the soil but no deeper or the frame starts to become too heavy; ours measured 80 x 60 x 5cm (31½ x 23½ x 2in). Screw brackets in the four corners of the box frame and two more in the centre of each long edge, for extra security if preferred.

2 Paint the box and front frame with a PVA and emulsion mix to help protect against the elements. Leave to dry, add another coat if required, then apply a finishing coat of clear yacht varnish for additional protection, if preferred.

3 Cut plastic liner so that it lines the insides of the box, right up to the edge of the frame. Measure and cut 2 pieces of batten so they sit parallel to the top of the frame.

4 Position the batten so they are evenly spaced and screw them to the box frame. This creates planting compartments to prevent the soil slipping down to the bottom once the frame is hung.

5 In a large bucket, mix up a free-draining growing medium for the succulent plants of 2 parts cacti potting mix to 1 part perlite. Do not use ordinary potting mix as it retains too much moisture which would eventually rot the roots of the plants.

6 Fill each of the planting compartments with the soil mix to just below the top edge of the box frame. Lightly tap down the whole frame so that the soil settles and the surface is level.

Project Steps

7 Squeeze out excess water from the sphagnum moss and put a thick layer over the top of the potting mix. The moss will help the succulent plants to root in.

8 Cut a piece of tulle fabric to overlap the edge of the box frame; this allows the fabric to be held in place when the front is screwed on.

9 Screw the front on to the box frame, ensuring the tulle fabric is held securely in place. Paint over the screws or, for a neater finish, drill a recess hole for each screw, cover the screw head with wood filler, sand smooth, then paint over.

10 Plan your planting design; we aimed to create bands of colour with blocks of each particular succulent. To make a planting hole, cut a cross in the tulle fabric with a pair of scissors.

11 Fold back the sides of the cross then insert your plant dibber to create a planting hole. Place your plant into the hole, firm soil around the roots and then fold back the edge of the fabric.

12 Plant succulents 3–5cm (1¼–2in) apart; over 4–6 months they will produce further plantlets to fill in the picture. Leave the frame flat for 1–2 weeks until the plants have put down roots, before securely screwing the frame to its final hanging position.

Care Advice

Where to site We used Echeveria, which isn't frost hardy, so our frame needs to be under cover somewhere cool and bright over winter. If all plants are frost hardy or grown in a frost-free region, leave the frame outside all year; if the winter is very wet move it somewhere protected from heavy downpours, like a verandah.

Watering and feeding Use a water mister to squirt water into the moss between the plants, trying to avoid getting water on the succulent leaves. Water every 10 days in summer and add a diluted liquid feed to the water in spring and summer, but do not feed in autumn and winter, and water only occasionally in winter.

General care Snip spent flowering stalks back to the base and remove any dead plant material before winter, as this could attract disease. Plants may need pruning as they grow larger. Simply snip off any excess plant material and use as cuttings.

Air Plants
Living Picture Frame

Make an eye-catching vertical display of plants that seem to float in the air. Tillandsia air plants get all their moisture and nutrients from the air, making them perfect for creating some living art.

TIME IT RIGHT Air plants aren't hardy to frost or heat so make your living picture frame during spring to give plants time to anchor onto the support wires. Put the frame outside in a warm but sheltered spot, bringing it under cover or indoors through winter.

A Rootless Life

Tillandsias are a type of bromeliad known as "air plants" because they are able to grow without soil, getting moisture and nutrients from the air through specially adapted leaves. Plants that are watered and fed well will develop flowers and new plants, which appear as offsets or "pups". Leave the pups to form clumps or remove when half the size of the parent plant to use in other displays.

Air plants grow short roots only in order to attach themselves to their "host" object.

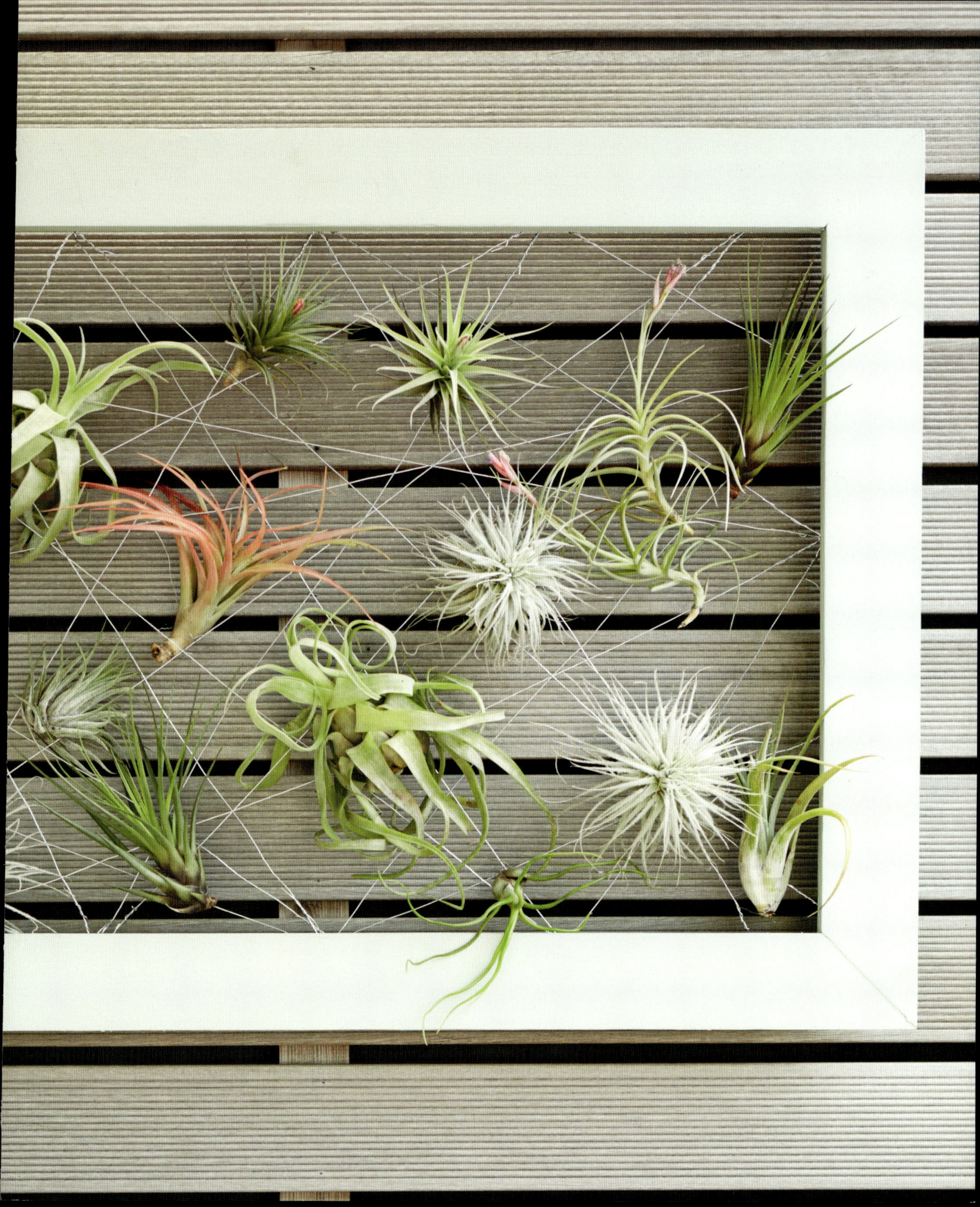

TOOLS & EQUIPMENT

wooden box-style picture frame, ideally 5cm (2in) deep and with an overlapping front, painted with a 2:1 mix of emulsion paint and PVA glue, and finished with a coat of clear yacht varnish (see page 120)

pencil & tape measure

electric drill & drill bits

screw eyes

strong metal hanging brackets

screws

galvanized wire

pliers

wire cutters

florist wire

PLANT LIST

selection of small air plants, such as:
 Tillandsia aeranthos
 Tillandsia bulbosa
 Tillandsia circinnata
 Tillandsia filifolia
 Tillandsia ionantha
 Tillandsia ionantha scaposa
 Tillandsia ixioides
 Tillandsia juncea
 Tillandsia melanocrater tricolor
 Tillandsia tectorum

Project Steps

1 Measure and mark points for holes for the screw eyes all the way around the inside edge of the box frame, about 2cm (¾in) behind the front frame and at 10–15cm (4–6in) intervals. Match a drill bit to the width of the screw eyes and drill shallow holes at each of the marked points.

2 Twist in screw eyes by hand at each of the drilled starter holes. Screw heavy-duty metal hanging brackets in the four corners of the box frame, plus a third bracket in the centre of each long edge, if preferred, for additional security.

3 Take one end of a coil of galvanized wire, thread a short length of 3–5cm (1¼–2in) through one of the screw eyes, and twist it back around the wire to secure it.

4 Uncoil enough wire to reach an eye hook diagonally opposite on the frame, leaving 3–5cm (1¼–2in) excess. Cut with wire cutters. Thread the loose end through the eye and, using pliers, pull it so that the length of wire is taut across the frame. Twist off and secure; there should be no slack.

5 Repeat to create an abstract "mesh" with areas of fairly closely overlapping wires where the air plants can easily be attached. Fix several wires to each screw eye, if required.

6 Wrap florist wire around the plant stems to secure them to the mesh structure. If a plant has a short stem, gently slide the wire between the bottom pair of leaves.

7 Attach plants by tucking the leaves between wires and tying off with the florist wire. The plant will eventually secure itself to the wire by anchoring with a root. Securely fix your frame onto a sturdy surface using the brackets.

Care Advice

Where to site Air plants like warmth but not direct sunlight and are happy outdoors in mild weather. Bring your frame inside when temperatures fall below 8°C (46°F), somewhere with good light levels and air circulation; do not place near heaters.

Watering and feeding Air plants absorb moisture and nutrients from the air through their leaves. Plants generally need spraying 2–3 times a week (ideally using rainwater), more frequently during summer or dry conditions. Feed with a diluted special air plant liquid fertilizer misted on leaves once a week in spring and summer, fortnightly in winter.

General care Remove dead, diseased, or dying foliage throughout the year. Do not let any water sit in the base of the plant.

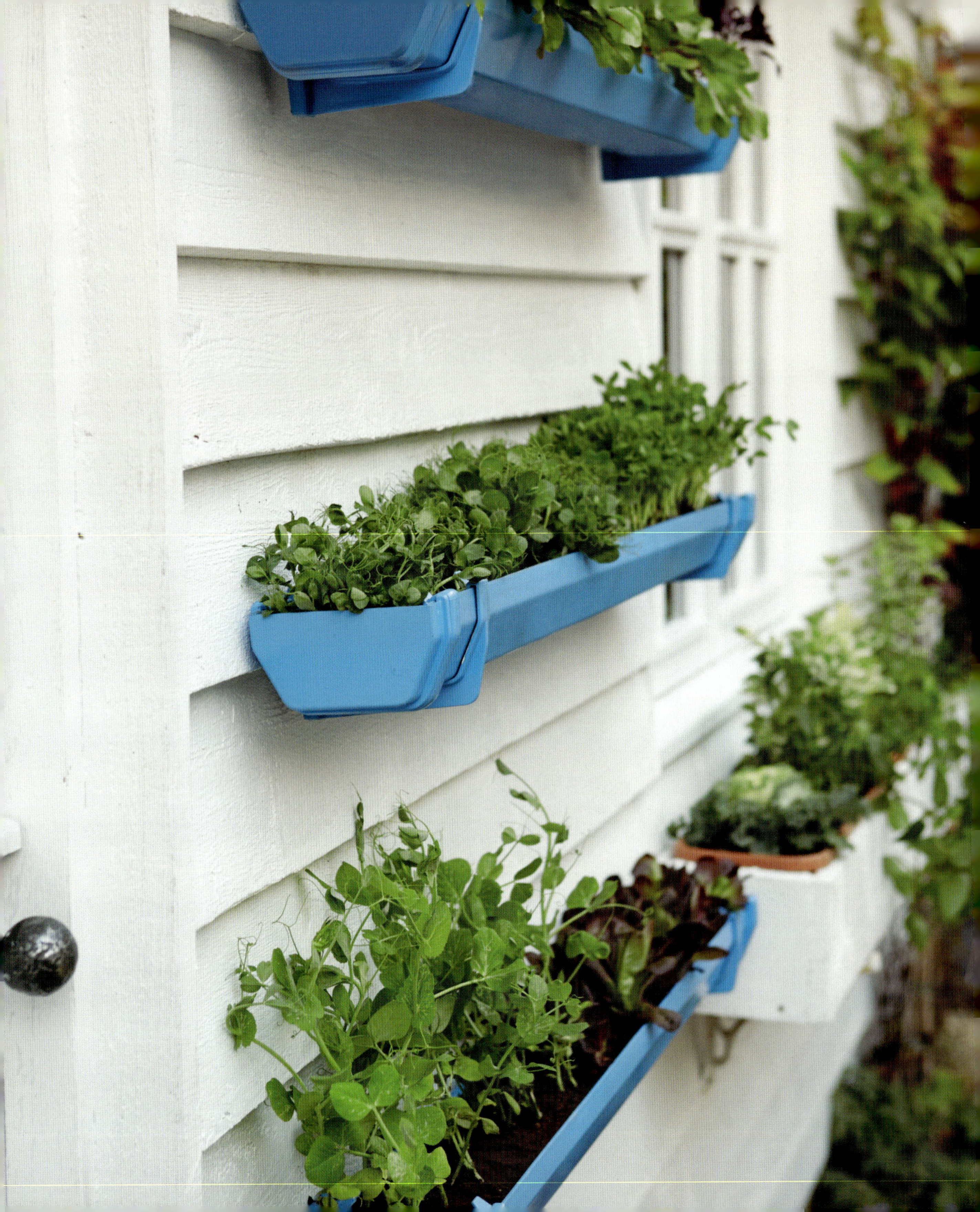

Pea and Broad Bean

Shooter Shelves

Transform ordinary plastic guttering into an attractive and innovative growing space for a tasty, nutritious crop of salad shoots – a fun way to use vertical space for growing vegetables.

TIME IT RIGHT Sow dried peas and beans from spring through to autumn. Protect emerging shoots from wind and hot sun. If conditions are right, you can expect to be harvesting shoots in 4–6 weeks.

TOOLS & EQUIPMENT

- non-PVC plastic guttering kit, including brackets & end pieces
- tape measure & pencil
- hacksaw or handsaw
- electric drill & drill bits
- face mask (optional)
- non-toxic spray paint (optional), marked as suitable for exterior use and safe for children's toys and furniture
- screws
- general-purpose potting mix & scoop
- well-rotted animal manure
- watering can

PLANT LIST

whole dried marrowfat peas & dried broad beans from a greengrocer's or supermarket, pre-soaked for 24 hours

1 Measure the guttering to your desired lengths, mark with a pencil, then carefully cut to size using a hacksaw or handsaw.

2 To provide some drainage, drill small holes in the base of each length of guttering, roughly 75cm (29½in) apart, using an electric drill and relatively thin drill bit.

Project Steps

PLANTING TIPS

Lots of vegetable plants have tasty young leaves. Try chard, beetroot, nasturtiums, cutting lettuce, parsnip, onion, spinach, kohl rabi, and herbs such as basil. Sow seeds at twice weekly intervals for a succession of tasty shoots.

3 If you like, paint the guttering in a colour of your choice. The easiest way to do this is using a non-toxic spray paint. Apply in a ventilated room or outside and wear a face mask to avoid breathing in any paint. Leave to dry completely.

4 Mark the position of the brackets on the wall so that they are carefully aligned. Keep in mind ease of access for watering and harvesting, and make sure the shoots have space to grow up to at least 20cm (8in). Screw the brackets to the wall, attach the end pieces, and then click into place.

5 Make a soil mix of manure and potting mix in equal proportions, then fill the guttering to a little below the top lip, leaving space for watering. Water the soil in well.

6 Sow the pre-soaked peas and beans in separate planting blocks. As you are only growing them for shoots, you can sow much closer together than for mature plants.

7 Cover thinly with more of the soil mix. Green shoots should start to appear after 1 week, depending on conditions and temperature.

8 The optimum time to harvest shoots is when they are 10–20cm (4–8in) high; any longer and the shoots start to get tough. Carefully pinch shoots off halfway to two-thirds down the plant, just above a leaf joint; this will encourage the plant to grow more shoots for a second harvest.

Care Advice

Where to site Preferably in a sheltered location, the shoots will need some sunlight but will be happy in a semi-shade position.

Watering Water frequently or daily, depending on conditions, once shoots start to appear. Never let the potting mix dry out, which can easily happen with a shallow container. Feeding is not required.

Vertically Mounted Miniature Greenhouse

Recycle wooden boxes into a useful little space-saving greenhouse. This makes a handsome feature on a wall and gives you the chance to grow, with some protection, your own plants from seed.

TIME IT RIGHT You can make this project at any time of the year but it's great to have it ready in early spring for seedlings or in autumn for winter-flowering annuals.

TOOLS & EQUIPMENT

- 2 wooden boxes, such as wine gift boxes
- strong outdoor adhesive
- metal clamps
- electric drill, drill bits, & screws
- small handsaw
- wooden batten
- pencil, pen, & ruler
- wooden rounded architrave
- additional piece of wood, for lid
- 4 metal hinges
- exterior wood paint & paintbrushes
- clear yacht varnish (optional)
- sheet of Perspex & silicone glue
- cupboard door knob
- square wooden batten
- 4 mirror fixing plates
- 2 door hooks
- newspaper & aerosol can with good recess at the base, for seed pots

PLANT LIST

easy seedlings to try are: lettuce, beans, and annual flowers – start seeds in recycled clear plastic food trays (add drainage holes), then grow on in newspaper pots

Alchemilla mollis, *Digitalis purpurea*, *Dryopteris filix-mas*, and *Primula vialii* are planted underneath

1 Take an empty wooden box and apply outdoor adhesive down one of the long sides. Place the second box on top and use clamps to hold in place until dry.

2 Screw the boxes together with two screws at either end of the central "shelf", screwing diagonally so that they penetrate through to the sides for a stronger fix.

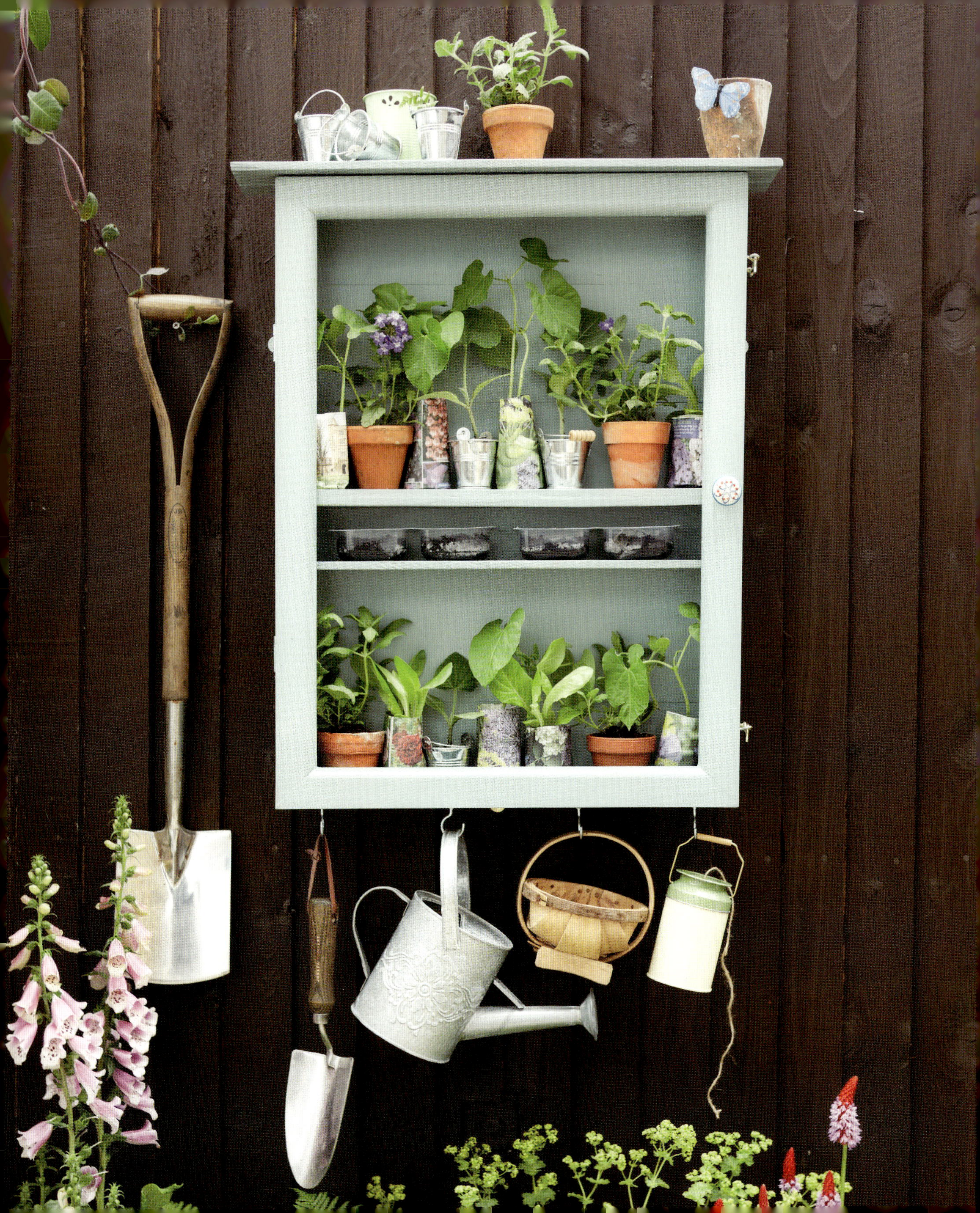

Project Steps

3 With a handsaw, cut out one of the long sides of the boxes; this will be the top of the greenhouse. Use this spare piece as a shelf and template for cutting further shelves.

4 Cut a piece of batten to fit the gap. Place it flush along the front edge, thin side facing out, and screw in place from the sides. This will be the top of the greenhouse; a lid will be fitted in its place that can be propped open.

5 Cut another piece the same size for the back of the gap, this time with the thick side facing out, and screw it in place.

6 Fit another piece of batten on the front edge of the bottom shelf, thick side facing out, to form a lip for the bottom of the greenhouse.

7 To make additional shelves, first measure and mark guidelines for where you would like the top edge to rest, bearing in mind the size of seedling pots and the height of seedlings.

8 Cut short pieces of batten for the shelves to rest on and screw them in position so that the top edges are level with the pencil guidelines.

9 Make the door frame from the architrave. To achieve a 45° mitre joint in each corner, first position one piece on the corner of the box flush with the sides and draw a diagonal guideline.

10 Cut out and use the diagonal edge as a guide for cutting the second piece of the joint, but draw the line on the reverse of the architrave. Repeat for each corner.

11 Glue and screw together the mitred sections. Use thinner screws and screw at an angle to pass through both pieces. Cut a piece of wood for the lid that will be slightly wider and deeper than the greenhouse when the door is in place. Attach to the back with two hinges, one near either end. Paint the box and door frame and leave to dry. You could also apply a coat of yacht varnish for extra protection.

Project Steps

> **RECESSING SCREWS**
>
> Recess screws for a neater finish. After making the pilot hole with the correct size of drill bit for the screw, change to a thicker, short drill bit to create a small recess. Once the screw is in, fill with wood filler and sand when dry.

12 For the window, measure a piece of Perspex to cover the whole of the door frame. Cut out carefully with a handsaw and fix it to the back of the frame using silicone glue. Fix two hinges at either end of one of the long sides on the back of the door frame.

13 For the pilot holes, use a drill bit slightly wider than the screws for the Perspex, then switch to the correct size for the wood. Fix a door knob to the front.

14 Hang the greenhouse body. Fix lengths of square batten to the back horizontally near top and bottom. Screw 2 mirror fixing plates either side of the battens and securely attach the greenhouse to your fence or wall. Additional fixing items, e.g. rawlplugs, may be required depending on the surface. Finally, attach the door frame to the front and fix a couple of small door hooks to keep it shut.

Grow Up **137**

15 To make seed pots, cut strips of newspaper 30 x 13cm (12 x 5in). Lay the aerosol can at the edge of a strip, 5cm (2in) in from the bottom. Roll and wrap the paper around the can to form a tube. Tuck the loose paper into the base.

16 Remove the pot, then fold in the top edge for strength and a neater finish. Pots will biodegrade, so place them straight into the ground when the plants are ready and all risk of frost has passed.

Care Advice

Where to site Choose somewhere which has sunlight for most of the day. You can add some shade for part of the day in summer if the sun is too strong.

Ventilation Air circulation is crucial for pest and disease control. Keep the door open for part of the day in spring, summer, and autumn, depending on the weather, closing it at night if temperatures are cooler. Prop the flap at the top of the greenhouse open with wooden blocks for extra ventilation in warm weather or minimal ventilation in cooler weather. In harsh winter conditions you may need some extra protection for the greenhouse such as bubble wrap around the outside.

Funky Abstract
Bamboo Trellis

Get creative with bamboo canes. Make your own abstract-design trellis and use it to support climbing plants. This contemporary feature also makes an arty screen for a small space.

TIME IT RIGHT You can grow trailing squash and pumpkin vines vertically – it's a good use of space. Plant seedlings from late spring to early summer, when the danger of frost is over; the other plants can go in at the same time.

TOOLS & EQUIPMENT

bamboo canes
exterior wood paint & paintbrush
large rectangular planting trough with drainage holes
tape measure
handsaw or lopper
green garden wire
wire cutters
gravel or crocks
general-purpose potting mix
garden twine
scissors
watering can

PLANT LIST

butternut pumpkin
climbing summer squash
Rudbeckia laciniata 'Herbstsonne'
Thunbergia alata 'Lemon Star'

1 Paint the bamboo canes with exterior wood paint; we chose black gloss for a bold, modern look that would contrast strongly with the plants. Leave to dry completely.

2 Start with two long upright canes positioned at either end of the trough. Measure the distance between them and cut two canes to size with a good overlap.

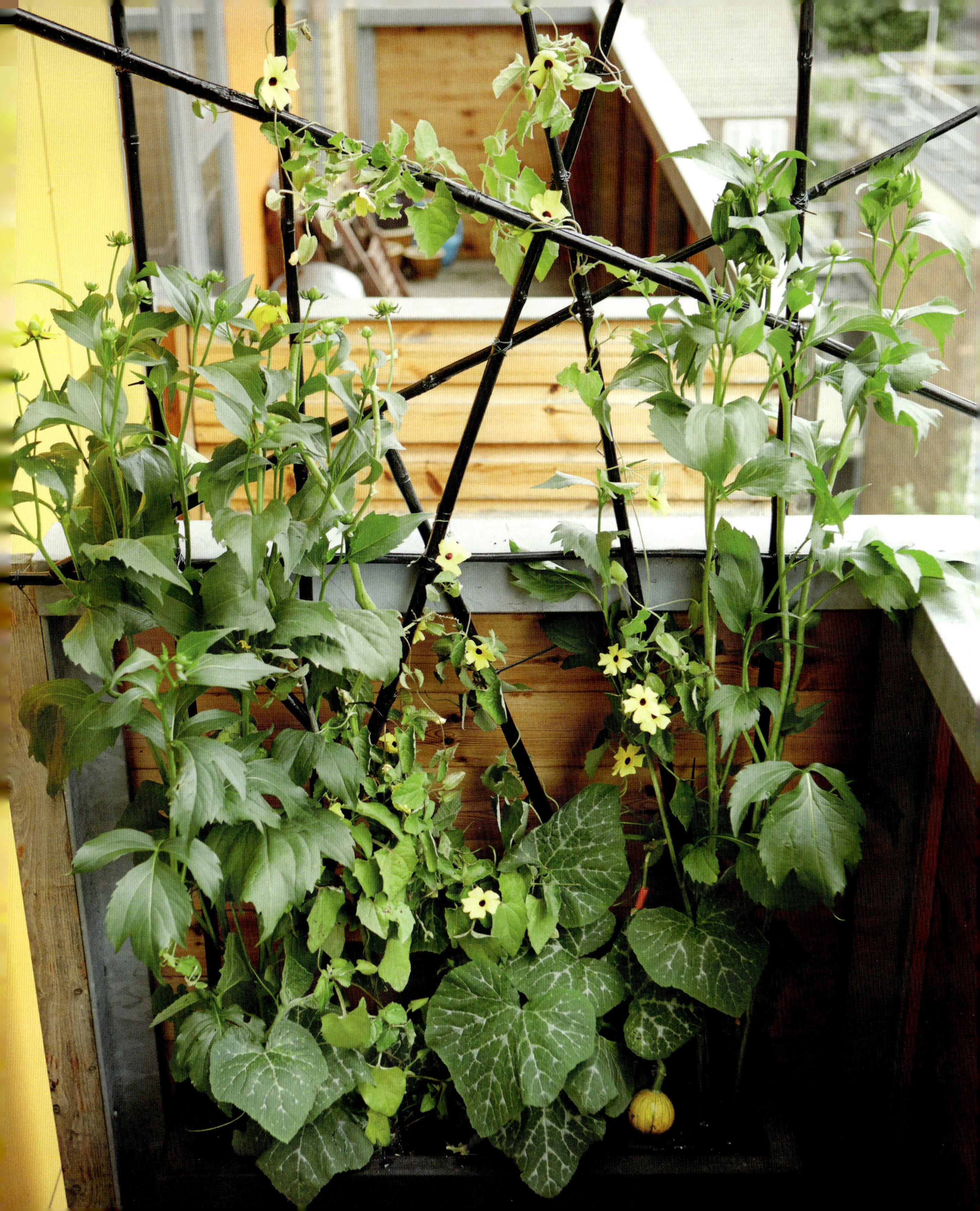

140 Grow Up

Project Steps

3 Tie these shorter canes at right angles to the uprights, one near the top and one in the middle. Do this securely by wrapping green garden wire several times around the cane junctions, then twist the ends together and cut off any excess wire.

4 Add a long cane running diagonally across the base frame from bottom left to top right, tying securely with garden wire as before.

5 Add canes of various lengths, attaching them to the frame at different angles; allow overlap and create abstract shapes, keeping the design asymmetric. Paint over the garden wire to match the canes and leave to dry.

6 To plant up, add a layer of gravel or crocks to the base of the trough for drainage, then fill about two-thirds with potting mix. Remove plants from their pots and position them in the trough, digging planting holes if they sit too high, then fill around with more mix and firm in. Water thoroughly.

Grow Up **141**

PLANTING TIPS
Try French climbing beans as an alternative to squash. French bean pods can be green, yellow, purple, or mottled deep pink and cream, and will also provide an appealing contrast to the background colour of the bamboo canes.

7 As the plants start to put out climbing tendrils, give them a helping hand by lightly tying them onto the canes with garden twine.

Care Advice

Watering Containers above ground level are more exposed, so water often in the growing season, especially if hot and sunny, and while plants are establishing.

Feeding Add diluted liquid feed to the water monthly in the main growing season as pumpkins and squash need high nutrition levels for fruit production; try misting them with diluted feed as well, but not when in direct hot sunlight as the leaves might scorch.

General care Remove damaged foliage in the growing period. Most summer vegetables are annuals, which die back in winter. Reduce watering as the weather cools and replace plants the following spring.

Pumpkins and squash need plenty of water and feed to produce a good, tasty crop.

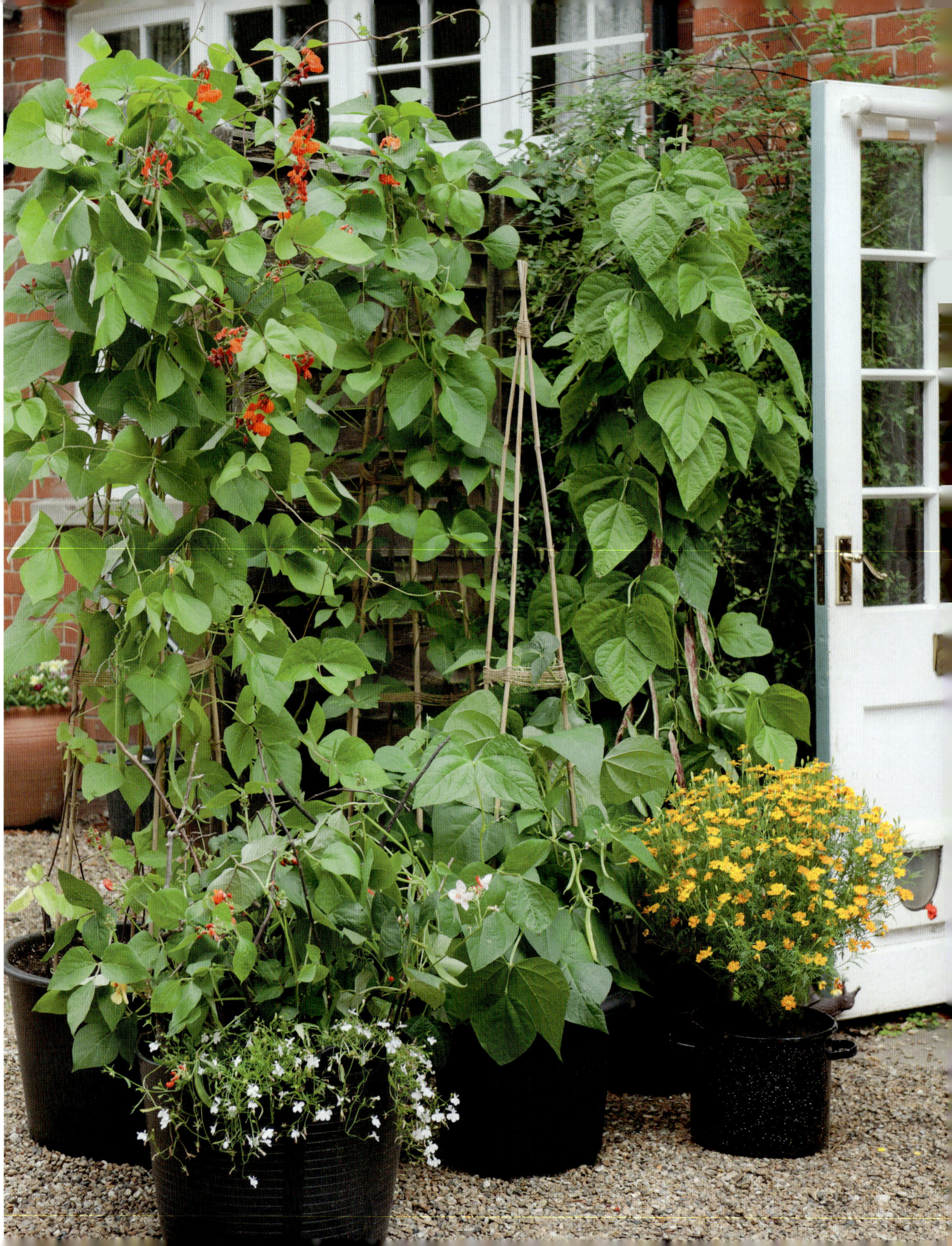

TOOLS & EQUIPMENT

small pots with drainage holes
general-purpose potting mix
seed-raising mix
large containers with drainage holes
gravel or crocks, for drainage
general-purpose fertilizer
tall bamboo canes or wooden stakes
garden twine
scissors

PLANT LIST

borlotti climbing bean 'Blue Lake'
French climbing beans 'Purple King' and 'Yellow Wax'
runner beans 'Painted Lady' and 'Scarlet Runner'

Homegrown Bean Feast

Nutritious, fast growing, and with attractive flowers and lush foliage, climbing beans are easy to grow from seeds and perfect for planting in pots for an edible container garden or to decorate an entrance.

TIME IT RIGHT Sow seeds under cover from mid-spring or outdoors in late spring. Beans are frost tender so only plant outside when spring weather warms. Expect to be harvesting 2 months after sowing.

1 To get your beans off to an early start, sow seeds 5cm (2in) deep from mid-spring in individual containers filled with seed-raising mix. Water well and keep under cover or in a greenhouse (see pages 132–37) for this sowing, as the seeds need warmth to germinate.

2 Climbing bean seed can be direct sown in small pots (1 per pot) for potting up into tubs later or sown directly into larger pots (3 per pot), spaced evenly.

Project Steps

BEAN TIPS

It is important to keep the potting mix moist at all times; for best results mulch at the beginning of summer. Harvest runner beans when they are 15-20cm (6-8in), and French beans at 10cm (4in). Keep picking regularly.

3 When your beans are ready for planting out, take a large deep container and add a layer of gravel or crocks to aid drainage. Fill with potting mix mixed with a little general-purpose fertilizer. Put tall bamboo canes or wooden stakes all around the outside edge. Secure together at the top with twine to make a wigwam.

4 Water the beans well, remove from their pots, and place in planting holes at the base of each stake, one per stake. Fill in around, firm the mix, and water again.

5 Encourage your beans to climb up the bamboo by lightly tying stems to the stakes. Once established, the plants will find their own way to grow up the poles.

Care Advice

Where to site Beans like a sunny but sheltered site, however they will also do well in semi-shady conditions.

Watering and feeding Beans need humidity to produce a good crop, so spray the plant foliage regularly and water frequently, especially in very hot weather. Never let the potting mix dry out. They need lots of food, too. Add liquid fertilizer, such as tomato feed or seaweed extract, once a week when flowers appear.

General care Pinch out the growing tips of plants once they reach the top of the canes, as this encourages a larger yield and keeps the tops of the plants less congested. Pick beans every 2–3 days to encourage lots more pods to form.

French climbing bean 'Yellow Wax' is a butter bean, which needs poles for support. Ideal for early sowing, this vigorous bean crops throughout the summer.

This borlotti climbing bean has attractive red-and-green stripy pods. Beans can be picked young or left to dry and stored for later.

Runner bean 'Scarlet Runner' produces attractive red flowers followed by long, tasty pods throughout summer and into early autumn.

Brightly Painted
Terracotta Pot for Climbers

Create a vibrant and welcoming display of climbers by simply painting a terracotta pot in bright colours. We've used two colours here: a sunny yellow and a warm purple, with climbing stakes in a soft grey.

TIME IT RIGHT You can paint your pot at any time of year but, in cold conditions, paint somewhere warm and dry. Plant up in early spring or autumn so the plants can get established.

TOOLS & EQUIPMENT

- large terracotta pot & drip tray
- small plastic container
- PVA glue
- measuring jug
- paintbrushes
- 2 colours of paint, ideally made for exterior use
- bamboo canes or wooden stakes
- crocks or gravel
- general-purpose potting mix
- garden twine
- scissors

PLANT LIST

- grape 'Black Muscat'
- *Lonicera sempervirens* 'Trumpet Honeysuckle'

1 You need to seal your terracotta pot first as the container is porous. In a small plastic container, mix up a solution of PVA glue and water at a ratio of 1:10 and then brush it all over the pot. Leave to dry for a couple of hours or overnight. Once dry, paint the top section of the pot yellow (you may need to do two coats), including some of the inside to below soil level, and leave to dry for a few hours or overnight.

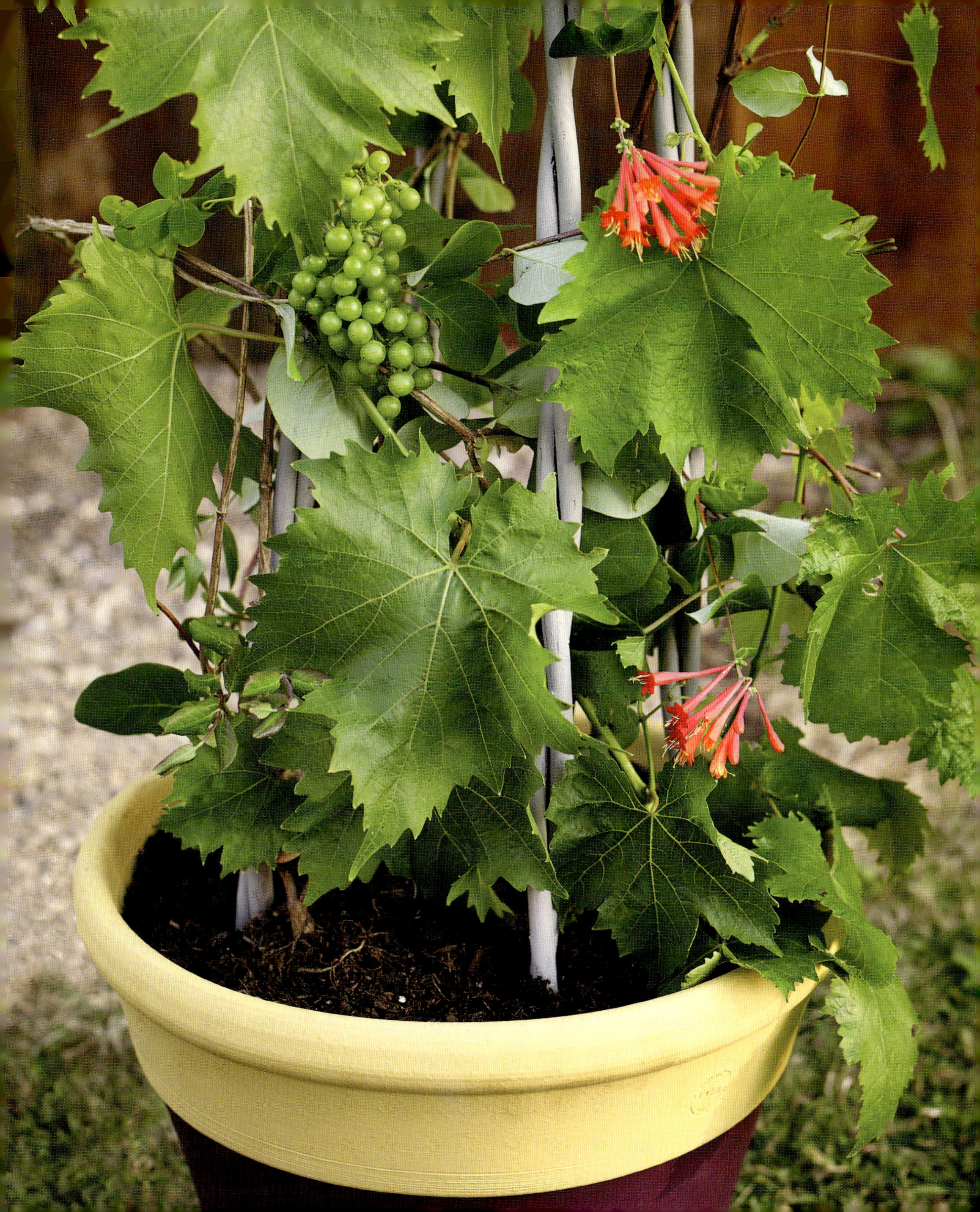

Project Steps

2 Using the rim moulding as a guide, carefully paint the darker colour on the remainder of the pot. Add a second coat if required. If you are not using exterior paint, seal with a coat of the diluted PVA solution.

3 Paint the pot's drip tray, too, and then paint your support stakes (we used four) in a complementary colour. We used one coat of paint to let some of the stick show through for a more decorative look. Seal with the PVA and water mix, if required.

4 Cover the drainage hole with some crocks or gravel to stop potting mix from spilling out and to help with drainage for the plant.

5 Fill your container halfway with potting mix, then position your climbing stakes around the edge of the pot, making sure they are evenly spaced.

6 Before planting, tie your stakes together with garden twine near the top to secure them in a sturdy position, then plant your grapevine.

7 Lightly tie the grape stems to the stakes to encourage them to attach. Then plant the honeysuckle – this will self-twine around the stakes but needs some help, so tie lightly, too.

Care Advice

Watering and feeding Water plants regularly from mid-spring to early autumn, and frequently in hot, dry weather – twice a day if exceptionally warm. It's best to water in the evening and use a drip tray underneath for extra moisture. Use liquid feed diluted in water every 2–3 weeks or put slow-release plant food tablets in the soil during the growing season. Do not water or feed from late autumn to late winter. Never overwater.

General care Keep your grapevine and honeysuckle to size by pruning above a bud in late winter, but bear in mind that grapes have particular pruning requirements if you're aiming for a bumper crop. When pruning the honeysuckle, try to encourage branching for shape and flower production. You may need to repot both plants after a few years to a larger container.

Container care Keep sheltered to protect it from toppling in strong winds. Clean the surface in spring with a damp cloth.

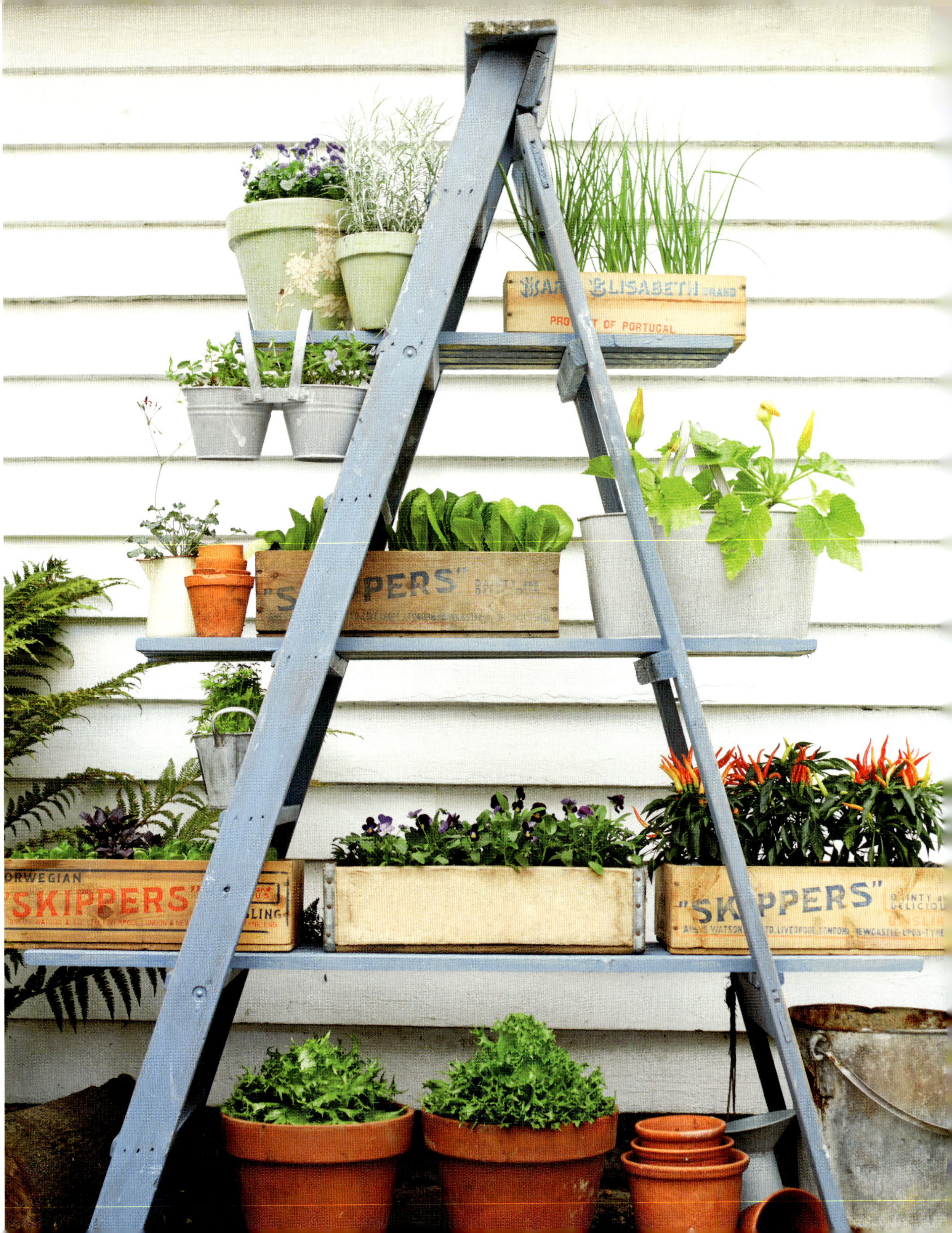
"SKIPPERS"

Upcycled Stepladder Tiered Planter

Upcycle an old stepladder into a tiered planter by adding shelves across the steps. Paint in a snazzy colour, plant up vintage crates and, hey presto, you've got an eye-catching, space-saving feature.

TIME IT RIGHT You can paint your stepladder at any time of the year, but colder weather may slow drying time. Aim to plant containers with a mixture of seasonal plants and crops for year-round interest.

TOOLS & EQUIPMENT

old stepladder
tape measure & pencil
wooden batten
handsaw
spirit level
electric drill & drill bits
wood screws
sandpaper in a selection of grades
exterior wood paint & paintbrush
clear yacht varnish (optional)
vintage wooden crates, galvanized metal tubs, terracotta pots
thick black plastic liner & scissors
PVA glue or staplegun
gravel or crocks
general-purpose potting mix

PLANT LIST

basil 'Purpleleaf'
carrot baby round 'Paris Market'
chilli 'Jalapeno'
Helichrysum italicum
lamb's lettuce
lettuce cos 'Parris Island'
loose-leaf lettuce 'Lollo Rosso', 'Green Coral', 'Royal Oak'
Pelargonium sidoides
spring onion 'Evergreen Bunching'
Viola 'Blue Beacon', *cornuta*, 'Trailing Lavender', 'Trailing Violet'

1 Take your stepladder and, starting at the second rung down from the top, measure and mark a piece of batten so that it will fit across the full width of the ladder inside the frame, directly opposite the rung. Cut the batten to size with a handsaw. Hold a spirit level against the top edge of the rung and mark this point on the opposite side of the frame.

152 Grow Up

🛠 Project Steps

2 Position the batten so the top edge is level with the mark just made, then screw to either side of the frame. This provides a second supporting rung for a planting shelf.

3 Measure and cut to size 4–5 battens to create a slatted shelf. They should extend 20cm (7¾in) beyond each rung with an extra 3–4cm (1¼–1½in) of excess wood on both sides; this excess will be cut off later for a neat finish. Arrange the battens so that they are evenly spaced, then screw them in place to both rungs.

4 Once secured, measure and mark pencil guidelines along the battens at the point where they extend 20cm (7¾in) beyond each rung.

5 Cut along the guidelines to remove the excess wood, then sand the cut ends smooth. Repeat steps 1–5 to make further planting shelves. Position the shelves on alternate rungs to allow enough growing space for plants.

6 Paint the shelves and ladder with an exterior wood paint and leave to dry. If preferred, paint your tiered planter with a final coat of clear yacht varnish for extra protection against the elements. The vintage crates would also benefit from a coat of varnish.

7 Drill drainage holes in the crates, if required, then line with black liner, glued or stapled to the base and sides. Cut a few holes in the base of the liner for drainage.

8 Add a thin drainage layer of gravel or crocks, then half fill the crate with potting mix. Arrange your plants, fill around them with more mix, firm in, and water. If you are using galvanized buckets, there is no need to line them but drill drainage holes if they don't have any.

Care Advice

Where to site Most plants need some sunlight although many will grow in part shade. Put plants requiring more sun on the top rung or at the shelf ends.

Watering and feeding Water plants regularly during their growing season but less often during winter, depending on the plant's requirements. Add diluted liquid feed to the water in the growing season but not in winter.

General care Move the crates often so each gets enough sunlight. Re-pot any plants that outgrow their containers. You could grow some vegetables as "mini veg", planting them quite close together and harvesting when the crop is still small and tasty. Clean the ladder with a cloth after winter to keep it fresh and bright.

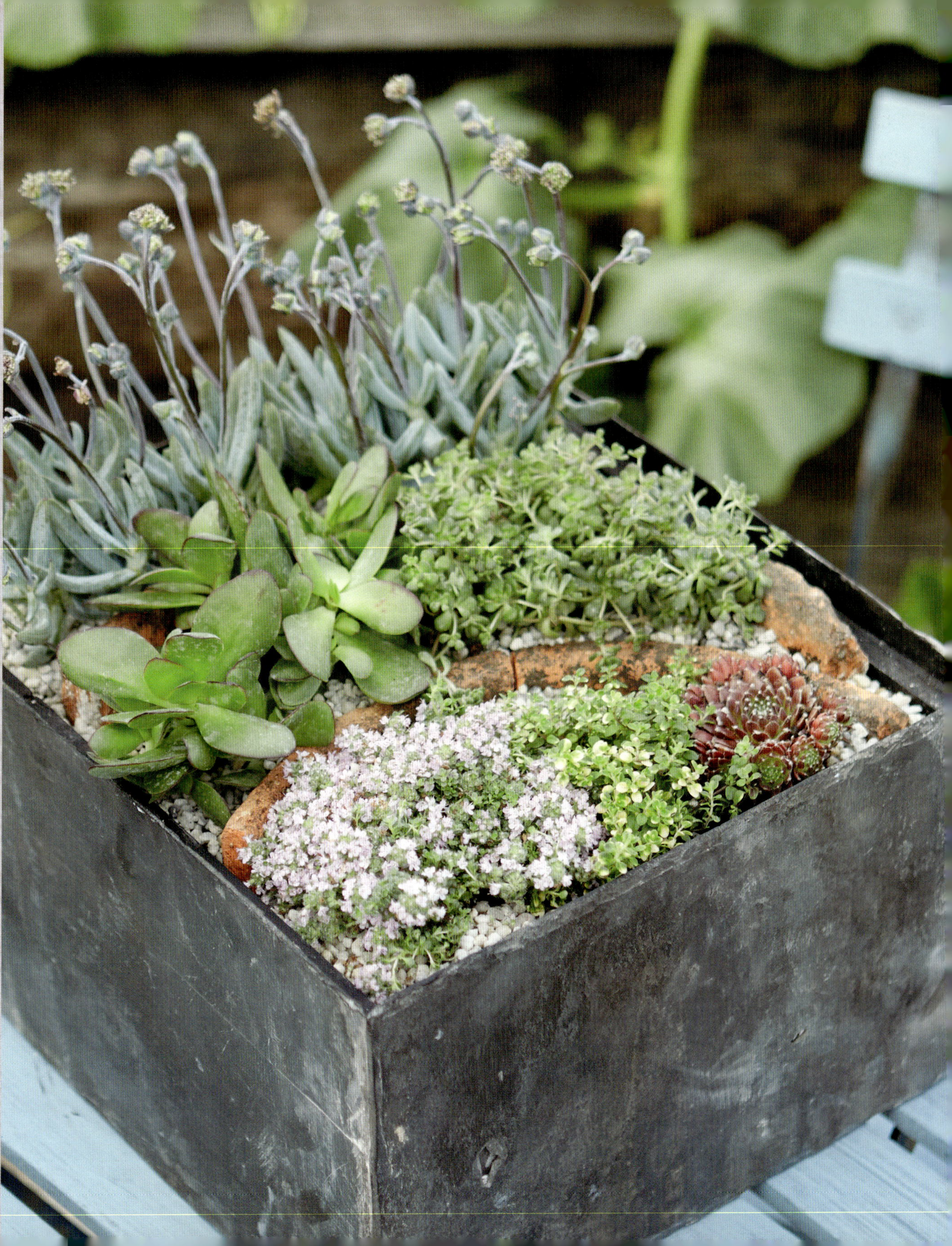

CONTAIN YOURSELF

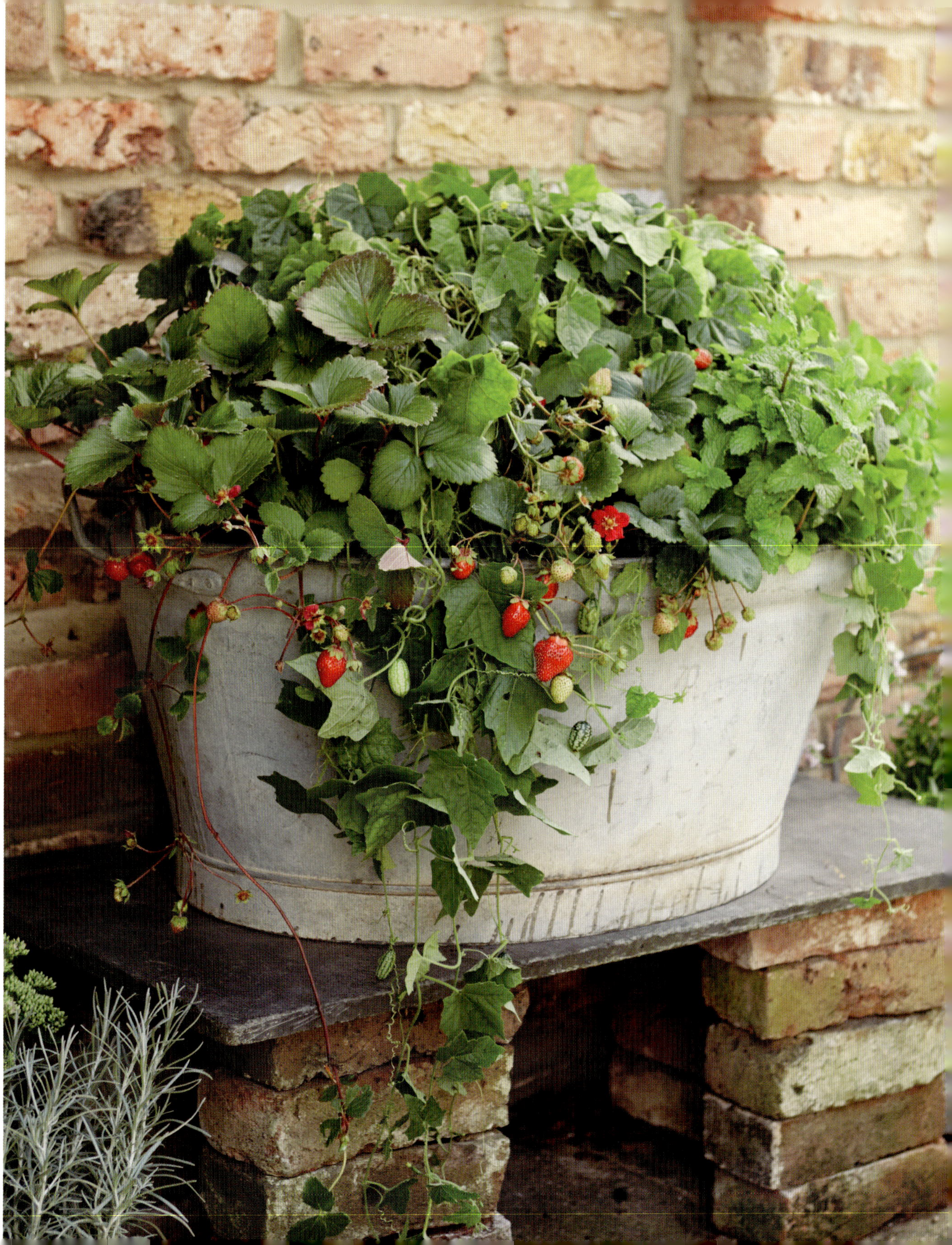

Summer Drinks
Tiered Planter

Pick your own garnish for thirst-quenching drinks while entertaining outdoors with this stylish tiered planter filled with fruit, vegetables, and herbs specially selected to complement summer drinks.

TIME IT RIGHT Plant in early spring so everything has time to grow and begin fruiting in time for summer. You could also plant alternative garnishes such as a small lemon tree, different herbs, and edible flowers.

1 If they don't already have them, drill several drainage holes in the bottom of each metal bath or bucket using an electric drill fitted with a metal drill bit.

2 Place the larger bath or bucket in its final position. Stack bricks in the centre to create a stable platform for the smaller bath or bucket to sit on.

TOOLS & EQUIPMENT

2 vintage galvanized steel baths or buckets, one small enough to fit inside the other and leaving ample planting space

electric drill & metal drill bits

bricks

gravel or crocks

general-purpose potting mix

scissors

trowel

watering can

PLANT LIST

apple mint (*Mentha suaveolens*)

peppermint (*Mentha* x *piperata*)

melon, such as 'Orangeglo'

mint 'Eau de Cologne'

strawberries, such as 'Sweetheart' and 'Strawberry Pink'

🪴 Project Steps

3 Add a thin layer of gravel or crocks at the base of both containers for additional drainage and to ensure air can circulate around the roots of the plants, keeping them healthy.

4 Now add a layer of potting mix, filling each container to two-thirds full.

5 Position the smaller container on the raised platform, then start to plant them up. Plant the lower tier with strawberries and mint, and the top tier with one or two melon seedlings grown from seed (see General care, opposite).

6 As mint is a vigorous grower and could otherwise crowd out the strawberries, restrict growth by keeping each plant in its plastic pot and simply cutting off the base.

7 Plant one side of the lower tier with mint and the other side with strawberries, leaving room for plants to spread. Make planting holes at a depth so the plants sit 2–3cm (¾–1¼in) below the rim of the bucket. Fill and firm in soil around the plants, then water thoroughly.

Care Advice

Where to site The strawberries and melon need good sun for crops to ripen, so place the planter in a sunny, sheltered site. Decide upon the final position before filling the planter as it is heavy to lift.

Watering and feeding Water often while plants are establishing and during the growing season. Add diluted liquid feed 1–2 times a month in the growing season, but do not feed the mint as it may grow too much. In winter, reduce watering and do not feed.

General care Remove any damaged, diseased, or dying foliage or fruits throughout the growing period. Keep mint in check by regular cropping and pruning back; remove plants if they get too big or invasive. Cut back strawberry plants after fruiting and pot up any "runners" (plantlets at the end of an extended shoot) by pegging them in a separate pot; once rooted, cut them from the main plant. Sow melon seeds under cover from early to mid-spring then plant out once danger of frost is over. Regularly trim the foliage of over-vigorous plants to prevent less vigorous plants being smothered. Alternatively, plant different types of plants in separate containers.

Try choosing different strawberry varieties that fruit at different times in the growing season for a successional crop of fruit.

Harvest sweet melons, which have a fresh and sweet flavour, when the fruit are mature.

Make-it-yourself
Slate Box Planter

Transform a wooden box into a stylish planter by enclosing it in slate. Inexpensive and easy to make, the planter can be filled with a range of plants – see pages 164–9 for an alpine-themed planting scheme.

TIME IT RIGHT Constructing your planter should not take more than a couple of hours, but remember that you will need to leave it overnight and then allow for the paint to dry before you can plant up.

1 Take your wooden box and drill drainage holes in the base using a large drill bit. You'll need several holes, so space them evenly across the base. Drainage is vital to prevent the plant roots from sitting in too much water and rotting.

TOOLS & EQUIPMENT
- wooden box or crate
- electric drill & drill bits
- slate roof or floor tiles
- white pencil or chalk
- protective goggles
- protective gloves
- angle grinder
- strong outdoor adhesive
- black epoxy filler
- paintbrush
- matt black exterior paint
- thick black plastic, for lining
- scissors
- metal skewer

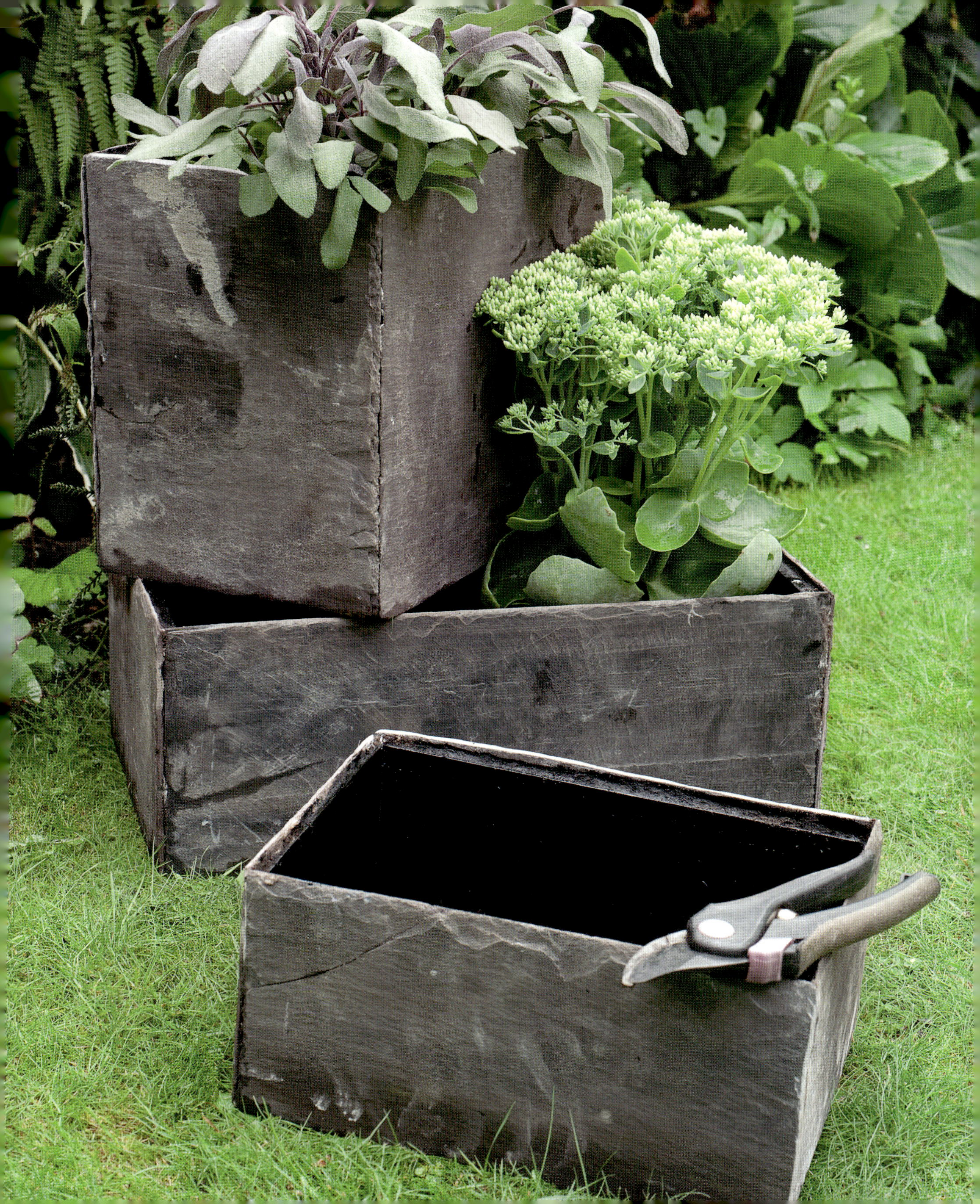

Project Steps

2 Lay your tiles flat and, using a white pencil or chalk, draw around each side of the box, so you end up with 4 separate pieces marked out. Include an excess of 2cm (¾in) to the depth of each piece to provide a "lip" at the top of the planter.

3 Wearing protective goggles and gloves, carefully cut out the 4 slate pieces using an angle grinder. Make sure you do this on a stable surface that will not be damaged by the angle grinder.

4 Spread a layer of adhesive on to one outer panel of the box, then attach a matching slate piece and hold it in place until slightly bonded. Continue to attach the remaining slate pieces one by one. Wipe away any excess glue before it sets. Fill any gaps between the slate panels with black epoxy filler.

Contain Yourself **163**

SELECTING SLATE

Reclaimed slate offcuts or roof or floor tiles are ideal for this project. Make sure they don't have any cracks in them or are too badly damaged. Clean up the surface with mild soap and water to bring out the natural patina of the slate.

5 Leave the slate-covered box overnight to allow the glue and filler to dry, then paint the base and the inside with black exterior paint; a matt paint blends better with the finish of the slate.

6 When the paint is dry, cut out some thick black plastic to fit the inside of the box and glue in place with adhesive. When the glue is dry, pierce some drainage holes in the base of the liner using a metal skewer.

Rock Strata
Alpine Planter

Low-growing succulents and other alpines are perfect for displaying in a box planter. This miniature alpine landscape makes a stunning centrepiece for an outdoor table and should be admired at eye level.

TIME IT RIGHT Early spring is the best time to plant up. You can also do this in summer, but it will require more watering. The plants will offer colour and interest all year round.

TOOLS & EQUIPMENT
Slate Box Planter (see pages 160–63)
gravel
cacti potting mix
general-purpose fertilizer
large pieces of broken terracotta pots or similar
horticultural grit or aquarium gravel

PLANT LIST
Crassula dwarf red form
Sedum species
Sempervivum tectorum
Senecio small leaf form
Thymus creeping form

1 Place a layer of gravel over the base of the box planter for drainage. Succulents need good drainage and do not like to be sitting in water as it will cause their roots to rot. Add a layer of cacti potting mix, mixed with a little general-purpose fertilizer, filling to halfway up the container.

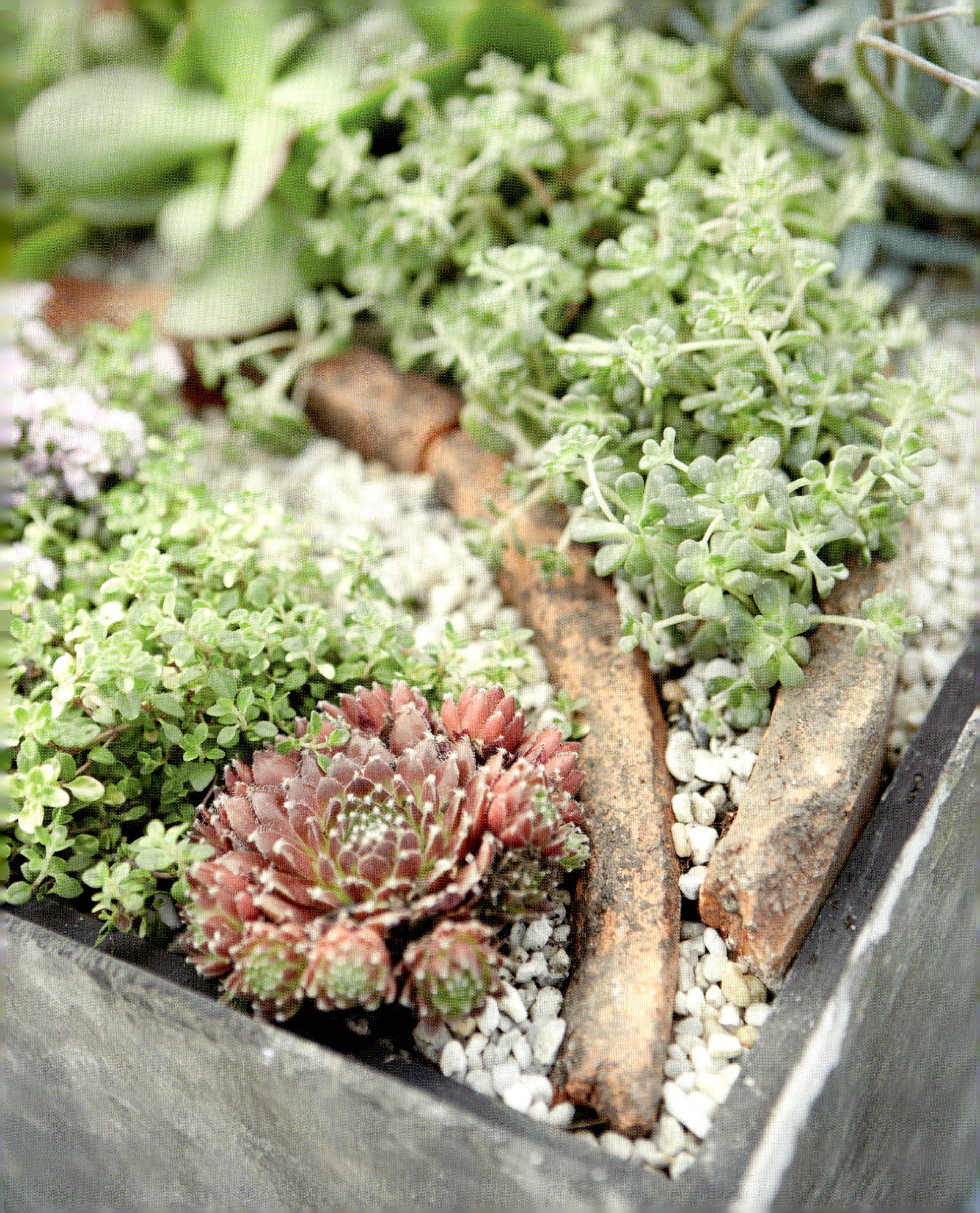

166 Contain Yourself

Project Steps

2 We used the broken rim of a terracotta chimney pot, or you can use large old plant pots, to create planting segments in the box for a natural landscape feature.

3 Lay out all your plants and roughly position them so you have a feel for how everything will look. Place taller plants at the back and lower, spreading ones at the front. Take them out of their pots, gently teasing out any compacted roots, and start to plant up. Top up with a layer of potting mix.

Create a miniature alpine landscape for your planter by using broken terracotta pot rims or pieces of slate to simulate rock strata in a natural environment

PLANTING TIPS

Choose to put plants with different leaf textures and foliage colours next to each other to create interest and depth to the planting. Taller plants add different layers and height to the arrangement.

4 To finish off your alpine planter, dress with a layer of contrasting small grit, which helps to keep moisture in the soil and shows off the details of the plants.

Care Advice

Where to site Succulents need a sunny, warm site to thrive. They will need to be sheltered from hot sun and heavy rain and protected from frost in winter. Move under cover on a verandah during the dormant season or place on a sunny windowsill in a warm room.

Watering and feeding Water regularly in spring and summer, with just occasional watering in autumn. Do not water in winter and do not overwater at any time of year. Fertilizer added at planting time will keep plants fed for their first year and, after that, add a little diluted liquid feed to the water in spring and summer, but not in autumn and winter.

General care Remove any spent flower stalks at the base of plants and remove any dead plant material before winter, as this attracts disease if left on during this period. Small scissors or secateurs are useful for keeping plants pruned. Some plants will produce offsets, which can be snipped off and grown as cuttings; leave for 1–2 days to dry out and then pot in free-draining potting mix.

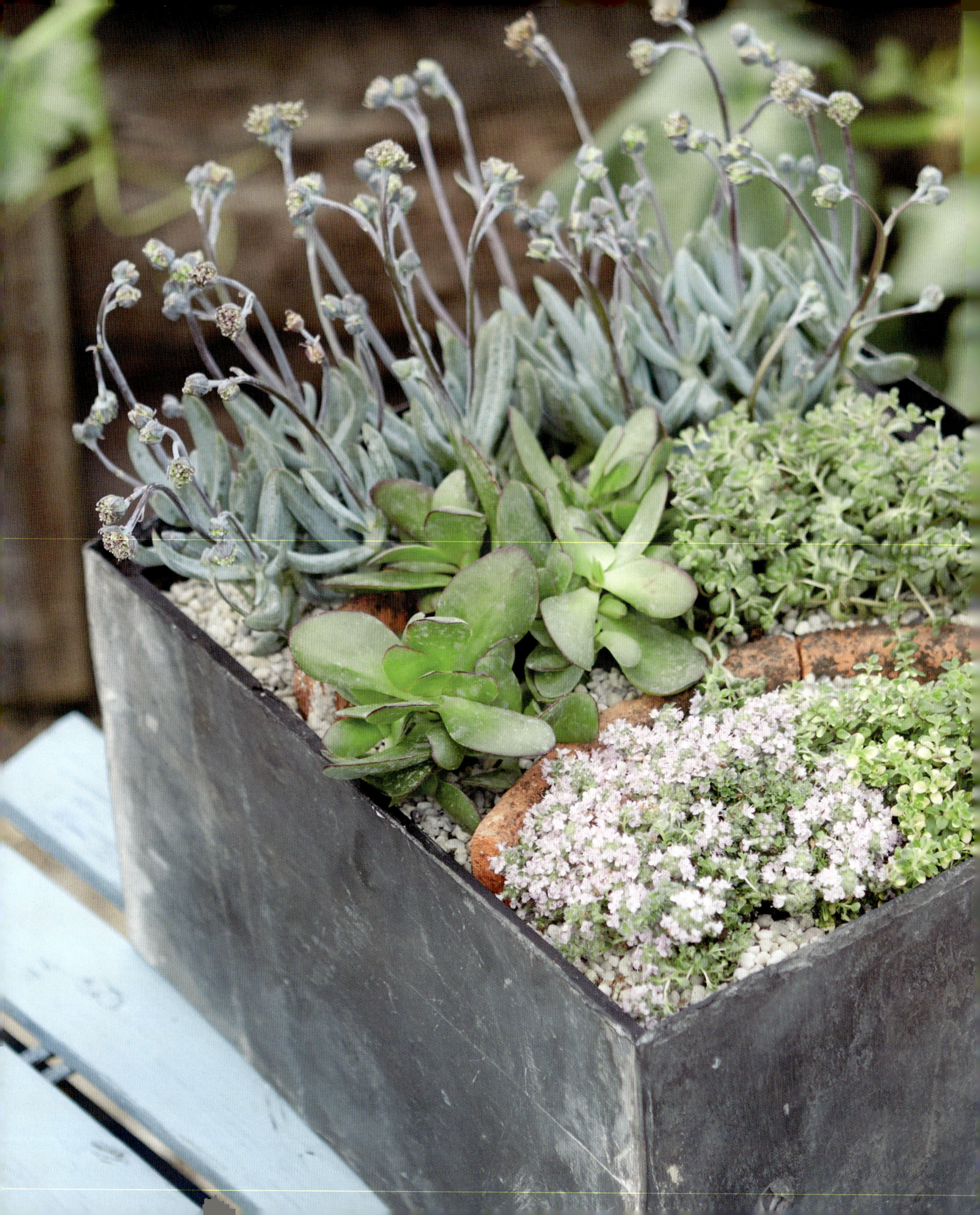

Put your alpine planter on a table to appreciate the textures and patterns of the plants. A gravel mulch shows off plants and helps to retain moisture.

Grow Your Own
Fruit in Tubs

You don't need a big garden to grow fruit trees and bushes, as many can be grown in pots. As well as producing a crop, many fruit trees are ornamental, with pretty blossom and colourful fruit.

TIME IT RIGHT You can plant container-grown fruit trees and bushes at any time of year, but be prepared to water frequently if planting in summer. Don't plant in very hot or very cold weather.

TOOLS & EQUIPMENT

- vintage zinc containers in a range of sizes
- electric drill & metal drill bits
- crocks or gravel
- general-purpose potting mix
- horticultural grit (for gooseberries)
- trowel
- slow-release fertilizer granules (optional)
- wooden stakes & ties (optional)
- watering can
- gravel or well-rotted manure, for mulch
- netting, bamboo canes, & toppers

PLANT LIST

- apple, grown as a vertical cordon
- blackcurrant 'Baldwin'
- blueberry 'Bluecrop'
- fig 'Brown Turkey', grown as a half-standard tree
- golden marjoram
- gooseberry, grown as a half-standard shrub
- sage 'Tricolor'
- strawberry, small fruit variety such as 'Sweetheart'

1 Drill several drainage holes into the bottom of your container, if it does not have them already.

2 Place a layer of crocks (pieces of broken terracotta pots), gravel, or small pebbles in the base of the container, which will prevent the drainage holes from getting clogged up and ensure that air can circulate around the plant's roots.

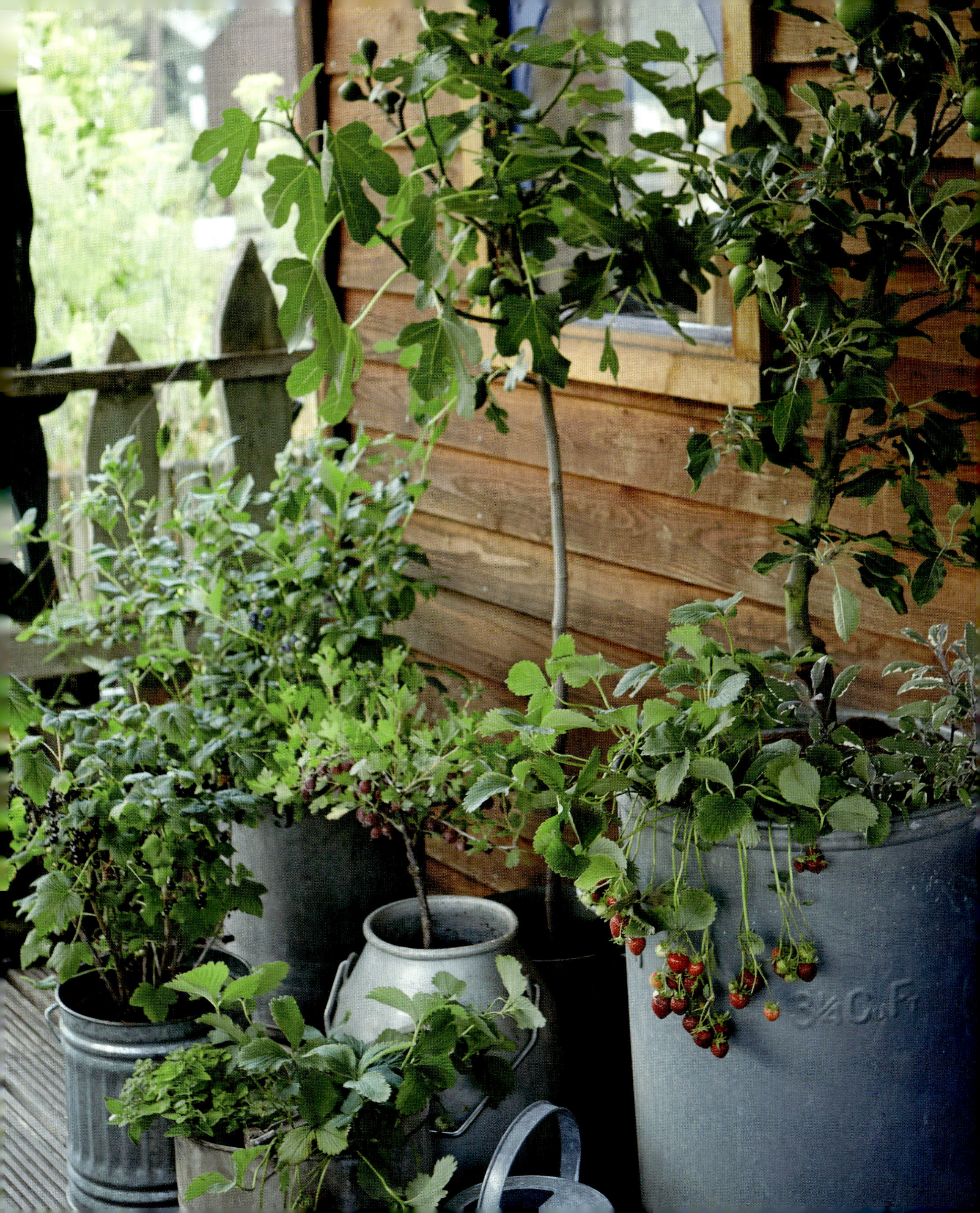

Project Steps

3 Gooseberry bushes, shown being planted here, do not like to be waterlogged and will benefit from a relatively free-draining soil made of 2 parts potting mix to 1 part horticultural grit. Mix with a trowel and add to the container. You can also add slow-release fertilizer granules into the mix.

4 Add the potting mix to the container, building up a base layer of soil to the correct height so that the top of the root ball will be 3–4cm (1¼–1½in) below the rim of the pot. Remove the bush from its container and tease out the roots, especially if it has become pot-bound and the roots have spiralled.

5 Position the plant in the container and fill in around it with your soil mix, keeping the bush level and centred as you do so. Add a stake to support a standard plant and tie it in if needed. Thoroughly water the bush after planting.

6 Add a 3cm (1¼in) layer of decorative gravel or another kind of mulch, such as well-rotted farmyard manure, which will help to retain moisture in the container.

7 Protect buds and fruit from hungry birds with netting draped around canes using cane toppers, making sure none of the fruit presses against the mesh.

Care Advice

Where to site Fruit trees and bushes prefer growing in direct sun in a sheltered site. Turn pots regularly so that growth is balanced and the fruit ripens evenly. Some fruit may need their blossom protected from early frosts, so cover with horticultural fleece or similar. Containers may need shadecloth protection from hot sun in summer.

Watering Water regularly from spring to mid-autumn, reducing to minimal levels in winter. Containers may need watering twice a day in summer. Water when the surface of the potting mix is dry and use a watering can with a long spout or hose to get water directly into the mix. Do not overwater and do not let the potting mix dry out completely. Place a container under the pot to catch excess water.

Feeding Add diluted liquid feed to the water monthly from spring to autumn. Replace general feed with liquid tomato fertilizer weekly from mid-spring until late summer to encourage formation of fruit, then change back to general-purpose fertilizer from late summer to early autumn and from early to mid-spring. Do not feed deciduous or evergreen trees in winter. Alternatively, you can add a controlled-release fertilizer tablet to the potting mix in early spring, although additional tomato feed is also beneficial.

General care Keep the pots clear of weeds and add an annual mulch in early spring of well-rotted manure, leaf mould, or garden compost after watering containers thoroughly. Remove any dead, diseased, or dying foliage during the growing season. Prune fruiting trees immediately after harvest and repot larger specimens every 2–3 years.

An elegant and space-saving method of growing fruit trees is to train them into an espalier (right). Formed around a single verticle stem, pairs of lateral shoots are pruned and trained along canes at 45° to the main stem in the first year, and then at right angles in the second year, when a second tier is added. Several tiers can be formed this way, growing flat against a wall to make the most of a small space.

Specific Fruit Advice

Blackcurrants These plants have high chill requirements and are grown only in cold regions. Prune in winter, removing to ground level all weak, damaged, or diseased growth and thin the bush to promote good air circulation.

Blueberries Use ericaceous potting mix, as blueberries prefer acidic soil. Keep mix moist, and water with rainwater. Use fertilizer for ericaceous plants. Prune as blackcurrants.

Figs Prune in spring and regularly pinch out the growing point of the side shoots to encourage fruits. Bring the pot into a frost-free place when young, then place in a sheltered place once established.

Gooseberries Like blackcurrants, they require a cold winter to fruit well. Prune in summer by cutting back new growth to five leaves, then remove congested branches in winter to create better air circulation.

Strawberries Place containers off the ground for better air circulation. Pot up runners in late summer.

Apples Choose plants grown on dwarf rootstock. Columnar forms such as 'Ballerina' are perfect for smaller spaces and containers, and only require light pruning each year in summer.

Fruit Gallery

Fruit trees in containers can be moved around so that the plant gets the best site and sunniest aspect. Cordons, espaliers, and fan-trained fruit trees are particularly good for smaller spaces; they give a high crop yield and are very attractive.

Grow herbs under fruit trees and bushes to maximize space. Remember to feed containers regularly. Also shown here: strawberries and blueberries.

Pictured above: blackcurrants, gooseberries, and apples.

Make-it-yourself Concrete Planters:
Sleek White Bowl

Making your own concrete planters is quick, inexpensive, and surprisingly easy – give it a go! This stylish white bowl will add a lovely contemporary feel to your planting.

TIME IT RIGHT The bowl takes 1 hour to make and 48 hours to harden. Make it under cover on rainy days. Don't expose the hardening concrete to high temperatures, as this could cause the concrete to crack.

TOOLS & EQUIPMENT

- safety equipment: surgical or rubber gloves & face mask – these are essential as cement is mildly caustic
- 2 metal or plastic bowls that will comfortably fit inside each other to give a reasonable rim width
- 1 bag of pre-mixed sand and cement made with white cement
- weighing scales
- large plastic bucket
- measuring jug
- washing-up liquid (optional)
- cork bung, cut to the correct depth for the base of your bowl
- PVA glue
- cooking oil & brush
- additional sand or weights, to hold the top mould in place
- sheet of wrapping plastic, large enough to enclose the mould
- metal file &/or sandpaper in various grades
- water

PLANT LIST
Erica cinerea

Thymus x *citriodorus*

1 Source a pair of bowls, one fitting inside the other. Use plastic or metal mixing bowls, washing-up bowls, ice-cream tubs, etc.; note that bowls with an undercut or fluting in the wrong direction may be difficult to remove from the cast concrete. Carry out a water displacement test to calculate the quantity of dry mix: fill the outer mould with water, place the inner mould on top and press down gently, displacing water till the rims are level. Measure the volume remaining in litres; the total weight in kilograms of dry mix will be double that figure.

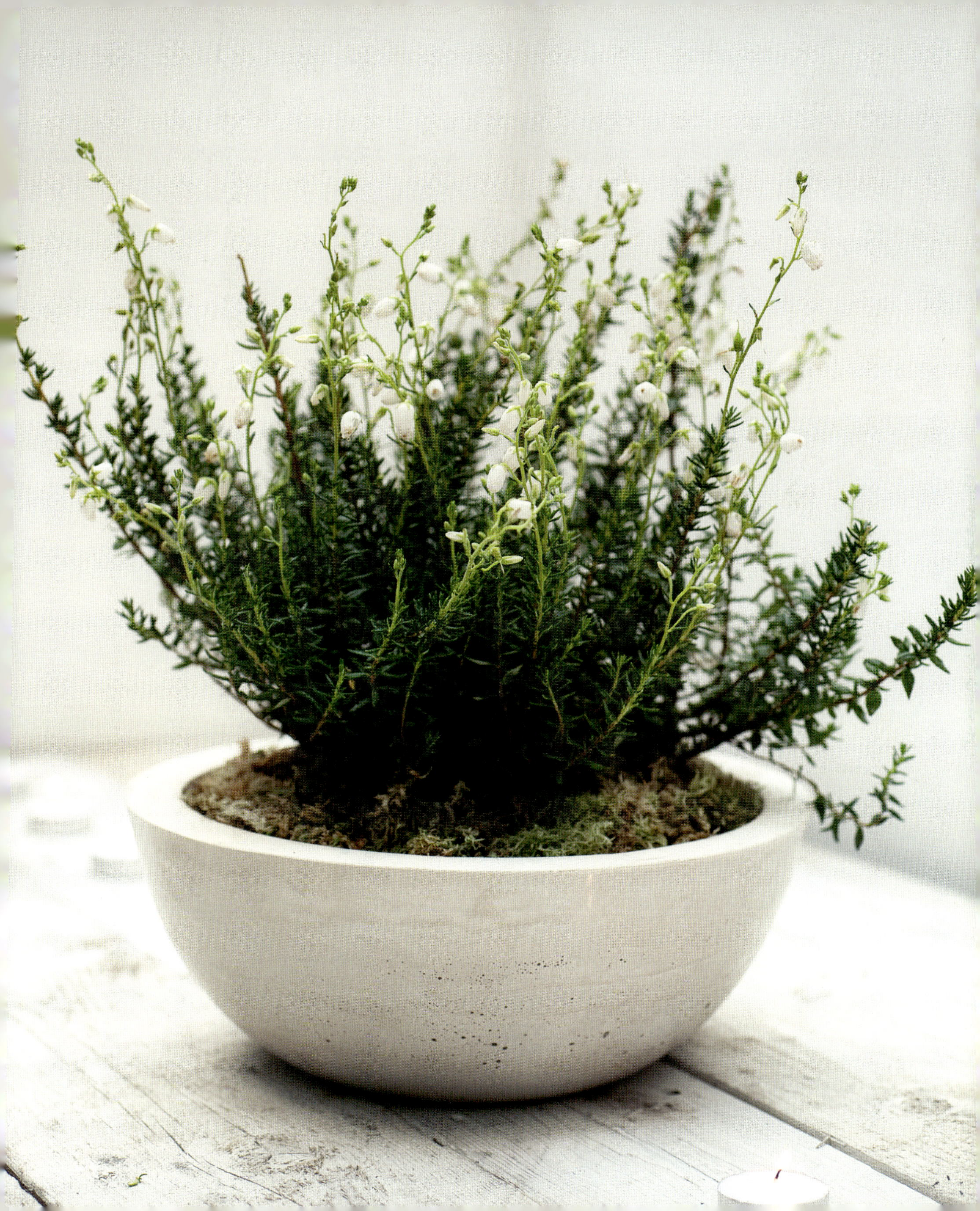

Project Steps

2 Follow packet directions for mixing pre-mix sand and cement. 1:3 is a recommended ratio of cement to sand. For a finer finish, stone dust can be combined with the sand at a 1:1 ratio. For the bowls we used, the volume of water remaining after displacement came to 2 litres, giving a total weight of 4kg dry ingredients, and because we used stone dust this broke down as 1kg cement, 1.5kg stone dust, and 1.5kg sand.

3 Wearing gloves and a face mask to protect against the caustic cement, measure out the dry ingredients and mix them together in a large plastic bucket until evenly combined.

4 The volume of water in millilitres needed will be 50–60% of the total weight in grams of cement. Our bowl required 1kg cement and 500–600ml water. Less water makes for stronger concrete but results in a more solid mix that can be more difficult to work with.

5 If you like, add a squirt of washing-up liquid, which will act as a plasticizer to make the concrete more malleable. Mix until there are no streaks of dry ingredients and the concrete forms firm, dough-like clumps.

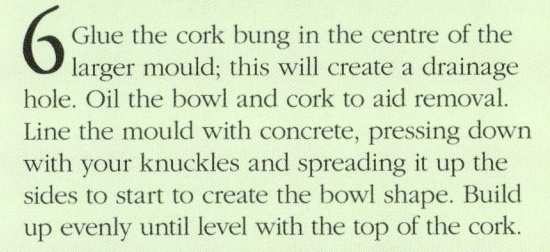

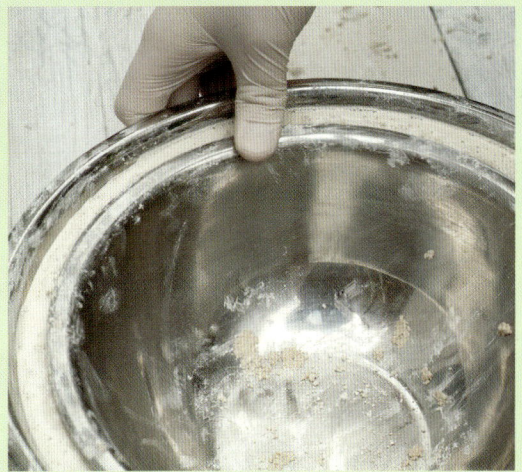

6 Glue the cork bung in the centre of the larger mould; this will create a drainage hole. Oil the bowl and cork to aid removal. Line the mould with concrete, pressing down with your knuckles and spreading it up the sides to start to create the bowl shape. Build up evenly until level with the top of the cork.

7 Oil the base (and lip, if it has one) of the inner mould and position in the centre. Fill in between the moulds until the concrete is level with the top. You may need to keep pressing down on the inner mould to ensure it sits on the cork, especially if the concrete starts to become more liquid.

8 Add sand or weights to hold down the inner mould and gently tap the sides of the outer mould to level the surface and release air bubbles. Place on a flat surface, wrap loosely in plastic, and keep out of direct sunlight to prevent it hardening too quickly. Leave for 24–48 hours. Remove the inner bowl and cork, then turn upside down to remove the outer bowl. Pouring boiling water on metallic moulds will help to release them.

9 Smooth any sharp edges with a metal file and finish off the surface with sandpaper, working from rough to fine grades of paper, as desired.

Make-it-yourself Concrete Planters:
Carnivorous Garden

With their exotic and unusual appearance, and fascinating ability to obtain their nutrient needs by trapping and feeding on insects, carnivorous plants make a bold impact. They are also surprisingly easy to look after, once you understand their needs.

TIME IT RIGHT Plant mid-spring to summer to enjoy the carnivorous plants at their peak of interest. They will die back in winter, then start growing again in spring. If possible, allow 1 week for the potting mix to reach correct acidity before planting up.

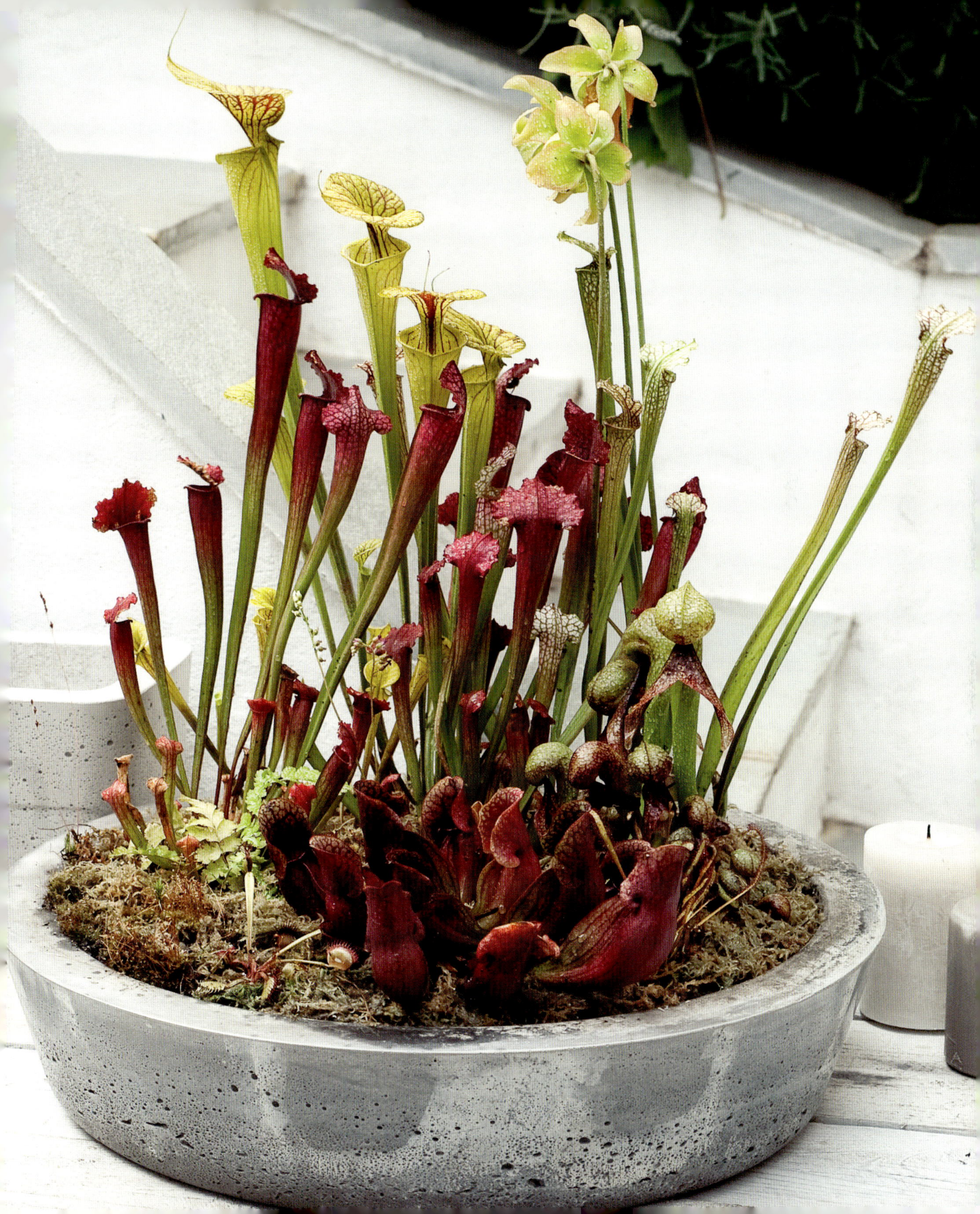

Project Steps

TOOLS & EQUIPMENT

wide, relatively shallow concrete planter, made as per instructions on pages 176–9; we used 2 large washing-up bowls for the moulds

gravel (optional)

organic coir mixed with perlite 3:1 (see step 3)

trowel

rainwater or distilled water

watering can

PLANT LIST

Darlingtonia californica

Dionaea muscipula

Drosera capensis

Sarracenia flava

Sarracenia purpurea subsp. *purpurea*

sphagnum moss (optional; if dried, soak for at least 1 hour and squeeze out excess water before using)

1 Clean the container before planting to remove any concrete residue, which may harm the plants. Plan your arrangement: place delicate, low-growing plants at the front where they can be appreciated, then continue building up the layers, putting taller plants at the back. Aim for a natural look that shows off each individual variety of plant.

2 As our concrete planter was made without a hole in the base, we added a very thin layer of gravel for drainage. This is not essential, however, and it is important to leave space so that the mix layer is deep enough to allow water to get under the roots of the plants.

3 Fill with a lime-free growing medium of three parts organic coir to one part perlite. Carnivorous plants need slightly acidic, nutrient-poor soil and the correct mix is essential for plants to thrive. You can replicate this with the organic coir and perlite mix, but check labels carefully on the coir product to ensure they don't contain any salt or added nutrients, which are likely to kill the plants.

4 Water the mix with rainwater or distilled water, and ideally leave for a week to allow the soil to reach optimum acidity. Never use tap water as carnivorous plants like acidic, nutrient-poor conditions and tap water is generally too alkaline with too many mineral nutrients.

5 Remove plants from pots and place them in their planting positions, making sure you leave room for plants to grow and expand without swamping each other. Plant so that the crowns of plants are just below the soil surface.

6 Water the plants well. They like to sit in damp conditions and a little water but not a huge amount, similar to a bog garden environment, so keep the soil mix moister than for other plants. Add a water-retaining mulch of sphagnum moss, if you like. In time, moss will also grow naturally on the surface.

Care Advice

Where to site Keep in a warm spot protected from wind and hot sun. Protect from frost in cold regions by bringing them into a more sheltered spot like a verandah in winter.

Watering Keep water levels topped up and never let the soil mix dry out. When watering, water at the base of plants directly into the soil, so as not to wash off any sticky coating that plants have or cause stress, e.g. flytraps can close in alarm if watered overhead. Make sure any pitchers on plants have a little water in them, too. Reduce watering in winter when plants are dormant, but still keep the mix slightly damp. Carnivorous plants thrive on poor, nutrient-free soil and you should not need to feed them as they get all their nutrients from insects they catch.

General care Remove any dead foliage and pitchers to keep plants neat. The foliage will die down in winter, particularly in cold regions, and plants would benefit from a plastic cover or being moved into a greenhouse. In spring, prune off old foliage at the base of the plants as new buds and tips emerge. Move the container out into the warm sun but when summer heat arrives, move to a sheltered spot receiving afternoon shade.

Make-it-yourself Concrete Planters:
Slate-grey Window Box

The colour of this elegant window box planter was created by mixing black pigment with the cement. Experiment by adding different coloured pigments to the mix to create a unique work of art for your windowsill.

TIME IT RIGHT This project involves more effort than some others but is well worth it. Allow 1 day to construct the mould and cast the concrete, and 48 hours for the concrete to cure. Make under cover if raining and protect the curing concrete from extreme temperatures.

Size Matters
Concrete may crack without reinforcement if the edge width is too narrow for its size. Our box edges were 2.5cm (1in) wide; for boxes larger than the one in this project, include reinforcing mesh or rods in the construction. Melamine-faced chipboard makes a good mould as its surface aids unmoulding. MDF or plywood must be sealed with 2–3 coats of shellac (button polish).

Adapt the size of the planter to suit your space but consider the weight of the concrete.

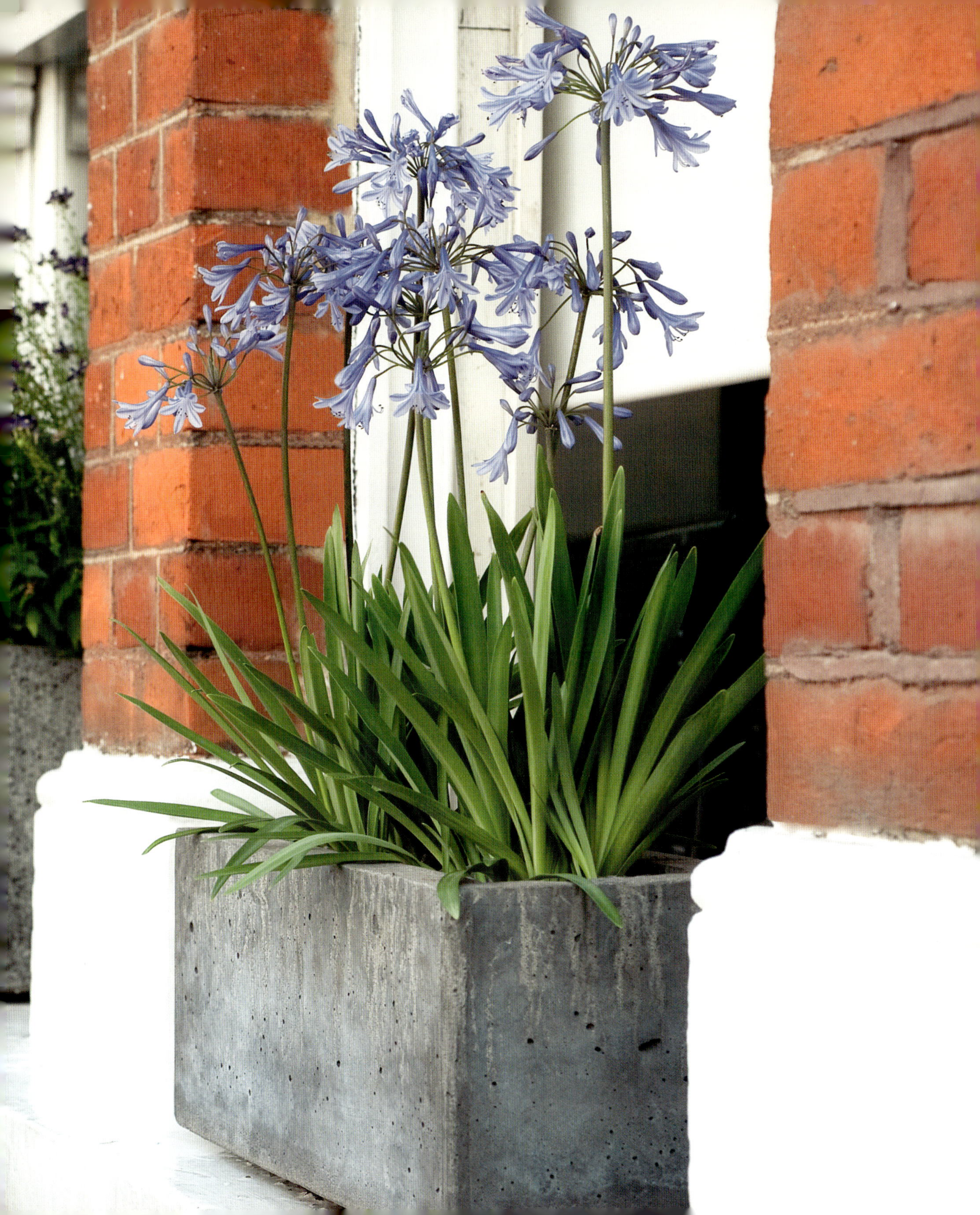

TOOLS & EQUIPMENT

- 1.5cm (½in) or thinner melamine-coated chipboard (see page 184)
- wooden batten
- tape measure & pen or pencil
- handsaw
- PVA glue & clamps
- electric screwdriver & screws
- safety equipment: surgical or rubber gloves & face mask
- 1 bag of pre-mix quick-set concrete mix
- black concrete pigment
- water
- weighing scales
- plastic buckets, bowls, & sieve
- measuring jug
- washing-up liquid (optional)
- cork bungs
- cooking oil & paintbrush
- trowel or metal scraper
- sheet of wrapping plastic, large enough to enclose the mould
- metal file &/or sandpaper in various grades

PLANT LIST

Agapanthus dwarf varieties, such as 'Peter Pan' or 'Blue Baby'

Project Steps

1 Calculate and measure up the pieces for the outer mould to achieve your desired box size, bearing in mind battens are fixed on the outside. Internal dimensions for our box were 46 x 19 x 19cm (18 x 7.5 x 7.5in). Using a handsaw, cut the pieces accurately to size; or you could opt to get them machine cut by a timber merchant.

2 Calculate the size of the inner mould to give a suitable width to base and sides of the box (see page 184), and cut pieces to size; ours measured 41 x 14 x 16.5cm (16 x 5½ x 8¼in). Note that battens are fixed to the inside and there is no base piece. When constructing the moulds, first glue the batten to the boards with PVA glue, clamp together, and leave for 1 hour before screwing it all together.

3 Measure out the concrete mix, adapting the quantities listed in proportion to the size of the box (see also page 178). To colour it, add pigment up to 10% of the weight of the cement; any more than 10% will weaken the structure. Sieve together the cement and pigment to ensure even distribution of colour. Add water, erring on a solid mix, and a squirt of washing-up liquid to aid plasticity, if you like.

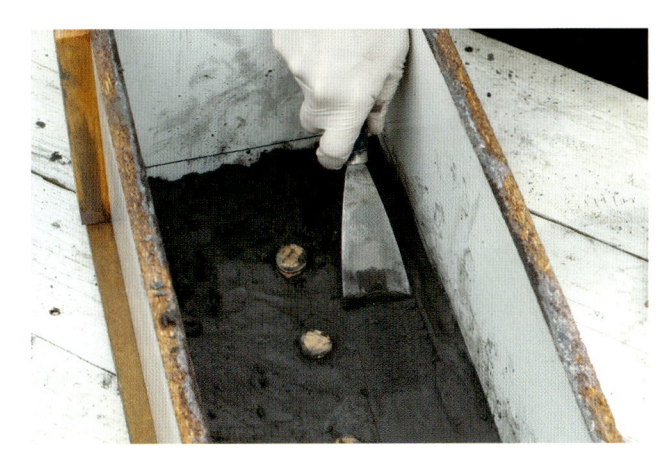

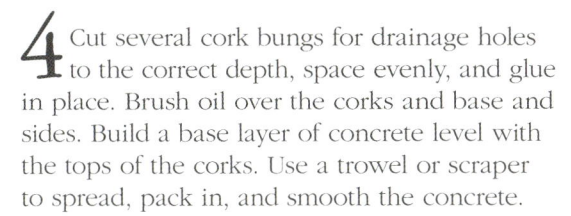

4 Cut several cork bungs for drainage holes to the correct depth, space evenly, and glue in place. Brush oil over the corks and base and sides. Build a base layer of concrete level with the tops of the corks. Use a trowel or scraper to spread, pack in, and smooth the concrete.

5 Rest the inner mould on the base layer. Pack concrete into the cavity between the moulds to build up the sides. As you fill, check you're maintaining consistent width all round using batten spacers.

6 Once you have filled the mould, tap all round to help remove air bubbles and then smooth the top edge of the concrete with a trowel. Loosely cover the mould with a sheet of plastic and leave to harden on a level surface, out of direct sunlight, for 48 hours.

7 Remove the inner mould by unscrewing the batten and then easing out the pieces of chipboard. Disassemble and remove the outer mould and finally remove the corks. Finish off by smoothing rough edges with a metal file and/or grades of sandpaper.

Why not try...

Make concrete containers in different sizes, shapes, and colours, and group together for a feature effect. Great for small spaces like tops of walls, steps, shelves, and corners.

PLANTING TIPS

Create a changing display of plants for year-round interest. Partner evergreen plants, such as variegated ivy, which give structure, with seasonal plants for interest at different times of the year. Candles create an ideal nocturnal display.

Two Ways to Decorate Your Terracotta Pots

Readily available and inexpensive, terracotta flowerpots are perfect for decorating with paint, decoupage, and other craft materials. Group your decorated pots together for a stylish effect that shows off your creativity.

TIME IT RIGHT You can create your decorated pots all year round, but prepare them under cover to avoid heat, wind, and cold. Paint and glue may not dry properly in very cold conditions. As well as plants, you can fill your pots with other items; try fir cones for a festive look in December.

Decorated pots look great when grouped together. The plants we used here (from left to right) are: *Cynara cardunculus*, *Echeveria* sp., *Laurus nobilis*, *Echinacea purpurea* 'White Swan', *Thymus* × *citriodorus* 'Argenteus', *Helichrysum italicum*, *Sedum spectabile* 'Autumn Joy'.

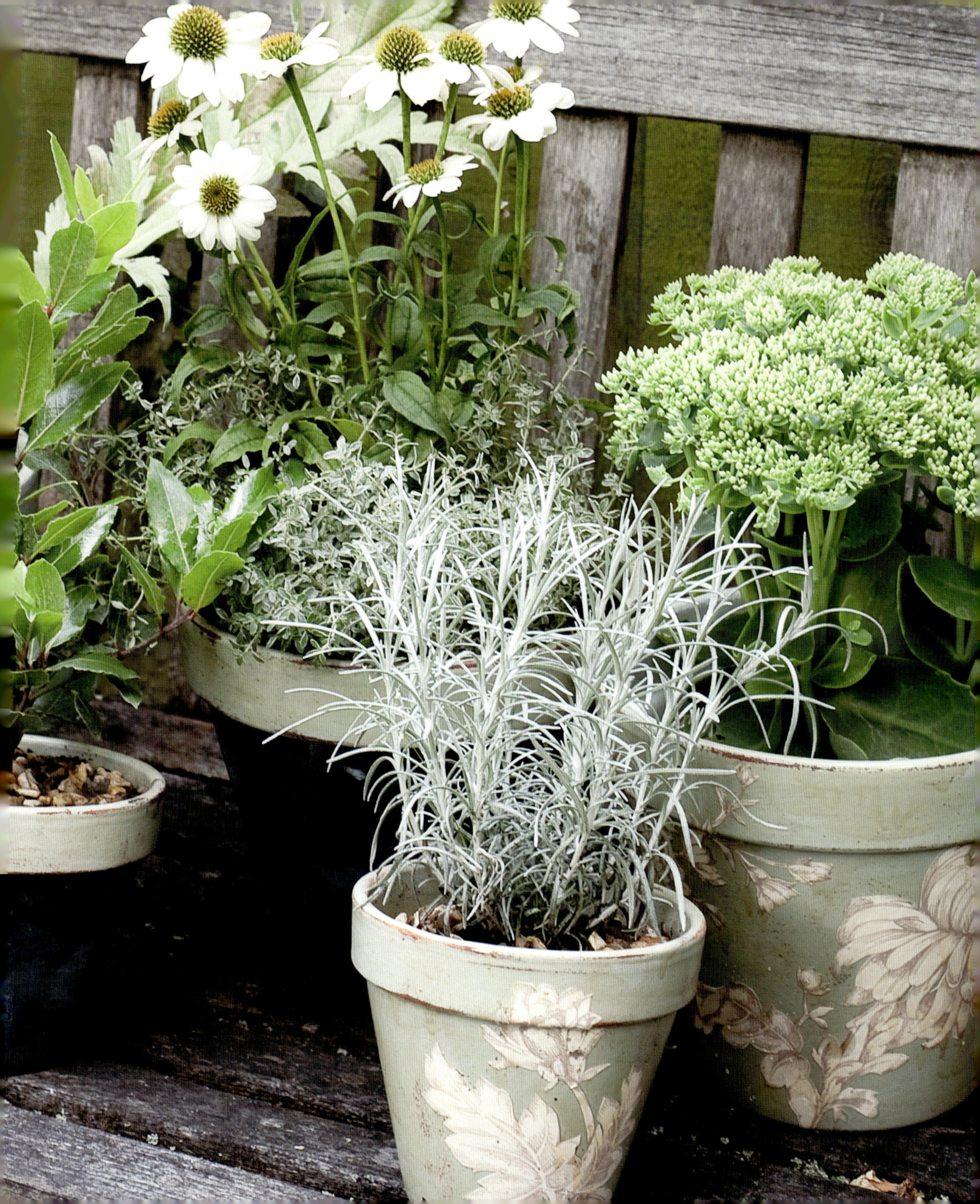

TOOLS & EQUIPMENT

terracotta pots – these can be sealed first with a 1:10 solution of PVA glue & water; leave to dry for a couple of hours or overnight before painting

acrylic or exterior paint

paintbrushes

sandpaper in various grades

decoupage material: choose prints and photos cut from wallpaper, wrapping paper, magazines, paper napkins, newspapers

scissors

PVA glue

small paintbrush or glue spreader

clear yacht varnish

PLANT LIST

Helichrysum italicum

Sedum spectabile 'Autumn Joy'

Project Steps

1 Paint the pot outside and halfway down the inside, then leave to dry. Lightly sand all over, but sand more at the rim and base, taking off a little of the paint along the edges for an aged effect.

2 Take one of your decoupage sample pieces and carefully cut around the outline with scissors. We used floral and leaf motifs cut from wallpaper.

3 Turn your decoupage pieces over to the non-patterned side and apply a thin covering of PVA glue with a paintbrush or glue spreader. Stick the pieces onto the sides of the pots until you have created a pleasing design all the way round. Leave to dry.

4 Finally, brush over a thin layer of clear yacht varnish to protect the decoration from the elements and also to add a further vintage look to the design. When dry, plant up your decorated pot.

Wallpaper is a good source for decoupage material, and floral designs complement the planting arrangement.

TOOLS & EQUIPMENT

terracotta pots – these can be sealed first with a 1:10 solution of PVA glue & water; leave to dry for a couple of hours or overnight before painting

blackboard paint

paintbrushes

acrylic or exterior paint

sandpaper in various grades

clear yacht varnish

white chalk

cloth

PLANT LIST

Echeveria species

Laurus nobilis

Project Steps

1 Paint blackboard paint around the sides of the pot but not the rim. Leave to dry.

2 Paint the rim of the pot and halfway down the inside in an attractive contrasting colour. Leave to dry, then lightly sand areas of the rim for a weathered look.

3 Paint clear yacht varnish over the rim area only for extra protection. Rub white chalk all over the blackboard paint, creating an even, fairly solid covering.

4 Take a dry cloth and rub off most of the chalk so that the pot is left with an appealing slate-coloured tinge. This also cures the blackboard paint, which is necessary if you wish to write on the pot, otherwise the writing will be indelible.

Contain Yourself **195**

These slate-effect pots looks stylish left just as they are, but you may find it a useful and attractive addition to write the plant's name and care instructions on the pot in chalk.

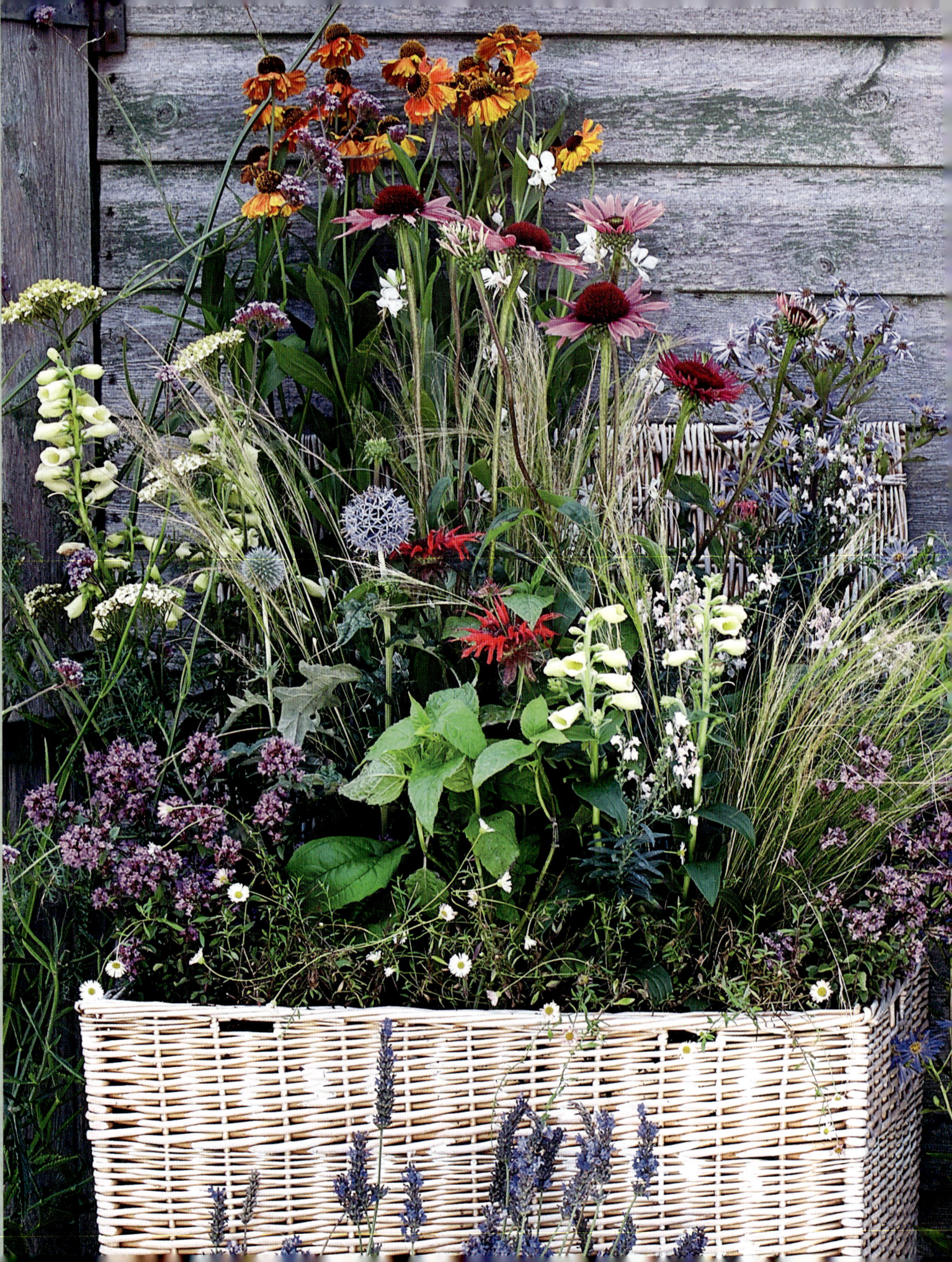

GO WILD

TOOLS & EQUIPMENT

- wooden box, such as a single-bottle wine box with slide-out lid, plus the lid from a second box
- paintbrushes & exterior paint
- yacht varnish (optional)
- metal ruler & set square
- pencil
- small handsaw
- strong outdoor adhesive
- pond liner or similar
- craft knife
- capillary matting or hanging basket liner
- scissors
- nails & sturdy brass picture hook
- hammer
- cacti potting mix mixed 3:1 with horticultural grit
- garden wire
- wire cutters

FOR THE INSECT ROOMS

- bamboo canes & pruning shears
- small logs, electric drill, & drill bits
- bark & sticks
- pine cones
- corrugated cardboard
- terracotta pots
- woodland moss

PLANT LIST

Sedum album
Sedum dasyphyllum
Sedum hirsutum
Sedum sexangulare
Sedum spurium 'Variegatum'
Sempervivum arachnoideum 'Hookeri'
Sempervivum tectorum

Portable Hanging Insect House with Green Roof

With its living succulent roof, this desirable insect house has lots of different rooms to encourage helpful, beneficial insects likes bees, ladybirds, and lacewings to seek shelter in your garden.

TIME IT RIGHT Make your insect house from spring to early autumn, when the plants for the green roof will be actively growing so they can root in, and before insects start looking for places to hibernate.

1 The insect house is made out of a single-bottle wooden wine box. Remove the lid and then paint the box; you could also apply yacht varnish to protect it further.

2 Take the lid and measure 2 roof pieces 20cm (8in) long. Divide the rest in half diagonally to form 2 triangular pieces for the sides. Cut out with a handsaw.

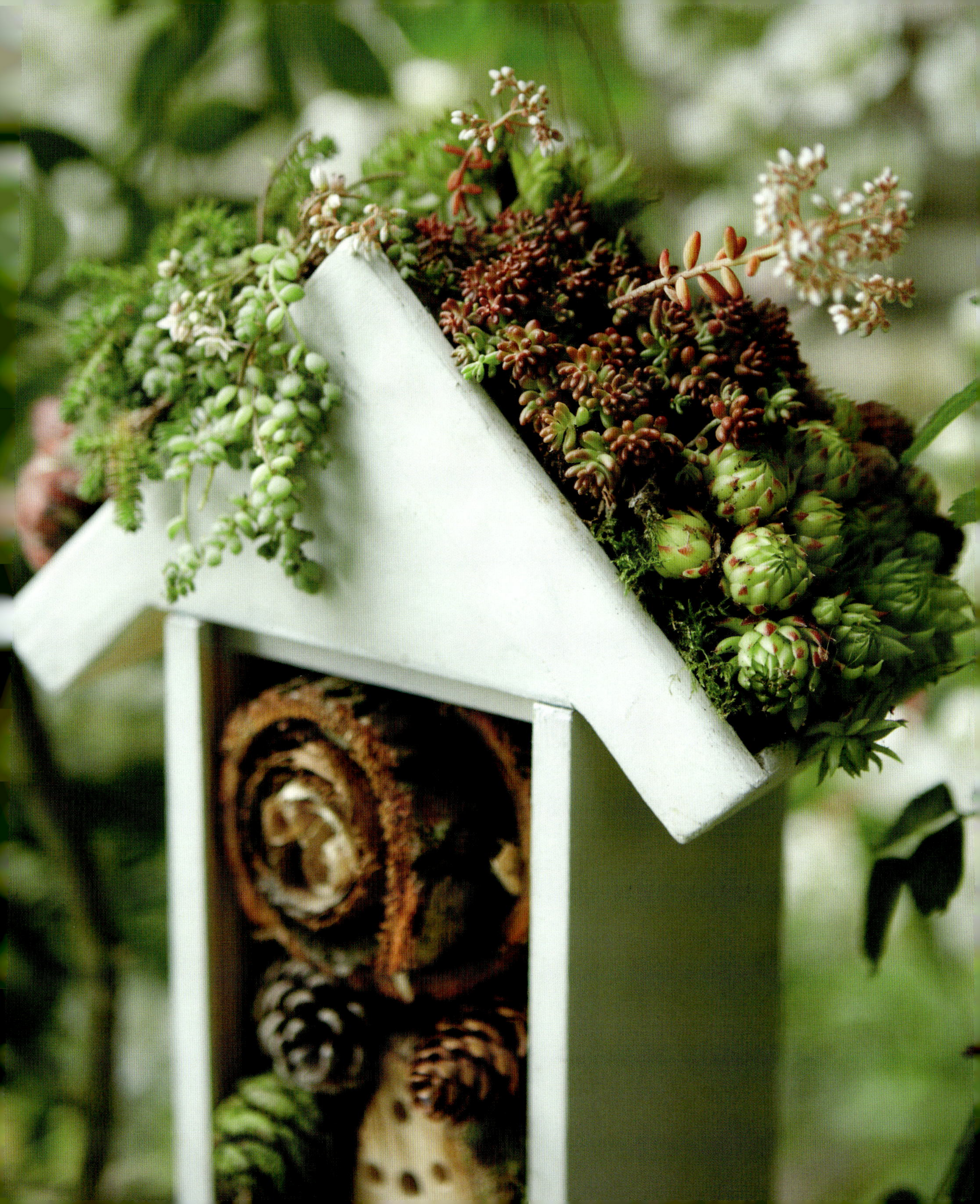

Project Steps

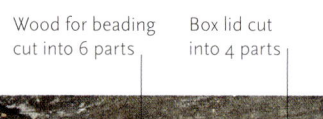

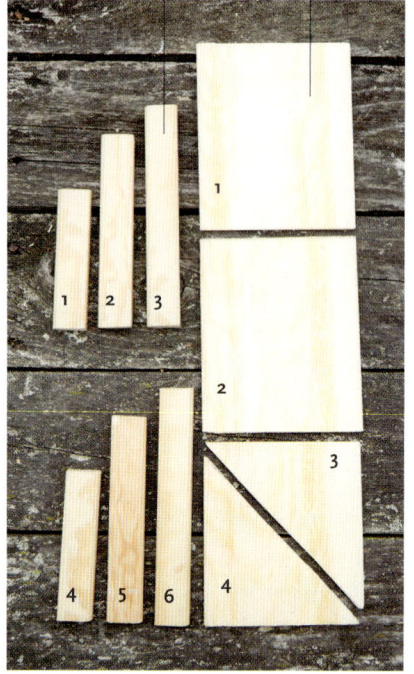

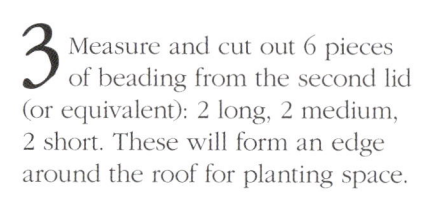

Wood for beading cut into 6 parts

Box lid cut into 4 parts

3 Measure and cut out 6 pieces of beading from the second lid (or equivalent): 2 long, 2 medium, 2 short. These will form an edge around the roof for planting space.

4 Glue the main roof pieces in a pitched shape using a strong outdoor adhesive. Glue on the triangular side pieces flush with the roof edge. Glue the beading around the edges. Paint the roof and leave to dry. Apply a layer of yacht varnish, if using.

5 To provide waterproofing for the green roof, line it with some pond liner (you could also use a heavy-duty black garbage bag). Using a sharp craft knife, cut it so that it lines the exposed roof and also comes up the sides of the beading, then trim off any excess and glue in place.

6 Now add a piece of capillary matting on top. This acts as a wick for the plants, holding moisture so that the water doesn't all run off. Cut the matting to size with scissors; it needn't cover the beading.

7 Nail a brass picture hook near the top of the box with a hammer. Glue the roof in place with strong outdoor adhesive.

8 Collect items for the insect rooms. Cut pieces of bamboo cane to the depth of the box with pruning shears and drill holes into the end of a log to create homes for solitary bees. Bark, sticks, and pine cones provide habitats for beetles, centipedes, ladybirds, spiders, and woodlice. Rolled-up corrugated cardboard or stacked terracotta pots are ideal homes for lacewing.

Little crevices are perfect places for insects to hibernate

Go Wild **203**

🛠 Project Steps

9 Build up different layers of insect rooms to create your 'hotel', filling any larger gaps with moss.

✂ Care Advice

General care The green roof doesn't need feeding, but needs occasional watering, particularly at the start while plants are establishing and in hot, dry weather. Just cut off spent flower stalks and dead leaves every now and then. You can leave your insect house outside all year round in a sheltered position shaded from hot sun. If the winter is very wet, move the insect house somewhere more sheltered from downpours. Leave the insect rooms to settle and be inhabited by your beneficial friends, topping up materials occasionally as needed.

10 For the green roof, remove plants from their pots, cut off the root ball to match the beading depth, and place snugly in the planting space, filling gaps with a mixture of potting mix and grit. Thread wire through the picture hook and hang securely outside.

Vintage Drawer
Wildflower Meadow

Create your own patch of wildflower meadow in an old vintage drawer. Your wildlife haven will attract lots of beneficial insects and is both simple to make and easy to maintain.

TIME IT RIGHT Plant up in early spring so that insects coming out of hibernation have an early nectar source. If you want to grow wildflowers from seed, sow these in either early spring or early autumn.

TOOLS & EQUIPMENT
- drawer from an old chest of drawers
- exterior wood paint & paintbrushes
- clear yacht varnish (optional)
- electric drill with wood drill bits
- scissors, thick black plastic, & glue
- gravel
- seed-raising mix
- large scoop or trowel
- butler tray table (optional)

PLANT LIST
- anise hyssop
- betony
- *Campanula* species
- carpet moss
- corncockle
- cornflower
- everlasting daisies
- lady's bedstraw
- love-in-a-mist
- small scabious
- sweet marjoram
- *Verbascum speciosum*
- wild oregano

1 Paint your drawer with exterior paint and finish with a coat of yacht varnish for added protection, if you like. We painted our drawer to contrast with our display table.

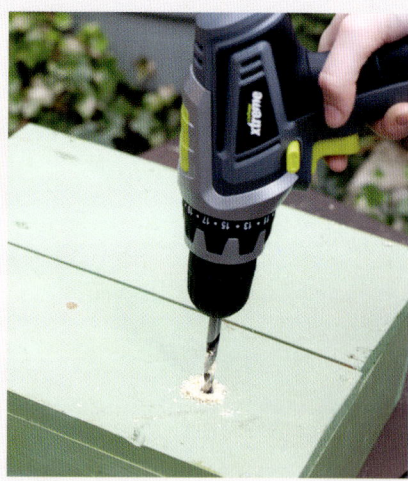

2 Drill several drainage holes in the base of the planter, spacing them evenly across the area.

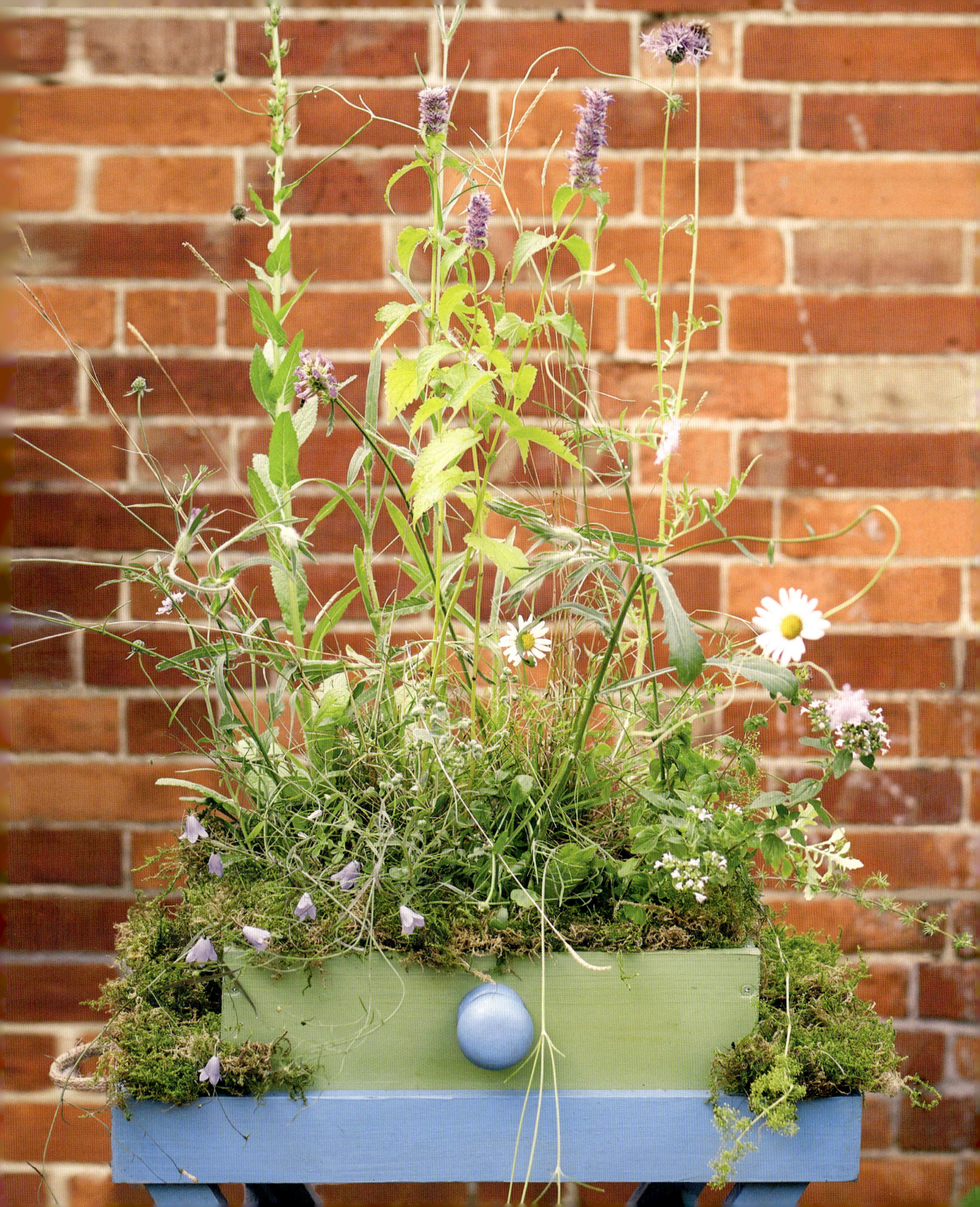

Project Steps

3 Cut to shape some thick black plastic to line the drawer, which will protect the wood and prevent it from rotting. Glue the liner into place around the sides.

4 Cut drainage holes in the base of the liner. Next, put a thin layer of gravel over the base of the plastic, which will also help with drainage.

5 Add seed-raising mix and fill to about two-thirds of the height of the plastic liner. It is important to use seed mix, as potting mix is too rich in nutrients.

6 Plan your arrangement before planting, seeing which plants fit best together. Aim for a natural look that is not regimented.

7 Start to plant up. Gently tease pot-bound roots to give them a good start. Fill any gaps between plants with seed-raising mix.

Project Steps

PLANTING TIPS

Always buy wildflower plants from specialist nurseries or grow from seed, as it's illegal to dig them up from the wild. We used native wildflowers for a sunny site, but you can choose plants for shade, semi-shade, or boggy conditions, too.

8 Water your wildflower arrangement well and finish by mulching with carpet moss for decoration and to keep in moisture. Display the meadow on a butler tray or small table, where the plants can be enjoyed up-close.

Care Advice

Where to site Keep your meadow outdoors in a sheltered sunny or shady position, depending on the plants chosen. Perennial plants do not need protection from cold weather, but annual flowers are less tolerant of temperature extremes.

Watering Water regularly from spring to mid-autumn, reducing to a minimum in winter. Do not overwater the container but nor should you let it dry out. You need not feed the meadow at any stage as wildflowers prefer soil low in nutrients.

General care Remove any dead, diseased, or dying foliage during the growing season, but leave seedheads on until early to mid-autumn so that plants self-seed naturally. Thin out or pot up any excess seedlings in mid-spring. You will need to cut every plant down to just above soil level in late autumn so that stems and foliage are not left on over the winter. For best results, remove all plants and replant into fresh seed-raising mix the following spring.

For a smaller space or alternative wildflower meadow, plant up a large metal garden sieve. Simply line (adding drainage holes if needed), cover the base with gravel, then add seed compost and plants.

TOOLS & EQUIPMENT

- rubber or surgical gloves
- wicker hamper
- dish cloth or old rags
- exterior paint & clear yacht varnish
- scissors, thick black plastic, & glue
- gravel
- general-purpose potting mix

PLANT LIST

- *Achillea* species
- *Agastache* species
- *Aster macrophyllus* species
- *Centranthus ruber* 'Coccineus'
- *Digitalis grandiflora*
- *Echinacea purpurea*
- *Echinops ritro* 'Veitch's Blue'
- *Erigeron karvinskianus*
- *Gaura lindheimeri*
- *Helenium autumnale*
- *Lavandula* species
- *Linaria purpurea* 'Canon Went'
- *Monarda* 'Cambridge Scarlet'
- *Origanum* species
- *Stipa tenuissima*
- *Verbena bonariensis*

Bee and Butterfly
Wildlife Hamper

Planted with nectar-rich plants, this hamper will keep bees and butterflies supplied with food. You'll enjoy watching the different species of beneficial insects that come and tuck into this fast-food feast.

TIME IT RIGHT Early spring is a good time to plant up your hamper so that insects coming out of hibernation have an early food source. Add spring and autumn bulbs to the planting to extend the season.

1 Wearing protective gloves, give the hamper a light paint wash by dipping a cloth or rag into paint and rubbing it all over the wicker. Leave to dry, then add a layer of yacht varnish in the same way, for extra weather protection.

2 Cut the plastic to line the hamper; this both protects and helps retain soil and moisture. Glue in place and, when dry, cut several holes in the liner for drainage.

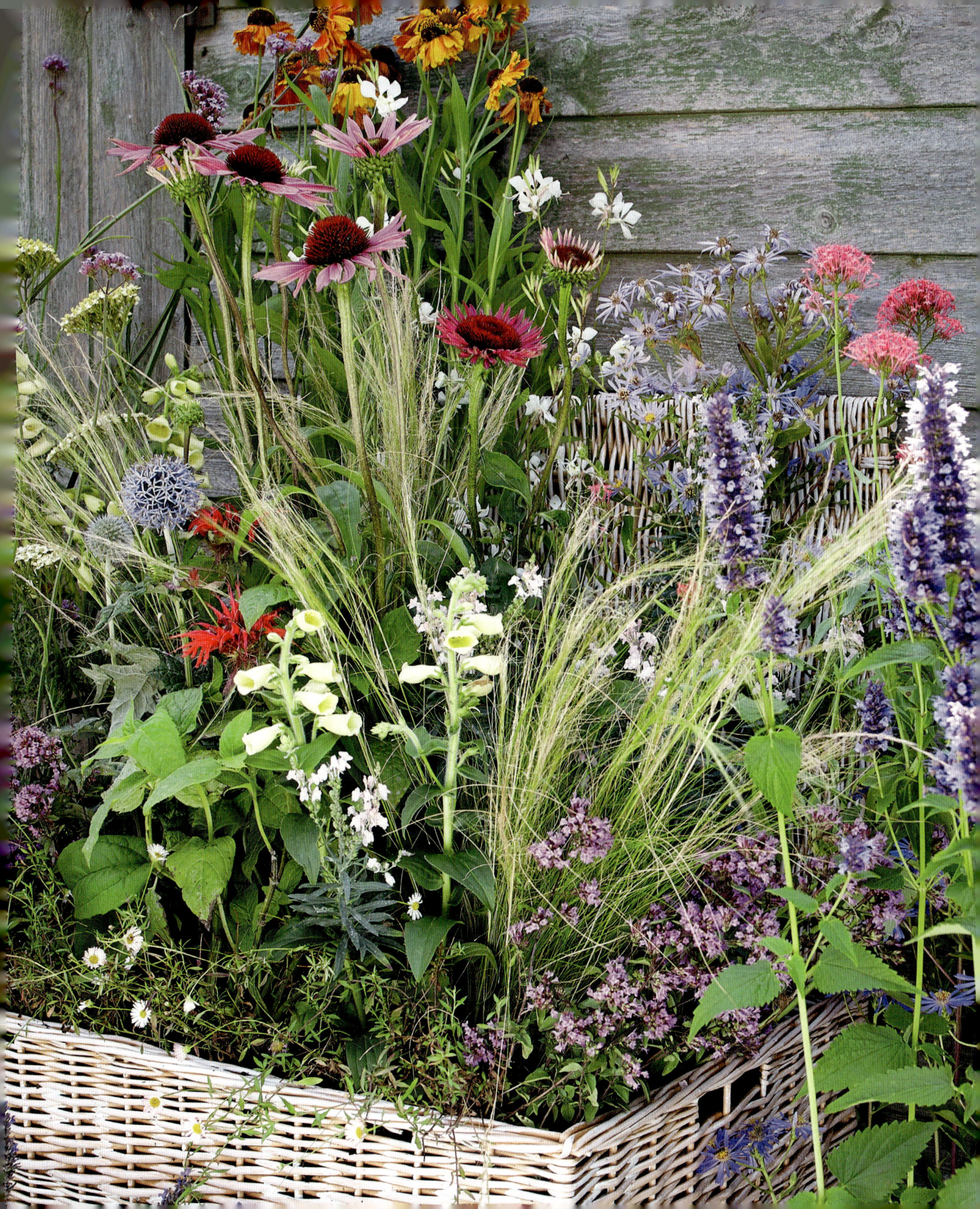

Project Steps

PLANTING TIPS

Bees and butterflies prefer to gather nectar in the sun, so choose sun-loving plants. Add year-round interest with bulbs for spring and autumn. Leave seedheads on plants over winter for birds to enjoy and insects to hibernate in.

3 Put a thin layer of gravel across the base of the plastic, which will help with drainage.

4 Add the potting mix and fill to about half the height of the plastic liner to leave room for the root balls of the plants.

5 Plan your planting arrangement, seeing which plants fit best together. Aim for a natural arrangement and dot grasses between flowering plants to add texture and movement.

Bees prefer single flowers, rather than double ones, while butterflies like small tubular flowers and those with a large central area

6 Plant up your hamper, gently teasing out any pot-bound roots to help get them off to a good start. Fill any gaps between plants with potting mix and water in thoroughly.

Care Advice

Where to site Place in a sheltered, sunny position that is shaded in the afternoon. The hamper is planted with outdoor perennials that do not need protection from cold weather.

Watering and feeding Water regularly from spring to mid-autumn, reducing to minimal levels in winter. Do not overwater or let the potting mix dry out. Add diluted liquid feed to the water monthly from spring to autumn.

General care Remove any dead or dying foliage during the growing season. You will need to cut every plant down to just above soil level in late winter or early spring. When the plants outgrow the hamper, split them into more plants, and replant the hamper at the same time.

A watering can with a long spout gets water directly into the potting mix.

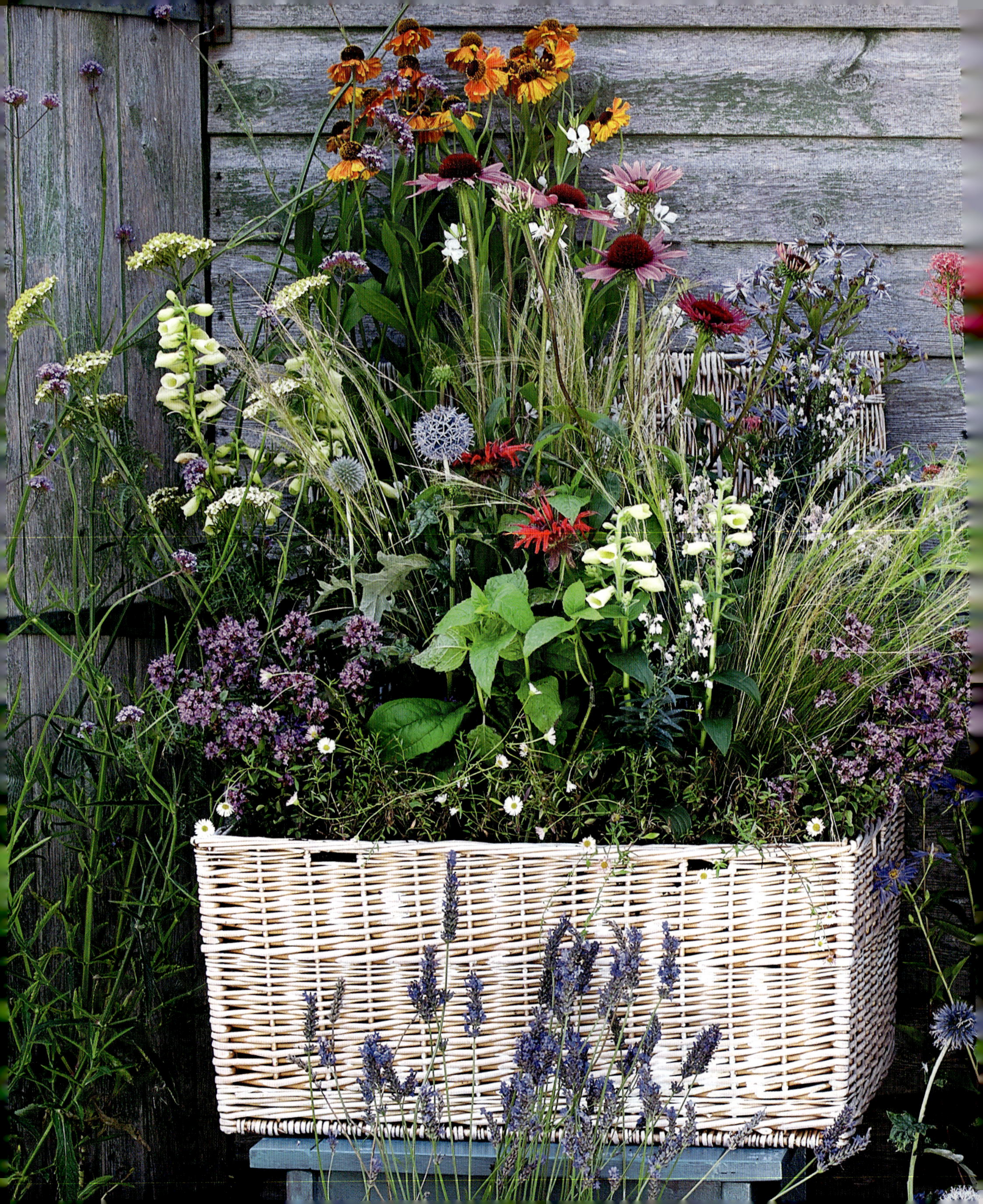

A bee enjoying *Agastache* cv. (top).
Digitalis grandiflora, *Achillea* cv. and *Verbena bonariensis* (centre).
The large central cone of *Echinacea purpurea* cv. (bottom) is perfect for bees and butterflies.

Cup-and-Saucer Bird Stations

Watching birds in your outdoor space is both fascinating and relaxing. Add a decorative touch while looking after your feathered friends with these delightful feeders made from cups and mugs.

TIME IT RIGHT Make these feeders in time for autumn when birds need to find extra food supplies to see them through the winter. Garden birds feed all year round, however, so keep seed topped up.

TOOLS & EQUIPMENT

- terracotta drip trays
- bamboo canes, cut to slightly different lengths
- acrylic or exterior paints
- paintbrushes
- clear yacht varnish (optional)
- selection of large ceramic or enamel cups, mugs, or small bowls
- masking tape
- electric drill with ceramic & metal drill bits
- exterior glue
- cane toppers or rubber caps
- bricks or large stones (optional)
- bird seed such as sunflower seed

1 Paint the drip trays and canes in a variety of colours. Think how they will work with your cups and mugs when choosing your colours, and try matching or contrasting the colours of the trays and canes. Leave to dry and then add a coat of yacht varnish, if you like, for extra protection against the elements.

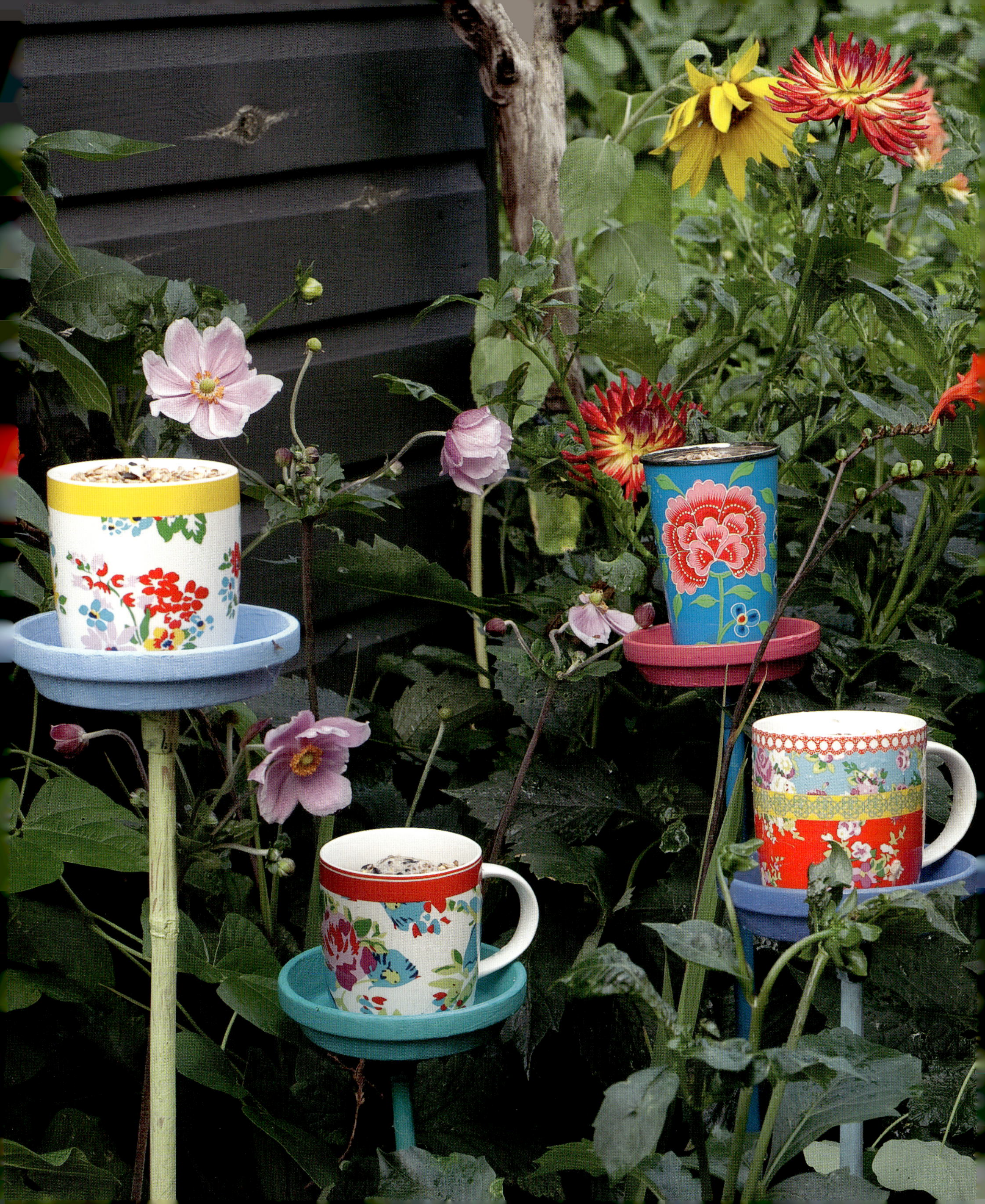

Project Steps

2 Drill a hole in the base of each of your seed holders. This will help rainwater to drain away so that the bird seed doesn't get too waterlogged. Make a masking-tape cross where you want to drill for a neat finish and to prevent slipping.

3 Glue a cane topper onto one end of each cane and leave to dry.

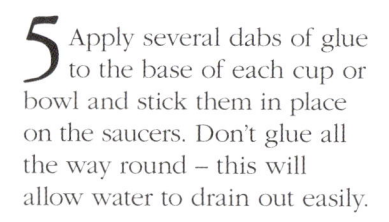

5 Apply several dabs of glue to the base of each cup or bowl and stick them in place on the saucers. Don't glue all the way round – this will allow water to drain out easily.

4 Apply glue to the tops of the cane toppers, then glue these to the middle of each of the painted terracotta saucers. Leave to dry completely.

6 Insert the canes firmly into the ground. Support them with bricks or large stones if they still feel a little loose.

220 Go Wild

🛠 Project Steps

NO GROUND?
If you don't have a patch of ground where you can insert your feeders, try cementing them into a flowerpot instead. Simply place the cane with feeder in the centre of a pot, fill around with concrete mix, and leave it to dry.

7 Fill the cups with bird seed and the bowls with water. Keep both regularly replenished and watch the birds flock to your garden!

✂ Care Advice

Where to site The ideal position for your bird feeders and bath is somewhere quiet so the birds won't be disturbed, relatively open and sunny so that they have a good field of view, but also near a large shrub or other plants where they can escape from cats. Several feeding stations allow smaller birds lower down in the pecking order to get a look in.

General care Clean out feeders and remove any debris regularly, particularly after long spells of wet weather. Use a cloth to clean the inside of the feeder and water bowl. Change the water in the bowl frequently.

More Ideas for
Hungry Birds

1 Seedcake hangers are useful for garden birds in winter, when other food may be scarce. Measure half the weight of fat to bird seed; use a hard fat such as lard or white vegetable fat. Melt the fat in a pan, stir in the seeds and spread onto a baking tray to the same depth as the cutters. Leave to cool slightly, then press the cutters into the mix.

2 Remove the filled cutters and leave to set. To hang them, cut lengths of garden twine, make a hole at the top of each cutter with a skewer, thread through the twine, and knot the ends together.

Tie seedcake hangers directly on to a suitable support or use clothes pegs for easy removal when the cutters need replenishing.

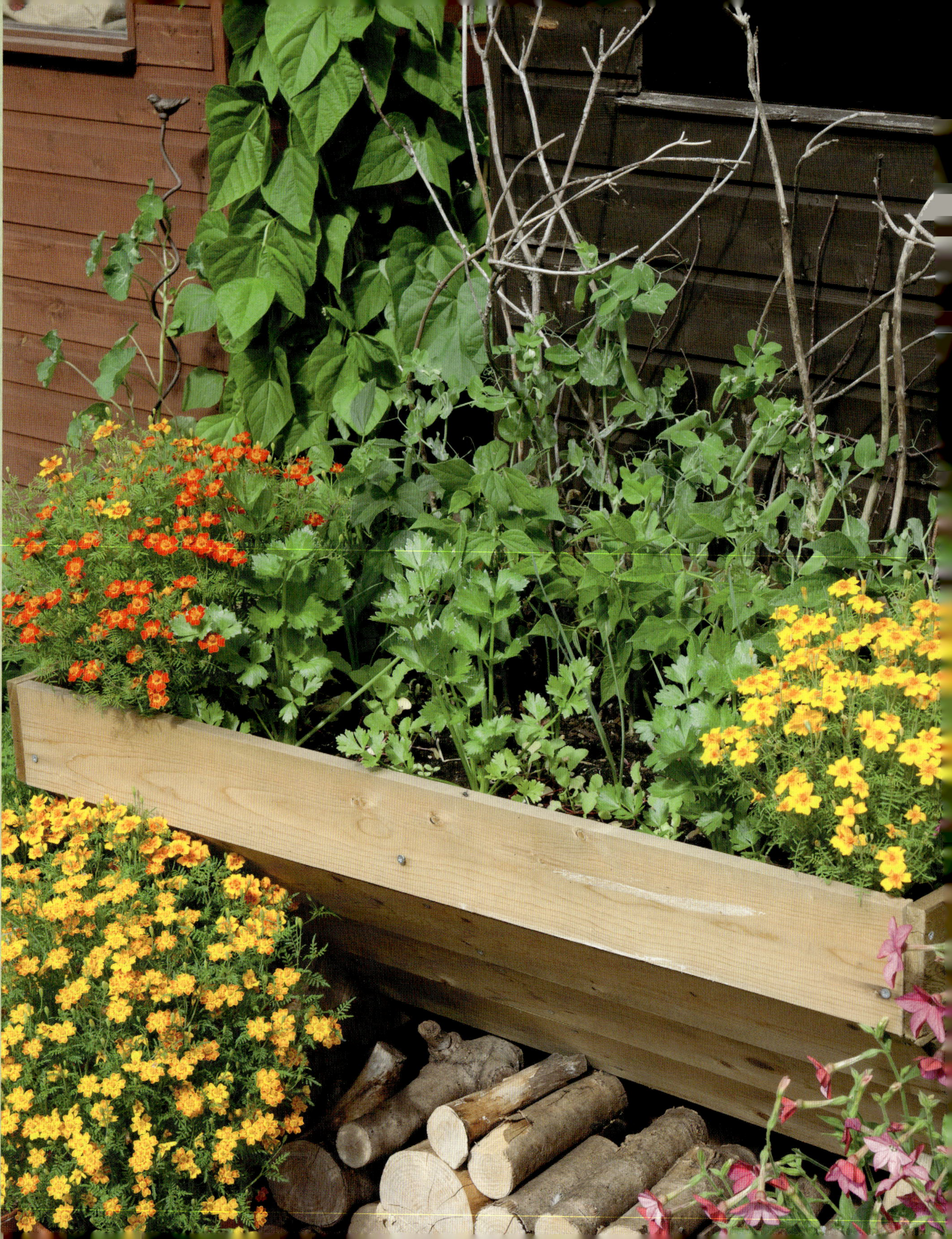

PLANT PRACTICAL

Choosing Plants

For your plants to survive and flourish, it is vital to match the right plants to the right conditions, so make sure you know what your growing space is like before buying. Is it sheltered, damp, and shady, or exposed, dry, and sunny?

Practical considerations

Think about what you want to grow and how much time you have to look after your plants. Some plants need less attention than others, but all plants require some care. Consider the time of year for your flowering display, too. Some plants look good when in flower but don't add anything else for the rest of the year. Combine these with other plants whose flowers, stems, or foliage add interest across other seasons. Look for plants with a good shape that can be used as a focal point to anchor a changing display. Consider what containers you are going to use. All containers need drainage and should be easily accessible for watering and care. Consider too how they might affect the overall look of your planting. Complex arrangements work best in less fussy containers where the focus is on the planting itself. Quirky, unusual containers add an element of fun too, so try anything suitable and adapt for drainage, if need be.

Be inspired

Seek inspiration for your garden style and explore planting ideas. Buy a big notebook and visit open gardens, jotting down what plants you like and different planting schemes. Don't be afraid to ask questions of garden owners and gardeners, who will usually be more than happy to tell you more. Have a look through gardening books and seek out magazines for ideas, keeping a note of anything that appeals. Don't forget the great outdoors for inspiration! Nature has a clever way of arranging plants and landscape features that blend perfectly: wildflower meadows; coastal planting; bushland; shady plants in gullies; or streams and ponds.

Finding your style

Do you want the planting to be ornamental or productive with herbs, vegetables, and fruit? Do you want to screen off neighbouring buildings? Do you want year-round interest? What style of planting particularly appeals to you? Planting styles can be re-created in smaller spaces by careful plant selection, so take time to really know what you want to achieve if you are planning a major design in your gardening space. As well as your growing conditions, take into account your home and how your planting will blend in with the building. Some planting styles may suit your home more than others, but don't be afraid to try something unusual for a different approach. Most of all, enjoy creating a garden space that is unique to you and reflects your own style and personality.

Although there are notable exceptions, such as succulents, most plants in containers will need a lot of watering, so make sure you have time to do this and easy access to water.

If the growing conditions of light, temperature, and exposure allow it, almost any style of planting, such as this cottage garden feel, can be adapted to fit a smaller space.

What sort of plant?

Sometimes it's obvious what type of plant you need to buy, like a tree, but sometimes it isn't, and it's useful to know the difference between the groupings so you can choose the correct plant for your needs.

Annuals complete their life cycle in one growing season. They will germinate, flower, produce seeds, and die in one growing season. Examples include annual bedding plants like pansies, zinnias, marigolds, forget-me-not, and sweet peas.

Perennials last more than three growing seasons, but the name is often used to cover herbaceous perennials, which are mostly border plants that survive year after year, with foliage usually dying back when the plant is dormant in winter. Examples include penstemons, asters, primroses, sedums, and hostas. Some perennials need a bit of protection from frost and stormy weather.

Bulbs are modified stems adapted to store food, and different bulbs can be planted in spring, summer, and autumn for year-round successional interest.

Shrubs and trees are woody perennials that add structure to planting. Some plants are evergreen, but most lose their leaves when the plant goes dormant.

Grow your own

Growing plants from seed is cost effective and fun for all the family. You'll need containers, seed-raising mix, and somewhere light and warm to start them off (see pages 132–7).

Some summer seedlings, particularly annuals and vegetable plants, will need protection from frost before they can be planted out.

Plants for sun

Key to symbols: ◊ Drought tolerant ◊ Water often ● Keep constantly wet ☼ Grow in full sun ☀ Partial shade ☀ Full shade

Echinacea purpurea
Outstanding late-summer display of large flowers with a prominent central cone. Easy to grow. Attracts bees and butterflies. Seedheads look good in winter. Flowering time: July–September.

Care: Cut back to encourage flowers, but leave some seedheads over winter.

◊ ☼–☀ ❄❄❄

Helenium autumnale
Upright plants with showy, daisy-like flowers from late summer through autumn. Rich flower colours range from buttery yellow to warm orange to bronzy red. The central cone is loved by bees.

Care: Deadhead, leaving some seedheads. Divide every 3–4 years.

◊ ☼ ❄❄❄

Sedum spectabile
Good for a dry, sunny spot. Late-summer flowers are adored by bees and butterflies, and fleshy leaves add interest year round. Some varieties have grey/green or purple/green foliage.

Care: Cut back after flowering or leave till spring for winter interest.

◊ ☼ ❄❄❄

Aster
Ranges from small alpine species to taller plants. Pretty daisy-like flowers, in white, pink, lilac, or blue, bloom in late summer. Loved by bees and butterflies.

Care: Choose mildew-free varieties for best foliage. Cut back after flowering or leave until spring for winter interest.

◊ ☼ ❄❄❄

Lavandula angustifolia
Small shrubs with aromatic leaves and spikes of fragrant blue, purple, pink, or white flowers in summer. Can grow quite large and lose its shape, so choose shorter varieties for smaller spaces.

Care: Trim after flowering. Shape in spring. Don't cut into old woody growth.

◊ ☼ ❄❄❄

Agapanthus
Excellent for containers. Upright funnel-shaped blue or white flowers create impact in summer and early autumn. Attractive seedheads in winter.

Care: Feed regularly during growing season and remove seedheads if self-seeding is a concern.

◊ ☼ ❄❄❄–❄❄

See also... *Aeonium* p228, *Agastache* p230, Bronze fennel p230, *Buddleja* p230, *Calamagrostis* x *acutiflora* 'Karl Foerster' p233, *Canna* p231, *Dianthus alpinus* p228, *Echeveria* p228, *Phlox douglasii* p228, *Rosa rugosa* p229, *Sempervivum* p228

Plants for shade and semi-shade

❄❄❄ Frost hardy   ❄❄ Can survive outside in mild regions/sheltered sites   ❄ Move inside for winter

Pulmonaria
Delicate blue, white, or pink flowers from late winter to early spring. Interesting blotchy leaves for most of the year. Lovely ground cover under other plants.

Care: Cut back old leaves before flowers appear, and again in summer.

💧 ☀–🌥 ❄❄❄

Hosta
Easy to grow, hostas come in a wide range of heights and leaf colours, some with variegation. The perfect foliage plant for light to part shade, with pretty upright flowers in summer.

Care: Feed monthly during growing season and protect from snails.

💧 ☀–🌥 ❄❄❄

Astrantia major
Dainty pin-cushion-style flowers ranging from white, pale green to pinks and reds. Can also be planted in sun, but needs moist soil. Good to plant under taller plants to add layers.

Care: Deadhead, and cut back to soil level in autumn or late winter.

💧 🌥 ❄❄❄

Ferns
Ferns add architectural interest to displays, thrive in shady conditions, and come in a variety of heights and leaf shapes. Great to plant under taller plants. Some are evergreen.

Care: Incorporate organic matter in planting area. Keep soil moist.

💧 ☀–🌥 ❄❄❄

Bergenia
Evergreen perennial with dark-green leaves, red tinted in winter, deep purple in some varieties. White or pink flowers in late winter and early spring. Easy to grow. Good ground cover plant.

Care: Remove faded flower spikes. Will grow in sun, but needs moist soil.

💧 ☀–🌥 ❄❄❄

Helleborus
Hellebores' elegant flowers brighten up late-winter days – they can be single or double, from pale pink to deep maroon. Large architectural leaves add interest.

Care: Cut back old foliage before flowers appear. Apply liquid or soluble feed in autumn and after flowering.

💧 🌥 ❄❄❄

See also... *Acer palmatum* p231, *Buxus sempervirens* p233, *Fothergilla major* p231, *Hydrangea* p233, *Photinia* p229, *Viburnum* x *bodnantense* p233

Succulents, alpines, and air plants

Key to symbols: ◊ Drought tolerant   ◊ Water often   ● Keep constantly wet   ☼ Grow in full sun   ☀ Partial shade   ✹ Full shade

Sempervivum
Tight rosettes of fleshy leaves with upright flowers in summer. Foliage in shades of green, mahogany, bronzy purple, and crimson. Plant in a shallow container with free-draining potting mix.

Care: Repot when roots fill container. Do not overwater.

◊ ☼ ❋❋❋

Echeveria
Thick, fleshy leaves in rosettes, which can be green tinged with red autumnal hints, or dramatic black/purple. Clusters of upright flowers in spring. Looks good in traditional alpine pots.

Care: Durable and withstands dry conditions. Do not overwater.

◊ ☼

Aeonium
Evergreen succulents. Rosettes of fleshy leaves. Star-shaped flowers in spring. Perfect for a sunny porch. Foliage is green with red tints in autumn/winter. Blackish-purple varieties also available.

Care: Tolerates hot, dry conditions. Do not overwater.

◊ ☼

Dianthus alpinus
Choose small alpine species with dainty and fragrant white or pink upright flowers in summer and evergreen foliage. Pretty in a tiny container. Use free-draining potting mix.

Care: Repot when roots fill container. Deadhead regularly. Do not overwater.

◊ ☼ ❋❋❋

Phlox douglasii
Makes a close-growing plant that will carpet shallow containers. Lilac, pale-blue, or pink flowers from late spring to early summer. Plant with free-draining potting mix.

Care: Repot when roots fill container. Deadhead regularly. Do not overwater.

◊ ☼–☀ ❋❋❋

Tillandsia
Air plants don't need soil to grow; they absorb all their moisture and nutrients from the air. Versatile in a variety of arrangements, including growing on bark and shells or in sand.

Care: Mist for humidity and shade from hot sun. Liquid feed in spring.

◊ ☀ ❋

See also... *Aster* p226, *Sedum spectabile* p226

Plants for screening

❄❄❄ Frost hardy   ❄❄ Can survive outside in mild regions/sheltered sites   ❄ Move inside for winter

Phyllostachys nigra

Vigorous, tall, upright bamboo with stunning blackish-brown stems. Wind rustling through leaves makes lovely sound, but plant can be invasive so grow in a large container.

Care: Remove older stems to thin out and show off newer stems.

Miscanthus sinensis

Ornamental grass with upright stems and arching silky flowers. Foliage has autumn colour or is evergreen. Good in containers and planted in groups.

Care: Leave flowers and stems over winter for added interest. Cut back to soil level in late winter.

Ceanothus 'Concha'

Dense evergreen shrub known as Californian Lilac due to its purple-blue flowers. It has twiggy branches, small deep green leaves and grows to 3m (9ft).

Care: Water regularly until well-established. Trim foliage after flowering to maintain a dense cover.

Rosa rugosa

Apple-green glossy foliage and single pink or white flowers in summer. Loved by bees. Huge red hips in autumn. Good hedging plant and easy to grow.

Care: Leave rose hips for winter interest. Feed in growing season. Prune in late winter. Cut older wood to base.

Callistemon viminalis

An excellent bottlebrush for screening. It grows to 3m (9ft) tall and the profuse blossom is loved by birds and bees.

Care: Water regularly in dry weather until well-established. Trim after flowering to promote dense foliage.

Photinia

Evergreen shrubs with glossy leaves. Newer growth is bright red. Creamy white flowers in spring. You can clip the plants into a formal or informal hedge, or grow as standard shrubs.

Care: Keep well watered and feed monthly in growing season.

See also... *Banksia ericifolia* p233, *Buxus sempervirens* p233, *Calamagrostis* x *acutiflora* 'Karl Foerster' p233, *Euonymous* p231, *Fatsia japonica* p231, *Lonicera* p230, *Pyracantha* p233

Plants for wildlife

Key to symbols: ◊ Drought tolerant   ● Water often   ● Keep constantly wet   ☼ Grow in full sun   ☼ Partial shade   ☼ Full shade

Buddleja
Known as the "Butterfly Bush" because the flowers, in shades of pink, mauve, blue, and white, provide a good source of nectar for butterflies. Some grow tall but can be kept smaller by pruning.

Care: Feed regularly in growing season. Prune after flowering.

◊ ☼ ❄❄❄

Agastache
Aromatic leaves and upright spikes of blue, orange, or pink flowers. The small, tubular flowers invite bees and butterflies. Adds height to planting.

Care: Remove spent flower spikes throughout the season. Feed during the growing season.

◊ ☼ ❄❄❄

Grevillea 'Robyn Gordon'
This wonderful free-flowering shrub provides nectar for birds and bees year round. It grows in a rounded form to 3m (9ft) but can be trimmed to control size.

Care: Flowers all year. Early summer is best time for pruning, as new growth is most rapid. Water in dry periods.

◊ ☼ ❄❄❄

Bronze fennel
Feathery bronze foliage with sulphur-yellow flat flowers in summer. Good seedheads for the birds in autumn/winter. Tall, architectural, with fragrant leaves. Looks good planted in gravel.

Care: Leave seedheads over winter. Cut back to base in early spring.

◊ ☼ ❄❄❄

Digitalis purpurea
Bees adore foxgloves! Flower colours on tall spikes range from traditional purple to white, apricot, and yellow. A woodland plant that enjoys an aspect receiving morning sun.

Care: Cut back spikes after flowering, but leave some to self-seed. Keep moist.

◊ ☼–☼ ❄❄❄

Lonicera
Honeysuckle is useful to grow up a trellis and as larger shrubs. Fragrant summer flowers are loved by bees and butterflies. Berries follow in autumn. Birds like to nest in thicker areas.

Care: Prune for shape in early spring. Tie in stems. Feed in growing season.

◊ ☼–☼ ❄❄❄

See also... *Aster* p226, *Calamagrostis* x *acutiflora* 'Karl Foerster' p233, *Echinacea purpurea* p226, *Helenium autumnale* p226, *Iris versicolor* p232, *Lavandula* p226, *Pyracantha* p233, *Rosa rugosa* p229, *Sedum spectabile* p226

Plant Practical **231**

Plants for foliage

✻✻✻ Frost hardy ✻✻ Can survive outside in mild regions/sheltered sites ✻ Move inside for winter

Heuchera
Slender stems have spikes of small bell-shaped flowers in late spring, and interesting, mostly evergreen foliage. Leaf colour ranges from pale bronze to green, and purple.

Care: Remove faded flower spikes. Feed in growing season.

💧 ☀–☼ ✻✻✻

Acer palmatum
Japanese maples have finely divided, palm-like leaves. Foliage colour varies from green to yellow to purple, turning a stunning fiery red in autumn. Choose a small variety for a container.

Care: Prune lightly in late winter for shape. Feed/water in growing season.

💧 ☀–☼ ✻✻✻

Fothergilla major
Easy-to-grow shrub with glossy, oval leaves that turn brilliant orange and crimson in autumn. Small, white, fragrant flowers in early spring. Brings charm and interest all year round.

Care: Lightly prune for shape in late winter/early spring. Keep moist.

💧 ☀–☼ ✻✻✻

Canna
A tropical-style plant with large, upright leaves, often with striped markings or good colour variations. Vibrant, showy flowers in late summer/early autumn. Adds a dazzling late-season display.

Care: Leave to die back in winter, then cut back to ground level.

💧 ☀ ✻

Fatsia japonica
Wonderful large, palm-like leaves that are glossy green all year round. A good architectural plant that needs a bit of space and can be under-planted with spring bulbs for seasonal colour.

Care: Prune to shape in early spring. Water well in growing season.

💧 ☀–☼ ✻✻✻

Euonymous
Dwarf shrub with evergreen foliage, which is often variegated yellow or creamy white with green. Good for planting under large shrubs/trees or for brightening darker corners.

Care: Prune to shape in early spring. Water well in growing season.

💧 ☀–☼ ✻✻✻

> **See also…** *Bergenia* p227, *Buxus sempervirens* p233, *Ceanothus* 'Concha' p229, *Ferns* p227, *Helleborus* p227, *Hosta* p227, *Photinia* p229, *Pulmonaria* p227

Water and bog plants

Key to symbols: ◌ Drought tolerant ● Water often ● Keep constantly wet ☼ Grow in full sun ☀ Partial shade ☀ Full shade

Baloskian tetraphyllum
Known as Tassel Rush for its attractive, tassle-like flowering stems, this Australian plant grows in shallow water or boggy situations to over 1m (3ft).

Care: Be sure to maintain moisture at all times. Also make sure container is large enough to allow for growth.

● ☼–☀ ❄❄❄

Iris versicolor
Upright, sword-like leaves from early spring to late autumn, with pretty blue and purple flowers in summer. Great for pond margins or boggy water features. Flowers are loved by insects.

Care: Remove dead foliage in late winter before new growth begins.

● ☼ ❄❄❄

Zantedeschia aethiopica
Elegant white or yellow funnel-shaped flowers in spring and summer. Dark-green arrow-shaped leaves add interest from spring to autumn.

Care: Remove dead foliage in late winter before new growth begins. Shade from hot sun.

● ☼ ❄❄–☀

Nymphaea
Water lilies have showy, bowl-shaped flowers that come in various colours. Floating rounded leaves create shade for submerged water plants.

Care: Deadhead flowers and remove old foliage regularly. Feed in growing season with aquatic fertilizer.

● ☼ ❄❄❄

Caltha palustris
Bright and cheery in early spring, the marsh marigold has clusters of deep-yellow flowers and heart-shaped leaves from spring to autumn. Vigorous grower that can spread widely.

Care: Cut back after flowering. Control spread by planting in a container or pond.

● ☼ ❄❄❄

Carex elata
This evergreen sedge is perfect for the edge of marsh or bog gardens. Leaves are upright and yellow, with small black flowers in summer. Adds interest all year round.

Care: Cut back stalks after flowering and remove any dead foliage regularly.

● ☼–☀ ❄❄❄

Plants for year-round interest

❄❄❄ Frost hardy ❄❄ Can survive outside in mild regions/sheltered sites ❄ Move inside for winter

Banksia ericifolia
With fine foliage and candle-like flower heads, Heath banksia offers a year-round display of flowers and seed cones loved by birds and bees. Grows to 3m (9ft).

Care: Water until well established, particularly in dry periods. Trim to desired shape and size in spring.

Calamagrostis x acutiflora
'Karl Foerster'
Ornamental grass with feathery flowers in late summer. The green foliage turns bronze in late summer, then provides interest during winter. Loved by birds.

Care: Leave stems and flowers over winter. Cut down in late winter.

Pyracantha
Evergreen shrub that can be grown as hedge or trained as specimens. Creamy-white flowers in summer; long-lasting red/orange berries in autumn. Loved by bees and birds.

Care: Prune to shape in early spring. Trim more often if used for hedging.

Hydrangea
For blue-flowered hydrangeas, plant in ericaceous soil. Pink ones prefer ordinary or alkaline soil. White-flowered species prefer some shade.

Care: Leave flower heads till late winter. Hard prune *H. arborescens* and *H. paniculata* to 5–7.5cm (2–3in) above soil.

Viburnum x bodnantense
Upright shrub with deciduous textured leaves. From autumn to spring, clusters of scented, light-pink and white flowers bring winter colour. Keep shrub height under control by pruning.

Care: Prune in late winter. Can be hard pruned if required.

Buxus sempervirens
Evergreen box is very versatile. It can be clipped as a hedge or into topiary for extra interest. Slow-growing. Only needs 1–2 cuts a year to keep its shape.

Care: Prune to keep shape in early spring, just before growth starts. Water well in growing season.

See also... *Carex elata* p232, *Fothergilla major* p231, *Grevillea* 'Robyn Gordon' p230, *Heuchera* p231, *Miscanthus sinensis* p229, *Photinia* p229, *Phyllostachys nigra* p229, *Rosa rugosa* p229, *Sedum spectabile* p226

Get the Look

Cottage garden

A mix of traditional flowering plants mingled with vegetables, fruit, and herbs makes for a gentle, romantic cottage garden look. Flowering plants are placed together in informal groups with different heights, shapes, and textures creating a tapestry-style effect. Plants are left to self-seed to soften the edges of gravel or natural paving paths.

Plants to try

- Alchemilla mollis
- Aster x frikartii 'Mönch'
- Auriculas
- Campanula lactiflora
- Dianthus 'Mrs Sinkins'
- Dicentra spectabilis
- Digitalis purpurea
- English Lavender
- Fuchsias
- Iris 'Jane Phillips'
- Primroses
- Rosa 'William Lobb'
- Salvia species
- Soft fruit and tree fruit
- Sweet Peas
- Viola odorata
- Wallflowers

Contemporary

Bold containers, formal lines, and architectural plants sum up the contemporary planting style. Use industrial materials for hard landscaping features – scaffold boards for terraces, stainless steel for containers and raised beds, fences painted in bold colours. Add lighting to show off your garden area at night and to highlight specimen trees and shrubs.

Plants to try

- Achillea 'Terracotta'
- Buxus sempervirens
- Colocasia species
- Dianella species
- Fatsia japonica
- Iris cultivars
- Lomandra species
- Phormium tenax
- Stipa gigantea
- Succulents e.g. echeveria

YEAR-ROUND STYLE
Focal plants with strong outlines help to define the area all year round. Combine plants that flower at different times for successional interest.

Naturalistic

Seek inspiration from the countryside, whether a wildflower meadow or bushland. Use ornamental grasses to soften the look and emulate planting in natural habitats. This style is informal, colourful, relaxed, and spontaneous. Leave seedheads on over winter as these add further interest and structure.

Eryngium alpinum 'Superbum' *Knautia macedonica*

Plants to try

- Agastache species
- Brachyscome multifida
- Calamagrostis x acutiflora 'Karl Foerster'
- Echinacea purpurea 'Ruby Giant'
- Eryngium alpinum
- Gaura lindheimeri
- Knautia macedonica
- Molinia caerulea
- Papaver species
- Phlomis russelliana
- Rudbeckia fulgida 'Goldsturm'
- Salvia x sylvestris
- Stipa species
- Verbena bonariensis

Mixed planting

Combining perennials with shrubs and trees will achieve a mixed planting style. Larger plants become focal points, while layers of perennials and bulbs add seasonal highlights. The style can be adapted for smaller spaces by choosing key structural plants and adding others in groups for a pleasing effect.

Plants to try

- Allium 'Purple Sensation'
- Artemisia 'Powis Castle'
- Convolvulus mauritanicus
- Cotinus coggygria 'Royal Purple'
- Geranium cultivars
- Hebe 'Red Edge'
- Heuchera 'Plum Pudding'
- Mahonia aquifolium
- Papaver orientale 'Perry's White'
- Penstemon 'Hidcote Pink'
- Perovskia 'Blue Spire'
- Philadelphus 'Belle Etoile'
- Rosa 'Iceberg'
- Sedum 'Autumn Joy'

KEEP IT SIMPLE

Keep things simple and don't place too many different plants together as this will create a congested and complicated effect.

Small Space, Big Harvest

Think big, think creatively, and think bountiful. Your growing space may be tiny, but that doesn't mean your harvest needs to be small as well. By matching the right plants with the right growing conditions, you'll enjoy a delicious crop.

Growing plants for an edible crop is easy. Some plants may require a bit more attention than others, but don't be put off trying something new and different. Before you start growing, do some preparation and decide what you want to grow and how you are going to do it. Consider your space, too, and how it can be maximized: can you put pots and containers onto paved areas and steps? Can you hang planters from railings or use a vertical space to grow plants up? Try tumbling bush tomatoes or strawberries in hanging baskets, herbs in window boxes, mini vegetables in patio containers, squashes and beans climbing up homemade wigwam structures, cutting lettuce in a kitchen colander. Be inspired by our projects, and have a go.

Luscious blueberries and strawberries are just some of the fruits that are easy to grow in containers.

Fruit and vegetable know-how
With a little careful planning, and by selecting plants that are reliable, don't take up too much room, or can be grown in a different way, you'll get the most out of your space, whatever its size.

Dwarf varieties are versions of plants that have been bred to be smaller, but still produce a good and tasty yield. Dwarf runner, French, and broad beans don't need support or a frame to climb, and small carrots can easily be grown in containers, while dwarf plums, apples, peaches, and other fruit take up less space than their full-size cousins. Mini vegetables are either bred to be tiny, full-sized varieties that are picked when the crop is young, or plants grown close together, which will produce smaller and tastier crops. Micro gardening is growing plants in a tiny space or container. Choose some of the mini or dwarf varieties, or, if your container is really small, you can even crop tasty salad leaves from sprouting seeds in a cup.

Fast-growing edibles can be sown or planted in between slower-growing types as a catch crop. Summer salad plants, like lettuce, basil, radish, beetroot, and spring onions, are quick growers, as are spinach and pak choi. Try pea and bean shoots, too.

Training fruit makes good use of a compact growing space as it will help to maximize yields and looks very decorative. Apples, pears, cherries, currants, figs, and peaches can all be trained vertically as espaliers, cordons, standards, or fans against a fence or wall.

Mixing edibles and ornamentals will create a garden area that is pretty, productive, and like a mini ornamental potager. Some flowering plants act as natural disease repellents; planting marigolds, with their strong scent, next to tomatoes will help to keep bugs away, for example. Add decorative features, like homemade wigwams for beans and peas, or use recycled containers for your plants. Consider how your plot will look as well as what is going in it.

Essential growing tips

Water well, and often Edible crops grown in containers need lots of water, sometimes twice a day in hot, dry weather. Give containers a thorough soaking – don't just water the top section of the pot. Adding a drip tray underneath is helpful so that the plant can take up water from the roots as well.

Protect Plants grown on balconies and high spaces will be more exposed to wind, rain, and sun than those grown at ground level. Foliage and potting mix will dry out more quickly in these conditions, so keep plants sheltered by adding screening.

Feed For a plant to produce a bountiful crop, you need to feed it first. Without the right nutrients, plants won't perform well and your crop will be small. Use diluted liquid feed when watering in the growing season, while diluted tomato feed is great for other plants besides tomatoes and helps to boost crop production. Mix slow-release general fertilizer granules into the potting mix for extra nourishment. Wear gloves when handling all fertilizers.

Drainage Make sure all your containers have drainage holes for excess water to escape, otherwise roots will rot. Add a layer of drainage material, like gravel, small pebbles, or broken terracotta pots (crocks), at the bottom of containers before planting.

Crop rotation Don't plant the same vegetable in the same container year after year, unless you have changed the soil, as soil-borne diseases will build up and affect the plant's health and the quality of the crop. Rotate vegetables where you can.

Disguise functional containers and grow bags with decorative cladding, and group planters together for an ornamental effect.

Feed and look after your edibles and they will reward you with a bountiful crop.

Summer vegetables

Key to symbols: ◊ Drought tolerant ♦ Water often ● Keep constantly wet ☼ Grow in full sun ☀ Partial shade ✸ Full shade

Eggplant
Perfect for containers. Mostly smooth, long, and slender with dark-purple skin, but can also be round or pear-shaped, and white, pale lilac, streaky, or red.

Care: Keep in a sheltered, sunny position, well watered and with high humidity. Mulch when in containers.

◊ ☼ ✸

Beetroot
Mostly round and purple, but can also be oval or long and bright red, golden yellow, and striped. Best eaten when young and sweet; leaves are also tasty.

Care: Sow successively for continuous supply throughout the year. Harvest plants while young and tender.

◊ ☼

Cucumber
Outdoor varieties are usually shorter than those grown under cover. Small, round cucumbers are sweet and tasty. Gherkins are preserved in vinegar or brine with herbs and spices.

Care: Grow up a wigwam. Plants prefer lots of well-rotted organic matter in soil.

◊ ☼ ✸

Lettuce
Lots of different types to choose from, with different shapes, textures, and colours. Loose-leaf lettuce is perfect for smaller containers and easy to grow.

Care: Sow in succession from spring to autumn; some varieties can be overwintered. Don't let soil dry out.

◊ ☼–☀ ✸✸✸–✸✸

Rocket
Peppery and spicy, rocket is easy to grow and lovely in salads and as a garnish. Wild rocket has narrower leaves than milder-tasting salad rocket. Plants can be kept through the winter.

Care: Pick a few leaves at a time or cut the whole plant back to allow regrowth.

◊ ☼–☀ ✸✸✸

Tomato
Vine tomatoes have a tall central stem that needs support. Bush types are smaller and may not need support; some can be grown in hanging baskets. Fruit can be red, orange, or yellow.

Care: Choose a sunny site. Bring green fruit inside to ripen in autumn.

◊ ☼ ✸

Also try... Beans (French), Capsicum, Chicory, Chilli, Gherkin, Radicchio, Radish, Sweet Corn

Cabbage and leaf vegetables

❅❅❅ Fully hardy   ❅❅ Can survive in mild regions/sheltered sites   ❅ Frost tender

Broccoli
Broccoli includes single-head and sprouting broccoli that crops for many months; the latter is usually green but a purple variety is also available.

Care: Can be grown year round but is best grown in cooler months when cabbage white butterflies are not pesky.

💧 ☼–☀ ❅❅❅

Cabbage
Autumn/winter varieties have denser heads and can be stored; spring/summer types, which are round or pointed, should be eaten straight away.

Care: Harvest spring/early-summer cabbages as spring greens. Net in summer from cabbage white butterflies.

💧 ☼–☀ ❅❅❅

Cauliflower
Most varieties can be grown year round, and have snow-white heads, but also try purple, green, or orange. Plant close together for a crop of mini cauliflowers.

Care: Harvest when curds are firm and tight. Net plants in warm weather to protect from cabbage white butterflies.

💧 ☼–☀ ❅❅❅

Kale
A tough, hardy vegetable that needs a bit of space and has decorative crinkly leaves in green, red, or black. Very tasty and nutritious. Young and tender leaves can be harvested through winter.

Care: Taller types may need staking. Net in summer from cabbage white butterflies.

💧 ☼–☀ ❅❅❅

Pak choi
This oriental vegetable can be cooked or eaten raw in salads. Green and red varieties available. Decorative and fast-growing. Flowering stems also edible.

Care: Plants can bolt if planted too early or they don't have enough water. Net in summer from cabbage white butterflies.

💧 ☼–☀ ❅❅❅

Spinach
Easy to grow in cool weather. Harvest while young and tender for salads; cook mature leaves. Nutritious and tasty. Sow in succession for continuous crops.

Care: Plants can bolt if weather is hot and soil is dry. Cover with net if birds are pesky.

💧 ☼–☀ ❅❅❅

Also try... Brussels Sprouts, Chinese Cabbage, Red Cabbage, Romanesco Cauliflower, Silverbeet

Beans, peas, and squash

Key to symbols: ○ Drought tolerant   ◐ Water often   ● Keep constantly wet   ☼ Grow in full sun   ☀ Partial shade   ❄ Full shade

Broad beans
Dwarf varieties are ideal for containers, but taller plants will need staking. Pick as a mini vegetable when pods are 3–4cm (1¼–1½in) long. Sow seeds in autumn for an early spring crop.

Care: Harvest and eat when young and sweet. Picking encourages more pods.

◐ ☼–☀ ❄❄❄

Borlotti beans
Pods are green at first, then mottled purple, red, and cream. Eat as whole pods when green; eat as beans when either half ripe or mature and dried. Climbing and dwarf varieties available.

Care: Direct sow or put out when frosts have passed. Need good rich soil.

◐ ☼ ❄

Climbing beans
Climbing French and runner beans have attractive flowers and are easy to grow up a wigwam of poles. French beans can be green, yellow, or purple, and dwarf varieties of all beans are available.

Care: Direct sow when frosts have passed. Need good rich soil.

◐ ☼ ❄

Zucchini
Can be various shades of green, stripy, or yellow, and either traditionally shaped, round, or curved. Easy to grow, but needs space. Best picked when young. The flowers can also be eaten.

Care: Water well when flowering. Do not let the soil dry out. Feed regularly.

◐ ☼ ❄

Peas
Decorative and very tasty, with pretty flowers as well. The whole pod is eaten for snow peas and sugar snap pea varieties. The growing tips and shoots can also be eaten and used in salads.

Care: Harvest and eat when young and sweet. Picking encourages more pods.

◐ ☼–☀ ❄

Pumpkin
An impressive range of sizes, colours, and textures. Trailing varieties need space, but can be grown up archways and trellis if fruit are not too heavy.

Care: Remove leaves to help fruit ripen. For extra large specimens, remove all except one or two fruits from plant.

◐ ☼ ❄❄❄–❄❄

Also try... Asparagus Pea, Butternut Pumpkin, Cannellini Bean, Gourd, Lima Bean, Pattypan, Round Squash, Soya Bean, Spaghetti Squash, Yard Long Bean, Yellow Zucchini

Roots and stems

❄❄❄ Fully hardy ❄❄ Can survive in mild regions/sheltered sites ❄ Frost tender

Carrot
Many shapes, sizes, and colours available, mostly suitable for deep containers. Needs free-draining soil. Can be sown in spring and summer, for almost continuous harvest.

Care: Sow directly in soil in mild weather so soil doesn't dry too quickly.

💧 ☀—☀ ❄❄

Garlic
Easy to grow as long as you remember two key things: water and food. Needs free-draining soil. Bulbs need a period of cold, so best planted in autumn.

Care: Water and feed well when leaves start to grow. Cut off flowering stems for bigger bulbs.

💧 ☀ ❄❄❄

Leek
Versatile winter vegetable. Can be used when young and mini, or as mature plants. Good to have during autumn/winter when little else is harvested.

Care: Best started in modules or seed trays in spring. Transplant into holes pre-filled with water in potting mix.

💧 ☀—☀ ❄❄❄

Onion
Easy to grow and comes in white or red – the latter is sweeter and perfect for salads. Onions are low-maintenance, take up little space, and store well.

Care: Grow from sets (special baby onions) in spring for harvesting from late summer into autumn.

💧 ☀ ❄❄❄

Parsnip
Sow in spring and summer for year-round harvest – tastes even sweeter when they have had some frost. Leaves die back in winter, but plants can be left in the ground until harvested.

Care: Sow direct in soil and keep well watered. Needs free-draining soil.

💧 ☀—☀ ❄❄❄

Potato
A huge variety available: large for jacket potatoes or smaller new or salad crops. Need space – they will grow in special large bags – and soil needs to be rich.

Care: Plant seed potatoes in spring and regularly mound earth on top of plants to keep them out of the light.

💧 ☀—☀ ❄

Also try... Elephant Garlic, Florence Fennel, Jerusalem Artichoke, Kohl Rabi, Pickling Onion, Shallot, Spring Onion, Swede, Sweet Potato

Fruit

Key to symbols: ◊ Drought tolerant   ◊ Water often   ◆ Keep constantly wet   ☼ Grow in full sun   ☼ Partial shade   ☀ Full shade

Apple
Huge range of varieties, but for smaller spaces choose plants grown on dwarf root stock, or cultivated "patio" or trained varieties. Needs large containers.

Care: Choose a sheltered site to protect blossom from frosts. Thin out tiny apples in midsummer for bigger fruit.

◊ ☼–☼ ❄❄❄

Blackcurrant
Packed with vitamin C, and easy to grow as bushes or standard shrubs. Prune in winter to get air to centre of plant. Feed well in growing season for a good crop.

Care: Needs a cold winter to fruit well. Prune back a third of the plant each winter.

◊ ☼–☼ ❄❄❄

Peach and nectarine
Quite easy to grow, with ornamental blossom. You'll need a warm, sunny, sheltered wall or fence to train your plants up. Prune in summer, not winter.

Care: Protect blossom from frost. Thin out small fruit in summer for a good yield at harvest time.

◊ ☼ ❄❄❄

Pear
Good for smaller spaces, but you will need to use large containers. Responds well to training; can easily be grown against a wall or fence.

Care: Choose a warm, sheltered site to protect blossom from frosts. Thin out tiny pears in midsummer for bigger fruit.

◊ ☼ ❄❄❄

Plum
Start harvesting in summer and through the autumn, depending on variety. Choose plants grown on smaller root stock and that are self-pollinating.

Care: Only prune plants when in active growth and not in winter, as this will help prevent fungal diseases.

◊ ☼–☼ ❄❄❄

Strawberry
The quintessential taste of summer. Plant in winter for summer harvest. Include several varieties to extend harvest. Mulch under plants with straw or mats to protect fruit from damp.

Care: Propagate new plants from runners (see page 159).

◊ ☼ ❄❄

Also try... Blackberry, Cherry, Cranberry, Fig, Gooseberry, Pomegranate, Quince, Raspberry, Redcurrant, Rhubarb

Herbs

❅❅❅ Fully hardy, blossom may need frost protection   ❅❅ Can survive in mild regions/sheltered sites   ❅ Frost tender

Basil
Easy to grow in a sunny sheltered spot or on a windowsill. Large-leaved is perfect for pesto; smaller and purple-leaved types are ideal for garnish. Also grows well with tomatoes.

Care: Sow under cover in spring; place outside in pots when risk of frost is over.

💧 ☀ ❅

Coriander
Distinctive flavour. Can bolt to seed in warm weather but holds well through winter. Leave some to flower to set seed, as these are also used in cooking.

Care: Sow seeds direct in growing position at intervals. Summer and autumn sowings are most productive.

💧 ☀ ❅❅

Florence Fennel
The whole plant is edible, but this variety is grown for its fleshy bulb. To avoid it bolting to seed, sow successive crops in summer and they will be ready to harvest in autumn and winter.

Care: Keep soil moist and mound soil to protect plants from wind.

💧 ☀ ❅❅❅

Mint
Comes in many interesting flavours, with common mint recommended for mint jelly and sauce. Some have variegated leaves and look ornamental.

Care: Can be very invasive; grow separately in a pot, or plant in a pot within another arrangement.

💧 ☀–☀ ❅❅❅

Sage
Attractive, aromatic evergreen shrub. Looks good in a flower border as well as a herb area. Green, purple, and variegated varieties add further interest. Leaves suit a wide variety of dishes.

Care: Choose well-drained potting mix for containers. Trim after flowering.

💧 ☀ ❅❅❅

Thyme
Pretty, low-growing plant – ornamental as well as edible. There are many different varieties and all have lovely flowers. Leaf stalks dry well for cooking.

Care: Choose a warm, dry, sunny site. Trim plant immediately after flowering to avoid woody growth.

💧 ☀ ❅❅❅

> **Also try...** Aniseed, Chervil, Lovage, Oregano, Parsley, Sweet Marjoram, Tarragon

Essential Garden Kit

There are a few tools and materials you'll need to look after your plants and garden area. Make the tools part of your garden display by storing them in a pretty cupboard or use a small table that could also double as a plant display area, and hang smaller items from hooks on a trellis.

Watering can
Use one with a detachable rose so that you can get the spout directly into pots and containers.

Trowel
Essential for planting, scooping potting mix, and removing weeds.

Hand fork
Useful to lightly dig in between plants and incorporate granular fertilizer.

Secateurs
Essential for pruning, cutting back plants, and harvesting.

Water mister
Great for spritzing moisture and humidity on to plants in warmer weather. Also good for liquid foliar feed.

Mini hoe
A useful tool to help with weeding between tightly packed plants.

Long-handled tools
These are perfect to use on larger containers and raised beds.

Plant Practical

TOOL MAINTENANCE

It is worth taking the time to keep tools clean by removing soil and compost after use. At the end of the main gardening season, lightly oil metal surfaces to stop any rust. If you look after your tools, they will last for years.

Tub trug
Very handy for collecting plant debris. Also useful for holding compost when planting, and for immersing plants for watering.

Horticultural fleece and shadecloth
Protects plants from frost and hot sun.

Gloves
Choose reasonably tight-fitting waterproof ones so you can still handle tools and plants.

Pots
Classic terracotta pots are attractive in themselves and can be customized with paint effects.

Crocks
Broken terracotta pots for drainage. Gravel and small pebbles can also be used.

Garden twine
For tying plants to structures as they grow and lots of other uses in the gardening space.

Drip tray
Put these under your containers so plants can take up water from their roots.

Kneeler
Choose a comfy one that will protect your knees when attending to low planting.

Bamboo canes
Available in lots of sizes, great for supporting plants and creating structures for climbers.

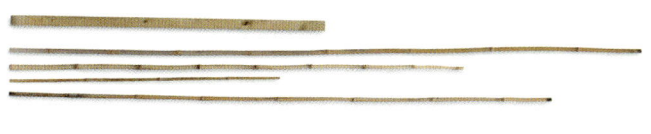

YOU MAY ALSO NEED

Garden tidy A plastic groundsheet is useful for spreading out to protect surfaces when you garden.

Garden wire Plastic-coated and stronger than twine, useful for weightier fixings.

Netting To protect edibles from birds and insects.

Plant markers So you never forget what you've planted!

Caring for Your Plants

Spend just a little bit of time choosing the right potting mix and meeting the watering, feeding, and care requirements of your plants and you will reap the rewards: healthy growth and a good, productive yield of flowers or crops.

Potting Mix

Most plants will grow well in general-purpose potting mix, but some have special requirements or are more suited to free-draining soil or acidic mix. You should always read plant labels for a guide to soil requirements, but it's also a good idea to do a bit of your own research before you plant anything, so that you can buy the correct potting mix.

Home composting
Add fruit and vegetable peelings to an outside compost bin where you can also put prunings. Mix plant matter with plenty of shredded paper and cardboard, and turn everything regularly to keep the air circulating and to aid decay. Don't add woody stems, weeds, diseased plants, or meat, fish, or cooked food. Keep the bin covered, but check it isn't too dry and add water if necessary. It should take 6–9 months to rot down.

A covered pot in the kitchen is handy for storing fruit and vegetable peelings before transferring them to an outside compost bin.

Free-draining soil Generally, anything that likes a lot of sun, such as succulents and cacti, prefers a free-draining, gritty mix, so choose one with horticultural sand already mixed in, or add perlite, granules of volcanic minerals, or horticultural grit.

Acidic soil All berries, azaleas, rhododendrons, and heathers need acidic or ericaceous soil and will die if planted in general-purpose potting mix.

Seed-raising mix This has no soil or nutrients and is also perfect for adult plants that require minimal nutrients, such as wildflowers.

Healthy additives
Incorporate homemade compost into your soil to help retain moisture, improve soil texture, and add plenty of healthy minerals. Mix into your soil or apply as mulch in spring. Not all plants need it, but edibles, shrubs, and trees will appreciate the boost. Whatever you use, make sure it is well-rotted as fresh compost produces too much heat as it decays.

Sun or Shade

Plants in containers are more susceptible to temperature extremes than plants grown in the ground. Place container plants in a position that is sheltered from wind, so that they are not blown over. Avoid a site exposed to hot summer afternoon sun or the plant – both above and below the potting mix – will over-heat and dehydrate. Always choose plant species that suit the available conditions.

Watering

Containers tend to dry out more quickly than plants in the ground; those on balconies or exposed above ground level need particular attention. Make sure containers have drainage holes; if not, make them yourself. If plants sit in too much water their roots will rot – unless they are bog or water plants, of course. Roots need air circulation, so add crocks (broken terracotta pots) or gravel to containers before adding potting mix. A drip tray underneath will protect surfaces from water and allow plants to soak up moisture via their roots. Plants that prefer moisture-retentive soil, such as ferns, still require drainage, but conserve moisture by mulching with organic material or sphagnum moss.

How and when to water

Water plants regularly and frequently. Plants will need more watering while they are establishing, and vegetables and fruit need plenty as flowers and crops form. In hot, dry conditions water twice a day. Fill the container to the rim, let it drain and water again. Watering just a little doesn't get moisture to the roots. You can give plants extra moisture by misting in hot weather. Make sure you water at the right time of day, too. Early morning or evening are best. Adjust watering frequency according to the season; greatest demand is during growth in hot, dry weather.

Watering help

Mix water-storing crystals into potting mix when planting. These expand to hold moisture and release it as the mix dries. Irrigation systems are also useful for larger areas or if you don't want to worry about watering every day. Many systems work on timers.

DIY weekend waterer Making your own simple irrigation system is easy. Drill a hole for a plastic tap near the bottom of a bucket. Attach a length of hose. Prick tiny holes in the hose and stopper the end. Place the bucket on a raised platform, then fill with water. Feed the hose over your plant pots and open the tap to let a small amount of water flow.

Watering requirements can vary dramatically depending on the plant. Some, such as air plants, are not watered at the roots at all; they are only watered by misting.

A simple weekend watering system is easy to make yourself and provides a gentle supply of water to your plants for several days.

Feeding

Plants, especially those in containers, need regular feeding in the growing season to keep them healthy and productive. Liquid feed, such as seaweed extract, is added to your watering can. You can also add diluted tomato feed to many ornamental and edible plants. Soluble granular fertilizers include fish, blood and bone, and general purpose; sprinkle into the potting mix at planting, or add around the plant base monthly. Ensure the granules do not touch plants. Wear gloves when handling fertilizers, and always check the manufacturer's instructions for dosage.

Only feed plants from spring to autumn; most do not need it when dormant in winter. Some require little or no feeding. Do not overfeed or you will have vigorous foliage at the expense of flowers or crops.

FOLIAR FEED

Boost plants by misting diluted liquid fertilizer onto foliage to keep them lush and healthy. The feed is taken up through the leaves.

Dilute liquid fertilizer in your watering can.

General care

Protect young plants and fruit blossom from frost in early spring by covering with horticultural fleece. Near to harvest time, fruit plants can be protected from birds by netting and from hot summer sun by shadecloth. Protect plants from wind damage by adding screening.

Keep plants looking healthy by removing any dead, diseased, or dying foliage regularly during the growing season. Don't compost diseased plant material as this could spread diseases to other plants. Some plants, such as succulents, need a good tidy up of spent flower stalks and old leaves before they go dormant, otherwise this dead material may rot the plant. Others, like echinacea, have lovely seedheads that add winter interest and provide food for beneficial creatures, so don't cut these back until late winter or early spring.

Protect fruit bushes from birds using netting.

Harvesting

Some fruit and vegetables need to mature fully before harvesting; others can be eaten while they are young and tasty. Apples, pears, strawberries, cauliflowers, and broccoli, for example, need time to develop and don't taste good when unripe, but peas, zucchinis, radishes, and beans are sweet and tasty when picked young and fresh. Many crops are best eaten straight away, but if you need to store produce, refrigerate or choose a cool, dry, dark place; don't store bruised or damaged crops. Fruit such as apples and pears can be refrigerated or individually wrapped for cellar storage, but check each one regularly for signs of decay. Many vegetables, herbs, and some soft fruit can be frozen, dried, or pickled – a lovely way to share your homegrown edibles with friends and family.

Homegrown seeds

Harvest seeds from flowers and vegetables at the end of their growing season. You may not get a "pure" offspring from the parent plant, depending on the variety and what was grown nearby, but it is fun to raise your own plants from homegrown seeds. Allow edible crops to fully ripen and flowers to set ripe seed before harvesting, and collect when the seed pod is dry. Use a paper or plastic bag to collect the seed, then store in an airtight container or paper bag until ready to sow. Depending on the plant, you can sow some seed straight away. The germination rate will deteriorate over time, so try to use your gathered seed within a year for best results.

> ### Easy-care edibles
> Choose fruit and vegetable varieties that have been selected by growers as good-quality crops that can manage pests and resist disease. Some examples are lettuce, spinach, and beetroot that don't bolt; potatoes and tomatoes that are blight resistant; fruit grown on dwarf rooting stock; and crops resistant to mildew.

Above: Radishes can be harvested while small, young, and tasty.

Left: Pears need to fully mature before picking.

Garden Year Planner

Spring

PREPARATION
- Tidy up containers and planting areas, replacing or topping up soil if required.
- Sweep up leaves and debris. Wash down areas as needed.

GROW
- Sow seeds from early spring. Some need to be sown under cover for cold protection.
- Buy young plants. Some of those for summer bedding displays are not frost hardy so will need protection until the danger of frost is over.
- Begin to water and feed plants in containers, increasing frequency as the weather gets warmer.

PLANT CARE
- Cut back old and dead foliage from plants in early spring before new growth begins to emerge.

OTHER WORK
- Mulch garden and potted plants to conserve moisture.

To find out when seeds need to be sown, check the information on the packet carefully.

Summer

PREPARATION
- Clean outdoor furniture.

GROW
- Continue sowing seeds of summer vegetables at regular intervals for successional crops and sow slow-maturing winter vegetables.
- Tie in climbing plants to frames and check if other plants need support.
- Water containers frequently in hot weather as soil will dry out quickly.

PLANT CARE
- Deadhead flowers regularly on ornamental plants to encourage repeat flowering.
- Harvest crops when ripe.

OTHER WORK
- Consider watering requirements if you are going away on holiday.
- Move potted plants to shaded area if there is a risk of sun scorch.

Tie in climbing plants, such as honeysuckle, that need support during the growing season.

Autumn

PREPARATION
- Give containers a clean and check soil levels, topping up with potting mix if required.
- Make sure all structures and climbing and larger plants are secure.

GROW
- Remove summer bedding schemes and plant autumn and winter plants and spring bulbs.
- Harvest edible crops and store excess produce. Remove plants after harvesting is finished.
- Start to reduce watering and feeding.

PLANT CARE
- Continue to deadhead flowers on ornamental plants to enjoy any late flowering displays.

OTHER WORK
- Keep walkways and terraces clear of leaves, twigs, and other debris.

Some edible crops, like pumpkins, store well in a cool, ventilated place.

Winter

PREPARATION
- Protect outdoor furniture.
- Move any frost-tender plants to a light, frost-free place.
- Move sun-loving plants to a sunnier spot, sheltered from wind.

GROW
- Do not water or feed dormant plants.
- Plant bare-root, fruiting, and ornamental specimens if weather conditions are favourable.

PLANT CARE
- Tidy plants up but leave some seedheads over winter for birds to enjoy and for ornamental interest.

OTHER WORK
- Order seed catalogues. Make notes of what you'd like to grow next year.
- Order and buy bare-rooted plants.

For winter colour, hellebores flower from mid-winter to spring, depending on the species.

Garden Doctor

Maintaining a healthy ecological balance and having a proactive approach helps with pest and disease control. Here are some simple and practical tips:

Look after your soil Add organic matter in spring; replace or renew potting mix in containers regularly.

Follow crop rotation Rotate edible crops to help reduce build-up of soil-borne diseases.

Choose resistance Use certified virus-free or disease-resistant seeds and plants, especially for edible crops.

Be vigilant Examine plants regularly and treat any pests or diseases as soon as signs of damage appear.

Encourage nature's little helpers Grow plants that attract beneficial insects (see pages 198–215).

Companion planting

By growing certain plants near to others you can help reduce pests and diseases. For example, the scent of French marigold discourages whitefly; basil can be planted with tomatoes to improve growth and flavour; and garlic planted near roses discourages greenfly.

A mixture of flowering plants and edible crops looks attractive and can deter pests and diseases.

Index

A
Abromeitiella sp. 26
Acer palmatum 231
Achillea
 A. sp. 210, 215
 A. 'Terracotta' 234
Aeonium 228
aeriums 103
Agapanthus 226
 A. 'Blue Baby' 186
 A. 'Peter Pan' 186
Agastache 230
 A. sp. 210, 215, 235
air plants 9, 228
 Air Plant Hangers 103
 Air Plants Living Picture Frame 124–7
 care of 21, 102, 127
 offsets 102, 124
 Plastic Cup Air Plant Chandelier 100–2
 Vertically Mounted Air Plant Canisters 18–21
Alchemilla mollis 132, 234
Allium 'Purple Sensation' 235
Aloe
 A. aristata 22
 A. brevifolia 22
alpine plants 228
 care of 94, 167
 Rock Strata Alpine Planter 164–9
 Vintage Teatime Alpine Planter 90–5
 watering 94, 167
anise hyssop 204
annuals 225
apple mint 157
apples 170, 175, 236, 242, 249
 'Ballerina' 173
Armeria dwarf variety 90
Artemisia 'Powis Castle' 235
Aster 225, 226
 A. macrophyllus 210
 A. frikartii 'Mönch' 234
Astrantia major 227
auriculas 234

B
Baloskian tetraphyllum 232
Bamboo Trellis 138–41
Banksia ericifolia 233
basil 28, 236, 243, 251
 'Purpleleaf' 151
beans 132, 249
 Homegrown Bean Feast 142–5
 Pea and Broad Bean Shooter Shelves 128–31
 see also borlotti beans; broad beans; French beans; runner beans
Bee and Butterfly Wildlife Hamper 210–15
beetroot 236, 238, 249
 'Bull's Blood' 28
Bergenia 227
betony 204
birds
 feeders 216–20
 seedcake hangers 221
blackcurrants 173, 175, 236, 242
 'Baldwin' 170
blueberries 173, 174, 236
 'Bluecrop' 170
bog plants 232
Bonsai, Instant 44–8
borlotti beans 145, 240
 'Blue Lake' 143
Brachyscome multifida 235
broad beans 129, 236, 240
broccoli 28, 239, 249
bromeliads 26
bronze fennel 230
Buddleja 230
bulbs 225, 235
busy lizzie 74
butternut pumpkin 138
Buxus sempervirens 233, 234

C
cabbage 239
cacti
 care of 23, 246
 Mexican-style Tin Can Cacti Planters 22–5
Calamagrostis acutiflora 'Karl Foerster' 233, 235
calendula *see* marigolds
Callistemon viminalis 229
Caltha palustris 232
Campanula
 C. lactiflora 234
 C. prostrate variety 80
Campanula sp. 204
Canna 231
Carex elata 232
caring for your plants
 compost 246
 feeding 15, 55, 173, 224, 237, 247, 248
 garden year planner 250–1
 general care 248
 harvesting 249
 pest and disease control 137, 248, 249, 1251
 potting mix 246
 sun or shade 246
 watering 247

carnivorous plants
 care of 41, 183
 Carnivorous Garden 180–3
 Closed Glass Terrarium 38–43
carrots 236, 241
 'Paris Market' 151
cauliflowers 239, 249
Ceanothus 'Concha' 229
Centranthus ruber 'Coccineus' 210
cherries 236
chillies
 dwarf varieties 97
 'Jalapeno' 151
 ornamental varieties 97
 Upside-down Lampshade Chilli Planter 96–9
choosing plants 12–13, 224–33
 air plants, alpines, and succulents 228
 inspiration 224
 planting styles 224, 234–5
 plants for foliage 231
 plants for screening 229
 plants for shade and semi-shade 227
 plants for sun 226
 plants for wildlife 230
 plants for year-round interest 233
 practical considerations 224
 types of plants 225
 water and bog plants 232
climbing beans *see* French beans; runner beans
climbing plants
 Brightly Painted Terracotta Pot for Climbers 146–9
 Funky Abstract Bamboo Trellis 138–41
 Homegrown Bean Feast 142–5
Colocasia sp. 234
companion planting 237, 251
compost 246
concrete planters 176–89, 188–9
 Carnivorous Garden 180–3
 Slate-grey Window Box 184–7
 Sleek White Bowl 176–9
containers 11, 15
 Carnivorous Garden 180–3
 Decorated Terracotta Pots 190–5
 drainage 237, 247
 Fruit in Tubs 170–5
 Rock Strata Alpine Planter 164–9
 Slate Box Planter 160–3
 Slate-grey Window Box 184–7
 Sleek White Bowl 176–9
 watering and feeding 15, 94, 167, 173, 224, 237, 247, 248

 see also concrete planters; terracotta pots
contemporary garden style 234
Convolvulus mauritanicus 235
cordons 174, 236
coriander 28, 243
corkscrew rush 64
corncockle 204
Cotinus coggyria 'Royal Purple' 235
Cotoneaster horizontalis 50
cottage garden style 234
Crassula
 C. dwarf red form 164
 C. sp. 26
crop rotation 237, 251
cucumbers 238
Cup-and-Saucer Bird Stations 216–20
Cyclamen hederifolium 50
Cynara cardunculus 190

D
Darlingtonia californica 182
Davallia
 D. humata tyermanii 'Bunny' 73
 D. sp. 69
decoupage 11, 192–3
Dianella sp. 234
Dianthus
 D. alpinus 228
 D. 'Mrs Sinkins' 234
Dicentra spectabilis 234
Digitalis
 D. grandiflora 210, 215
 D. purpurea 132, 230, 234
Dionaea muscipula 38, 182
diseases *see* pest and disease control
Drosera capensis 182
Dryopteris filix-mas 132

E
Echeveria 84, 112, 117, 123, 228, 234
 E. elegans 87, 115, 120
 E. schaviana 87
 E. secunda glauca 120
 E. sp. 22, 26, 190, 194
 E. 'Topsy Turvy' 87
Echinacea purpurea 210, 215, 226
 'Ruby Giant' 235
 'White Swan' 190
Echinops ritro 'Veitch's Blue' 210
edible plants 236–7
 Brightly Painted Terracotta Pot for Climbers 146–9

Index

crop rotation 237, 251
Cut-and-come-again Colourful Salad Colander 32–5
drainage 237
edible flowers 36
Edible Planted Wall 80–3
feeding 237
Fruit in Tubs 170–5
harvesting 249
Homegrown Bean Feast 142–5
Pea and Broad Bean Shooter Shelves 128–31
Pots and Pots of Gourmet Microgreens 28–31
protecting plants 237
Strawberry Picture Frame Planter 106–11
Summer Drinks Tiered Planter 156–9
Upcycled Stepladder Tiered Planter 150–3
Upside-down Lampshade Chilli Planter 96–9
Vertically Mounted Miniature Greenhouse 132–7
watering 237
see also fruit; vegetables
eggplants 238
English lavender 74, 234
Erica cinerea 176
Erigeron karvinskianus 69, 72, 90, 210
Eryngium alpinum 235
espaliers 173, 174, 236
Eucalyptus gunnii 64
Euonymous 231
everlasting daisy 204

F

fans 174, 236
Fatsia japonica 231, 234
feeding your plants 15, 55, 173, 224, 237, 247, 248
fennel 28
ferns 227
  fertilizers 237, 248
  aquatic fertilizer 55
  foliar feed 248
  granular fertilizers 248
  liquid feed 248
Festuca glauca 'Intense Blue' 64
figs 173, 236
  'Brown Turkey' 170
Florence fennel 243
foliage, plants for 231
foliar feed 248
forget-me-not 225
Fothergilla major 231
foxglove *see Digitalis*

frames
  Living Mirror Frame (Succulents) 112–17
  Living Picture Frame (Air Plants) 124–7
  Living Picture Frame (Succulents) 118–23
  Strawberry Picture Frame Planter 106–11
French beans 141, 236, 240
  'Purple King' 143
  'Yellow Wax' 143, 145
French lavender 74
fruit
  harvesting 249
  see also edible plants; individual fruits, e.g. apples
fruit bushes 173, 174–5, 242
fruit trees 234, 242
  cordons, espaliers, and fans 173, 174, 236
  easy-care 249
  feeding 173
  general care 173
  siting 173
  watering 173
Fruit in Tubs 170–5
fuchsias 234

G

Garden Sieve Wildflower Meadow 209
garden styles
  contemporary 234
  cottage garden 234
  mixed planting 235
  naturalistic 235
garden year planner 250–1
garlic 241, 251
garlic chives 80
Gaura lindheimeri 210, 235
Geranium cultivars 235
golden marjoram 170
golden oregano 80
gooseberries 170, 172, 173, 175
Gourmet Microgreens 28–31
granular fertilizer 248
grapes 'Black Muscat' 146
Graptopetalum 84, 112
  G. 'Paraguayense' 87
Graptoveria 84
  'Fred Ives' 87
Grevillea 'Robyn Gordon' 230

H

hanging gardens 9
  Air Plant Hangers 103
  Hanging Ball of Succulents 84–9

Hanging Plant Pot Mobile 64–7
Kokedama Hanging Garden 68–73
Plastic Cup Air Plant Chandelier 100–2
Saddle Bag Balcony Planters 74–9
Upside-down Lampshade Chilli Planter 96–9
Vintage Teatime Alpine Planter 90–5
Haworthia sp. 22
Hebe 'Red Edge' 235
Helenium autumnale 210, 226
Helichrysum italicum 151, 190, 192
Helleborus 227, 251
herbaceous perennials 225
herbs 174, 243
  see also specific herbs, e.g. basil
Heuchera 231
  H. 'Plum Pudding' 235
honeysuckle *see Lonicera*
Hosta 225, 227
  H. 'Blue Mouse Ears' 73
  H. sp. 38, 69
Hydrangea 233

I

Insect House with Green Roof 198–203
insects
  beneficial *see* wildlife
  pests *see* pest and disease control
Iris
  I. cultivars 234
  I. 'Jane Philips' 234
  I. versicolor 232

J

Japanese black pine 44
Japanese maple 231
Japanese sumac 50
Jovibarba hirta 198
Juncus
  J. sp. 52
  J. spiralis 64

K

kale 28, 239
Kids' Miniature Farmyard Garden 56–61
Knautia macedonica 235
Kokedama Hanging Garden 9, 68–73

L

lady's bedstraw 204
lamb's lettuce 151
Laurus nobilis 190, 194
Lavandula 74, 234
  L. angustifolia 226
  L. sp. 210
leeks 241
lemon thyme 80
lettuces 36–7, 132, 236, 238, 249
  cos 'Paris Island' 151
  loose-leaf 'Green Coral' 32, 151
  loose-leaf 'Lollo Rosso' 151
  loose-leaf 'Royal Oak' 32, 151
  loose-leaf 'Salad Bowl' 32
Linaria purpurea 'Canon Went' 210
liquid feed 248
Living Mirror Frame (Succulents) 112–17
Living Picture Frame (Air Plants) 124–7
Living Picture Frame (Succulents) 118–23
Lomandra sp. 234
Lonicera 230, 250
  L. sempervirens 'Trumpet Honeysuckle' 146
love-in-a-mist 204

M

Mahonia aquifolium 235
marigolds 36, 225, 237, 251
marjoram 170, 204
marrowfat peas 129
marsh marigolds 232
Marsilea drummondi 52
melons 159
  'Orangeglo' 157
Mentha
  M. suaveolens 157
  M. piperata 157
Mexican-style Tin Can Cacti Planters 22–5
micro-gardens 8
  Closed Glass Terrarium 38–43
  Cut-and-come-again Colourful Salad Colander 32–5
  Instant Bonsai 44–8
  Kids' Miniature Farmyard Garden 56–61
  Mexican-style Tin Can Cacti Planters 22–5
  Miniature Tabletop Water Garden 52–5
  Moroccan-style Lantern Garden 26–7
  Moss Pots 49–51

Pots and Pots of Gourmet Microgreens 28–31
Vertically Mounted Air Plant Canisters 18–21
Miniature Greenhouse 132–7
mint 159, 243
  apple mint 157
  'Eau de Cologne' 157
  peppermint 157
Miscanthus sinensis 229
  'Gold Bar' 69, 73
mixed planting style 235
mizuna 28
Molinia caerulea 235
Monarda 'Cambridge Scarlet' 210
Moroccan-style Lantern Garden 26–7
Moss Pots 49–51
mustard green 'Osaka Purple' 28

N

nasturtiums 36
naturalistic garden style 235
nectarines 242
Nemesia denticulata 'Confetti' 74
Nepenthes sp. 38
Nephrolepis
  N. exaltata 72
  N. sp. 69
Nymphaea 232

O

onions 241
Ophiopogon
  O. nigrescens 69, 72
  O. planiscapus 38
oregano 80, 204, 210
ornamental potagers 236–7

P

Pachyphytum 112
  P. sp. 22
pak choi 236, 239
pansies 225
Papaver
  P. orientale 'Perry's White' 235
  P. sp. 235
parsnips 241
pea and bean shoots 236
Pea and Broad Bean Shooter Shelves 128–31
peaches 236, 242
pears 236, 242, 249
peas 129, 240, 249
Pelargonium
  P. dwarf species 74

P. sidoides 151
Penstemon 225
  P. 'Hidcote Pink' 235
peppermint 157
perennials 225, 235
Perovskia 'Blue Spire' 235
pest and disease control 137, 237, 248, 249, 251
Philadelphus 'Belle Etoile' 235
Phlomis russelliana 235
Phlox douglasii 228
Phormium tenax 234
Photinia 229
Phyllostachys nigra 229
Pinus thunbergii 44
Plant Pot Mobile 64–7
Planted Wall 80–3
Plastic Cup Air Plant Chandelier 100–2
plastic milk bottles 36
Platycerium bifurcatum 69, 73
plums 236, 242
potatoes 241, 249
potting mix 246
Pratia pedunculars 90
Primula (primrose) 225, 234
  P. vialii 132
pruning 15
  see also individual projects
Pulmonaria 227
pumpkins 138, 140, 240, 250
Pyracantha 233

R

radishes 28, 236, 249
Rebutia sp. 22
Rhodanthemum 'African Eyes' 69, 72
Rhodohypoxis deflexa 90
Rhus succedeana 50
Rock Strata Alpine Planter 164–9
rocket 238
Rosa (rose) 251
  R. 'Iceberg' 235
  R. rugosa 229
  R. 'William Lobb' 234
rosemary 74, 80
Rudbeckia
  R. fulgida 'Goldsturm' 235
  R. laciniata 'Herbstsonne' 138
runner beans 236, 240
  'Painted Lady' 143
  'Scarlet Runner' 143, 145

S

Saddle Bag Balcony Planters 74–9
sage 243
  'Tricolor' 74, 80

salad plants
  containers 36–7
  Cut-and-come-again Colourful Salad Colander 32–5
  see also individual plants, e.g. lettuces
Salvia
  S. sp. 234
  S. sylvestris 235
  see also sage
Sarracenia
  S. flava 182
  S. purpurea subsp. *purpurea* 182
Scleranthus uniflorus 38
screening, plants for 229
Sedeveria 'Letizia' 87
Sedum 84, 112, 225
  S. album 198
  S. album 'Coral Carpet' 115
  S. birsutum 198
  S. brevifolia 114
  S. commixtum 87
  S. dasyphyllum 114, 198
  S. morganianum 87
  S. sexangulare 115, 198
  S. sp. 22, 58, 164
  S. spathulifolium 'Purpureum' 120
  S. spectabile 226
  S. spectabile 'Autumn Joy' 192, 235
  S. spurium 'Variegatum' 198
seed
  growing from 132, 225
  saving 249
Seedcake Hangers for Hungry Birds 221
Sempervivum 84, 95, 112, 228
  S. arachnoideum 'Hookeri' 198
  S. 'Atropurpureum' 120
  S. 'Blue Boy' 120
  S. 'Dark Cloud' 114
  S. 'Grapetone' 114
  S. 'Kelly Jo' 87
  S. 'Pippin' 87
  S. 'Rosie' 115
  S. sp. 22
  S. tectorum 120, 164, 187
Senecio small leaf form 164
shade and semi-shade 246
  plants for 227
shrubs and trees 225, 235
silverbeet 'Bright Lights' 28
Sisyrinchium
  S. angustifolium 52
  S. dwarf variety 90
siting plants 15
  see also individual projects
Slate Box Planter 160–3
Slate-effect Terracotta Pots 194–5

Slate-grey Window Box 184–7
Sleek White Bowl 176–9
small scabious 204
soft fruits *see* blueberries; strawberries
spinach 236, 239, 249
spring onions 236
  'Evergreen Bunching' 151
squashes 141
  climbing summer 138
standards 236
Stepladder Tiered Planter 150–3
Stipa
  S. gigantea 234
  S. sp. 235
  S. tenuissima 210
strawberries 159, 173, 174, 236, 242, 249
  alpine strawberry 80
  'Elan' 74
  Strawberry Picture Frame Planter 106–11
  'Strawberry Pink' 157
  'Sweetheart' 157, 170
succulents 228, 234
  care of 23, 89, 117, 123, 167, 203, 246
  cuttings 89, 117, 123
  Hanging Ball of Succulents 84–9
  Living Mirror Frame 112–17
  Living Picture Frame 118–23
  Mexican-style Tin Can Cacti Planters 22–5
  Moroccan-style Lantern Garden 26–7
  Portable Hanging Insect House with Green Roof 198–203
  Rock Strata Alpine Planter 164–9
  Summer Drinks Tiered Planter 156–9
sun 246
  plants for 226
sweet marjoram 204
sweet peas 225, 234

T

Tabletop Water Garden 52–5
temperature 246
terracotta pots
  Brightly Painted Terracotta Pot for Climbers 146–9
  decoupage decoration 11, 192–3
  slate-effect decoration 194–5
terrariums 8
  air plant hanger 103
  Closed Glass Terrarium 38–43

Thunbergia alata 'Lemon Star' 138
Thymus 243
  T. creeping form 164
  T. citriodorus 176
  T. citriodorus 'Argenteus' 190
Thymus creeping species 58
Tillandsia 124, 228
  T. aeranthos 101, 126
  T. brachycaulos multiflora 101
  T. bulbosa 19, 126
  T. caput medusae 19
  T. circinnata 126
  T. filifolia 126
  T. ionantha 19, 126
  T. ionantha scaposa 126
  T. ixioides 101, 126
  T. juncea 126
  T. melanocrater tricolor 126
  T. pruniosa 19
  T. streptophylla 19
  T. tectorum 101, 126
tomatoes 236, 237, 238, 249, 251
tools and equipment 244–5
  maintenance 245
  storage 15

U

Upside-down Lampshade Chilli Planter 96–9

V

vegetables
  beans, peas, and squash 240
  cabbage and leaf vegetables 239
  dwarf varieties 236
  easy-care 249
  fast-growing 236
  harvesting 249
  roots and stems 241
  summer vegetables 238
  see also edible plants; individual vegetables e.g. carrots
Verbascum speciosum 204
Verbena bonariensis 210, 215, 235
vertical gardening 10
  see also climbing plants; Stepladder Tiered Planter; walls
Viburnum bodnantense 233
Vintage Drawer Wildflower Meadow 204–8
Vintage Teatime Alpine Planter 90–5
Viola
  V. 'Blue Beacon' 74, 151
  V. cornuta 151
  V. 'Johnny Jump-Up' 80
  V. odorata 234
  V. prostrate variety 80
  V. 'Trailing Lavender' 151
  V. 'Trailing Violet' 151

W

wallflowers 234
walls
  Edible Planted Wall 80–3
  Pea and Broad Bean Shooter Shelves 128–31
  Vertically Mounted Miniature Greenhouse 132–7
  see also frames
water and bog plants 232
water gardens, tabletop 52–5
water lilies 232
watering 94, 167, 173, 237, 247
  frequency 247
  water-storing crystals 247
  weekend watering system 247
wicker balls 103
wicker baskets and hampers 36, 210–13
wild oregano 80, 204
wildflowers 14
  care of 208
  Garden Sieve Wildflower Meadow 209
  Vintage Drawer Wildflower Meadow 204–8
wildlife 14
  Bee and Butterfly Wildlife Hamper 210–15
  Cup-and-Saucer Bird Stations 216–20
  plants for 230
  Portable Hanging Insect House with Green Roof 198–203
  Seedcake Hangers for Hungry Birds 221
wind 246

Y

year-round interest, plants for 233

Z

Zantedeschia aethiopica 232
zinc containers 36
zinnias 225
zucchinis 240, 249

Suppliers

Antiques plus
Vintage ware
www.antiquesplus.com.au

Australian Succulents
Succulent plants
www.australiansucculents.com.au

Bonsai Shop
www.bonsaishop.com.au

Bloom Master Australia
Hanging baskets and planters
www.bloommaster.com.au

Cement Australia
Cement, blends and oxides
www.cementaustralia.com.au

Choice Succulents
Succulents and cacti
www.choicesucculents.com.au

The Diggers Club
Seeds, plants and containers
www.diggers.com.au

Exotica Plants
Carnivorous plants
www.exoticaplants.com.au

Gardenworld
Gardening sundries
www.gardenworld.com.au

The Green Life Soil Co.
Microgreen seeds
www.greenlifesoil.com

Masters Home Improvement
Tools
www.masters.com.au

modPlanters
Hanging planters
www.modplanters.com.au

Nurseries Online
Plant, nursery and gardening directory
www.nurseriesonline.com.au

Wildflowers Australia
Wildflowers
www.wildflowersaustralia.com.au

Watergarden Paradise
Native aquatic plants
www.watergardenparadise.com.au

About the author

Based near Cambridge, RHS medal award-winning garden designer and gardening journalist Philippa Pearson takes inspiration for her garden creations from the countryside, classical and contemporary architecture, and textiles. Her design portfolio covers many private gardens across the UK and her colourful planting style attracts much attention from visitors, the media, and photographers at RHS shows, and is greatly enjoyed by her garden design clients. Philippa enjoys the challenge of creating gardens in smaller spaces, as well as larger ones.
www.philippapearson.co.uk

Acknowledgements

Author's acknowledgements
The author would like to thank the following for their help supplying plants, equipment, information, and proofreading: Fiona Wemyss from Blueleaf Plants; Jo Woffinden; Mark Smith from Key Essentials; Luci Skinner from Woottens Plants; Peter Warren, Bonsai professional; Mark Haslett from Essex Carnivorous Plants; Chris Crow from Sarracenia Nurseries; and everyone who lent us their garden or balcony for photos.

The author would also like to thank especially the wonderful team at DK who have supported and helped her: Alastair Laing, Sonia Moore, Vicky Read, Holly Kyte, Penny Warren, Mary Ling, and Jane Bull.

Publisher's acknowledgements
DK would like to thank:

Katie Federico for project assistance; Geremia Federico for project consultancy and carpentry; Scott Flashman for design and carpentry on the hanging plant pot mobile; Peter Warren for his bonsai expertise, www.saruyama.co.uk.

The following people and organisations for generously allowing us to create projects and photograph in their garden spaces: Laura and Ed Buller, Satu Fox, Guy and Juliette Harvey, Rosemary Hignett, Hoa Luc, Sonia Moore, Philippa Pearson, Ron and Rita Saunders, Vauxhall City Farm, Chris Roos and Amy Wagner, Fiona Wemyss, Hin-Yan Wong.

Hand models: Katie Federico, Satu Fox, Alastair Laing, Max Moore, Harriet Stanton, Ciaran Webster, Fiona Wemyss.

Paula Johnson and the staff at Squires Garden Centre, Stanmore; Jacques Amand International Ltd, Stanmore, for plants and advice; Garden Brocante, Shiplake, for supplying galvanized metal planters; The Boma Garden Centre, Kentish Town; Tim Bailey at the Carnivorous Plants Society, for cultivation advice, www.thecps.org.uk; Alex Roberts at Chive.

Marie Lorimer for indexing.
Laura Nickoll for proofreading.
Nidhi Mathur for editorial assistance.

DK Australia would like to thank:
Max McMaster for indexing.
Erin Richards for proofreading.
Georgina Garner for editorial assistance.

Picture credits
The publisher would like to thank the following for their kind permission to reproduce their photographs:

(Key: a-above; b-below/bottom; c-centre; f-far; l-left; r-right; t-top)

225 Dorling Kindersley: Designed by Nilufer Danis / RHS Hampton Court Flower Show 2012 (t). **229** Jennifer Wilkinson (cb). **230 Dorling Kindersley:** RHS Garden, Wisley (cla). **230** Jennifer Wilkinson (tr). **232** Jennifer Wilkinson (tl). **233** Jennifer Wilkinson (tl). **236 Dorling Kindersley:** Alan Buckingham (cr, fcr). **237 Dorling Kindersley:** Designed by Heather Culpan and Nicola Reed (bl). **239 Dorling Kindersley:** Designed by Linda Fairman of Oasthouse Nursery / RHS Hampton Court Flower Show 2012 (ca). **242 Dorling Kindersley:** Alan Buckingham (ca, cra, clb, cb, crb). **243 Dorling Kindersley:** Linda Fairman of Oasthouse Nursery / RHS Hampton Court Flower Show 2012 (cra).

All other images © Dorling Kindersley
For further information see:
www.dkimages.com